THE GYPSIES IN POLAND

JERZY FICOWSKI

The Gypsies in Poland

HISTORY AND CUSTOMS

INTERPRESS PUBLISHERS

Translated from the Polish by Eileen Healey

Graphic design by Stanisław Szczuka

Production editor: Wiesław Pyszka

Illustrations selected by Jerzy Ficowski

On the jacket: tarok card
reproduced by W. Czapiński and T. Prażmowski

This book appears also in Polish and German

This is the two thousand three hundred and twenty-first
publication of Interpress

Copyright by Jerzy Ficowski

Printed in Yugoslavia

ISBN 83-223-2321-2

Contents

Introduction

Of all the ethnic groups that have lived in Poland over the centuries, the Gypsies are the most exotic and intriguing, and are at the same time the least well known to their fellow citizens and to folklore experts. Their closed tribal and clan communities, cultivating their traditional customs, ruled according to their own laws, and speaking a language known only to themselves, prevent the initiation of outsiders into their secrets. Their contacts with members of the outside world are limited to the area of employment and other money-making activities. This Gypsy apartness is guarded, as it were, from two sides: by their own distrust, borne out by experience, and by the antipathy frequently shown by society at large, which is in turn the product of fears both superstitious and justified, and also of downright xenophobia.

This state of affairs has developed over the centuries. We shall discuss below in more detail the historical and social factors that have magnified this mutual feeling of distance over the span of many generations, and have given deeper root to mutual animosities. The last decades, after the Gypsies ceased travelling around Poland, have begun here and there to show some softening of contrasts and in certain spheres some lessening of the social isolation of these ex-nomads. These developments can be discerned, but they as yet in no way represent a turning point; they are only the first symptoms, and there is no way of knowing to what extent they are signs of permanent and irreversible change; they are by no means generalized and they are meeting with a great deal of opposition. Gypsy social structures and the laws that govern them are still maintained, despite the changes in their way of life, and their settling in permanent homes.

The imperviousness of the Gypsy way of life, guarded by a system of taboos practiced by the members of the community, together with the language barrier, have effectively prevented Polish ethnographers from working in this little-known and highly attractive branch of folklore. The relatively small number of Polish studies of the Gypsies published over the past two centuries have on the whole been limited to historical information and some attempts to describe this people from the outside, without real familiarity with their life and customs. There have also occasionally been some more significant studies of the Romany language in the form of the dialects of settled groups, and a few transcriptions of Romany texts. The first to take up the subject of the Gypsies and pay some attention to them was Tadeusz Czacki, the distinguished historian, who wrote two treatises on the Gypsies, and was co-author of the beautiful Uniwersał względem Cyganów *(Proclamation on the Gypsies) of 1791, issued shortly after the proclamation of the May 3rd Constitution. Later, Ignacy Daniłowicz in 1824 and Teodor Narbutt in 1830 also published treatises on the subject. In the 20th century, apart from a series of minor historical contributions published before the Second World War, the main studies have been on linguistics: by Izydor Kopernicki (posthumously), Jan Michał Rozwadowski, and Edward Klich: and after the war, by Tadeusz Pobożniak, the present author and other authors.*

Only the latest studies attempted to go deeper and penetrate previously unfamiliar areas of Gypsy life and lore. The present author first turned his attention to Gypsy spiritual culture, which had not previously been examined, and found in the archives a wealth of documents on the history of the Gypsies in Poland. It was only possible to investigate living folklore by taking part in Gypsy life, and by going along with the Gypsies on their travels, for the Gypsies still maintained their nomadic lifestyle in Poland for almost twenty years after the war. It was by taking part in this way in their everyday life that observations could be built up on the Gypsy customs handed down from generation to generation, and still real, alive and practiced.

Traces of Gypsy history can only be found in Polish personal names, and in the attempts of the state authorities over the centuries to drive these nomads out of the country, or, later, in the nomination of certain members of the gentry as Gypsy overlords in what was called the Office of the Gypsy Kingdom in Poland. The task of writing the history of the Gypsies in Poland, even in part, is therefore a difficult one. It can only be an outline history of, in a sense, the official relations of the state with these wandering incomers. There is no Gypsy account of their own history, for it took place almost outside time, on the margins of major events, and – never having been written down – has fallen into oblivion. Even though, in the absence of Romany writing, something of this has been handed down in oral tradition, in legends, few of the events and facts that form the stuff of history can be found there. Perhaps there are some names of some of the early rulers of the Gypsy hordes, or some memories of the great migrations from country to country. But apart from this the Gypsy past differed little from the Gypsy present; it contains all the same elements: the cold winterings and roving summers.

The Gypsies are a singular people, continuing their age-old nomadic way of life in the midst of civilized Europe and through the industrial revolution. And not only the Gypsy people themselves have forgotten their past. History itself has overlooked the Gypsies, and has not even provided us with answers to such fundamental questions as what the original homeland of the Gypsies was, or when and how they came to Poland. The Gypsies themselves, shortly after their arrival in these hitherto foreign lands, tried to dispel this general ignorance in some way by telling a legend about their origin in Egypt. And although much later, comparative linguistics came to the aid of history and definitively established the original homeland of these peoples in quite a different place on the map of the world, and traced the path of their migrations, nonetheless there is a permanent relic of this Egyptian legend in their name: for example in English "Gypsies", in Spanish "Gitanos" and in French "Gitanes" – all words of which the etymology is clear.

Broadly based Gypsy studies, covering the results of ethnographic, philological, sociological and historical research, developed in Western Europe in the 19th century, and work in this field is still continuing and has already produced a considerable body of academic writing. However, the fact that the Gypsies were dispersed and created over the centuries specific varieties of their folk culture in individual, separate territorial groupings has meant that for example the lore of highland Gypsies, who arrived in Poland from the early 15th century, and that of the lowland Gypsies who arrived in the mid-16th century, require separate research, and abound in aspects which are unknown elsewhere or which appear here in varied form. Thus studies by foreign researchers cannot relieve Polish students of Gypsy lore of the task of carrying out their own investigations, for they are dealing with a separate field of research. Even so, the results of academic research are in the nature of things available mainly to specialists and a generally narrow audience, while in the world at large false and hackneyed views of the Gypsies are frequently held; three versions of these views are particularly stubbornly maintained: the "demonic", "criminal" and "operetta".

The "demonic" view arose from fear of the Devil, and sees in the Gypsies a tribe of sorcerers with supernatural powers, arousing superstitious fear. The "criminal" view treats Gypsy society as a collective of organized professional criminal groups. The mawkish and sentimental "operetta" view holds the Gypsies to be romantic nomads living by music and love of nature. Usually we are confronted by a mixture of all three of these views in varied proportions but usually marked by an absolute ignorance of the real nature of this people. It is therefore worth giving a wider account of their history and culture – not only to satisfy curiosity and fill a gap in our knowledge of the Gypsies, but also to prevent an acquiescence by silence in prejudice and superstition, and to allow the grimace of animosity that often still greets them to be replaced by a rational, although critical, approach. I should like this book to make a contribution here.

This is not my first publication on this complicated and fascinating subject, but it is in a sense a pioneering work, at least in Poland, in that it is planned as an album with a wide selection of Polish iconography on the subject of Gypsies, beginning with old engravings and paintings, through early photography, to contemporary photographs, some of which are in colour. These illustrations are historical documents in themselves: the majority date from the era of the Gypsy travels, which is a thing of the past, before the settlement campaign was carried out in Poland.

I should like to express my gratitude to the director of the District Museum in Tarnów, Adam Bartosz, who is an ethnographer and Gypsy specialist and who has set up the first permanent museum exhibition in Poland dealing with the Gypsies. He kindly made available to me his lists and files of iconographic material, compiled following research conducted by the Tarnów Museum, and this has made my selection of illustrations for the present book a much easier task. I should also like to thank the family of the late Jerzy Dorożyński, a photographer who died in 1972, for allowing me to use his pictures, which are undoubtedly the best black and white photographs in this book.

The First Migrations to Poland: Origins and Traces

We owe our present knowledge of the origins of the Gypsies to research carried out several hundred years after the first appearance of this people in Europe. These exotic newcomers, supposed to have been driven out of Egypt, made their appearance unexpectedly centuries ago, taking by surprise both the authorities and peoples of the countries where the first large caravans appeared. They travelled to the North and West from the East and South. Europe was long thereafter inclined to accept the version that they had originated in Egypt. And there were no completely reliable historical sources on the matter.

A pure accident provided the starting point for widescale and profitable research into Gypsy life and lore. In 1763, a Hungarian named Istvan Valyi, discovered when he came into contact in Europe with Indian students from Malabar, that there were many striking similarities between their language and that of the Gypsies. The Gypsies understood some words in the language of these foreign visitors. This discovery provided the basis for philological studies carried out initially by J.C.C. Rüdiger (1782) which confirmed and documented Istvan Valyi's observations, and discovered many more cases, by comparing particular Gypsy words with a Hindustani dialect. Rüdiger's work was taken up and continued by A. F. Pott in his study, *Die Zigeuner in Europa und Asien* (1844–45), which compared Gypsy expressions with Sanskrit and New Indian languages. The idea that the Gypsies had originated in India ceased to be an academic hypothesis and became an accepted fact, backed by a great deal of evidence. The great philologist F. Miklosich carried the research further, by compiling extensive lexical materials and attempting to locate the Indian aboriginal abode of the Gypsies more precisely. Since he discovered many similarities, mainly phonetic, between the European Gypsy dialects and the dialects of the Kafir and Dardic tribes in the North-West of East India, Miklosich put forward the thesis that this was the area that the Gypsies must have migrated from originally in about 1000 A.D., in a period after the individual New Indian languages had already developed.

It was not until 1927 that R. L. Turner proved that the phonetics of the Gypsy language had earlier been linked with the central group of Hindi languages, and that the Gypsies had only later migrated towards the North-West where the Dardic and Kafir tribes were to be found. It was from there that for unknown reasons they set out into the world and were over the centuries to wander into almost all its regions.

Miklosich not only pointed to the aboriginal abode of the Gypsies in India – a version somewhat corrected later by Turner – but also indicated the routes by which the Gypsies travelled from India right to the North and West of Europe. These conclusions were based on investigation of Gypsy dialects and lexical borrowings made along their way. He showed that almost all the European Gypsies initially followed a common route from India through Persia, Armenia and Greece, since all Gypsy dialects contained loan words from Persian, Armenian and Greek. Greek loan words are particularly numerous, which would indicate that the Gypsies spent a longer period of time in that country. In this way, linguistic research has proved fruitful where history remains silent. Next, anthropologists and ethnologists joined in the research, confirming the findings of the comparative linguists.

The first historical information on the Gypsies in Europe comes from the mid-11th century, and speaks of wanderers from Constantinople. These are mentioned in *The Life of George Mtharsmindel* of Mount Athos, which refers to people known as the "Asincan" as "well-known magicians and rogues". It is thought that these Asincan were in fact Gypsies. The second mention chronologically does not give the name of the people, but from the description given, it may be concluded that these were again the Gypsies. This is the account of the Franciscan Simon Simeonis, who made a pilgrimage to the Holy Land, of his meeting on Crete in 1322 with an unusual people. In about 1340 a priest of Cologne left a list of peoples that he had encountered during a journey to the East, and recalls a people that he called the "Mandopolos", describing their way of life and noting that they spoke a mysterious language: "These people use among themselves a speech which no-one is able to understand save themselves, while they can understand the speech of others." The presence of groups like these, differing from those around them, in the Peloponnese before 1350 is also confirmed by Ludolphus of Sudheim, who gave them a similar name: "Mandopolini". "Mandopolos" is almost certainly a corruption of the Greek "mantipolos" meaning seer, fortune-teller.

That these "Asincan", "Mandopolos" or "Mandopolini" were identical with the Gypsies is only a hypothesis. But the next mentions a few decades later appear to be certain evidence on the Gypsies. According to contemporary documents, a "feudum Acinganorum" existed on the island of Corfu in 1386. For the first time we meet the name for the Gypsies which was the prototype for the German *Zigeuner,* Italian *Zingaro,* French *Tsigane* or Polish *Cygan* etc. Still in the 14th century the Gypsies were leaving Greece in great hordes, heading northwards.

In 1384 a document was drawn up in which the voivode of Ugrovlahia Jan Mirca confirms the grant to the monastery at Vodica at the foot of the Carpathians of forty families referred to in the document as "Acigani" vel "Cigani". As a contemporary document reveals, in 1416 they are already in Bohemia. The great migration of the Gypsies to Central and Western Europe had begun – an extraordinary invasion of great hordes of unarmed people. In 1416 a chronicler noted that "Emaus from Egypt" appeared at Kronstadt in Transylvania together with 220 followers. On 30 August 1417 the Gypsies reached Zurich, Magdeburg and Lubeck; and in 1418 "poor people from Little Egypt" appeared in Strasbourg and Frankfurt. On 1 October 1419 they were seen at Sisteron in Provence, on 1 November at Augsburg; in 1420 "Master Andreas, the Prince of Little Egypt" appeared before the citizens of Deventer in Holland together with his followers and 40 horses. "Andrea, Duke of Egypt" rested on 18 July 1422 at Bologna before going on via Forli to Rome for an audience with the Pope; his followers set up a great camp outside the city gates. In 1422 a large horde with 50 horses led by one Michael arrived at Basle, before going on further to Italy, Alsace and France.

The contemporary chronicles noted not only dates, but also some colourful details about the appearance of these strangers and their way of life.

There is no similar evidence from Polish territories and so we must rely on these descriptions from abroad to provide an impression of the unarmed Gypsy invasion which must also at that time have affected Polish territories. We are told in other European accounts that the leaders of the travelling hordes rode on horseback and were dressed very colourfully, in red and green clothes decorated with large silver bosses. The leaders were followed by caravans of light carts drawn by donkeys or old nags; the women rode in oxcarts. Some of the Gypsies were leading bears or performing monkeys.

They claimed to be penitential pilgrims who had renounced the church. Sigismund of Luxemburg, King of Hungary and later Holy Roman Emperor, had, according to their story, occupied their country, forcing them to be baptized on pain of death. They told that this king had imposed a penance upon them: they were to wander the face of the earth for seven years, and seek absolution from the Pope himself. He had given them a safe conduct for this penitential journey, wherever they might wander. In this safe conduct dating from 1423 he had guaranteed not only freedom of movement and protection, but had also recognised their own Gypsy legal system: they were not to be brought before the courts of countries in which they committed crimes. Therefore at the beginning of their wanderings in Central and Western Europe they may have felt themselves immune from punishment as long as their story of the holy and penitential nature of their journey was taken in good faith. Their poverty, and the rags which the majority wore seemed to the local population to be attributes of penitents, and sometimes inclined them to help these alleged pilgrims. Nonetheless, the way of life of these visitors, and the thefts by which they tried to keep themselves, meant that five years after their first appearance at Bologna they were proclaimed unwelcome in that city.

At first, however, city gates were not closed to them. The fantastic version of their origins and the motivations for their travels, which they themselves had dreamed up, skilfully appealed to the ideas of contemporary Europe. We can see that this people which dabbled in fortune telling, and thus in meeting the needs and hopes of those who asked them what tomorrow might bring, were equally able to use their knowledge of psychology to create a past of their own for the consumption of the outside world. The titles of count or prince which these newcomers used were not an expression of Gypsy values but showed that the Gypsies were able deliberately to adapt to local and contemporary social hierarchies in order to add to their own prestige.

In this same period, if not a little earlier, the Gypsies must have arrived in Polish territories, although an absence of any written evidence makes it impossible to provide dates or details for this. The only traces to be found of this first migration come in personal or place name data linked with the word *Cygan* – Gypsy. The first piece of evidence of this kind dated from 1419, when the name of a settler at Trześniów in the Sanok region is given as Petrus Cygan; in 1428 the same name appears at Królikowa; at Berezówka in 1429, we find the name Nicolaus Czygan; in 1434, Mikołaj Czygan appears at Świerczów; and in 1436, Jan and Jakub Cygan at Królikowa.

In Długosz's *Liber beneficiorum* and in court records we can also find early traces of the presence of Gypsies in Poland in place and personal names. In 1487, a place called Cyhanowa Łuka existed in the Halicz region; in 1503 we can find evidence of the existence of a settlement named Cyganowo in the records of the Pyzdry region; and in the 16th century – or perhaps earlier – there was a village called Cyganowice, which belonged to a Poor Clares convent in the Sącz region.

Groups of these travellers almost certainly appeared in the South of Poland during the reign of Ladislaus Jagiello, and then shortly moved on northwards. Tadeusz Czacki claims that he found in "fragments of scattered Crown documents" which have today been lost, a mention dating from 1501 of Polgar, the leader of the Gypsies in the Kingdom of Poland. It was in the same year that King Alexander the Jagiellon issued a charter at Vilna to the "Gypsy Voivode" Vassili, which confirmed his authority over the Gypsies in the Grand Duchy of Lithuania and gave him the right to judge disputes among his subjects; it also conferred on all the Gypsies "freedom of movement in our lands... according to the customs of our ancestors, the Grand Dukes of Lithuania of blessed memory... according to the former laws, customs and ducal edicts". The way in which this was formulated indicates that this charter dating from 1501 was not the first document of its kind: it must have been preceded by others which have not been preserved and of which we today know nothing.

Thus from the beginning of the 15th century, exotic newcomers from the South-East were passing through Poland, practising their arts of blacksmithery and fortune-telling; they enjoyed the support of the rulers, and the superstitious respect of the local population. However, the situation gradually deteriorated. Belief in their penitential mission began to waver, and they became increasingly isolated from the host society. Doors were closed to the Gypsies because of fear of spells and theft, as fortune-telling and quack professions replaced the Gypsy handicrafts as their main source of livelihood. They wandered in great hordes from city to city, only rarely dividing up into smaller groups which roamed through the forests.

But when the first edicts banishing the Gypsies were promulgated in Germany, and they began to flee in a panicky rout to Poland, Poland also passed the first anti-Gypsy laws. The newcomers, who as a result of persecution had become accustomed to treating life as a bitter struggle for existence and who were full of desperate initiative, came into contact in Poland with their kinsmen who had arrived in the country a century and a half earlier. Until then no legal measures had been taken against the Gypsies, and no decisions had been taken to drive them out of the country. And so, they were able without harassment or discrimination to travel the length and breadth of the Polish Commonwealth. It was not only the Gypsies themselves who were responsible for bringing about a change in this situation. A radical change in the attitude of the authorities to the Gypsies took place in the mid-16th century, following the anti-Gypsy laws passed in Germany in 1496 and 1557. The German assembly ordered the Gypsies to be deprived of rights of citizenship and deported. Those who returned were hanged or burned at the stake. New hordes therefore appeared in the Polish Commonwealth. Deprived of their rights, they earned their living by robbery and violence, making raids from their inaccessible forest hiding places. In this same period, during the reign of Sigismund Augustus, the incidence of highway robbery began to increase on the borders of Silesia, and this was blamed on the Gypsies. In 1553, Przyłuski, writing of the Gypsies in his compendium of laws, condemned Polish hospitality, and said that they should be put in irons and sent to forced labour as convicts. The complaints to which the troubles in Silesia and the influx of Gypsies from Germany gave direct rise were ably seconded by Marcin Bielski, the author of the *Kronika wszytkiego świata...* (Chronicle of all the world..; 1551), his tone and argument full of impassioned prejudice. These anti-Gypsy views were accepted in good faith – all the more so that in addition to pure invention they did contain some well-founded opinions which were backed by the *vox populi,* whose unfriendly, or even openly hostile, attitude to the newcomers stemmed from several causes.

Apart from understandable dislike of their habit of theft, they also attracted the hatred of the peasants and impatience of the landowning classes because they were a free people, not tied to the land, not bound to any lord, not obliged to pay any feudal dues or services: they were therefore the object of envy of the oppressed common Polish people. Undoubtedly, one of the reasons why the Gypsies continued their nomadic way of life was their fear of being levelled down to the position of tied serfs if they allowed themselves to be persuaded to adopt a settled way of life. Another reason might have been the fear – by no means unfounded in an era when witches were drowned and burnt – of the great powers of the inquisitors searching for the Devil and all his servants, and the necessity of being able to escape from them quickly.

However, in Poland the verbal attacks on the Gypsies did not lead to persecution as so often happened elsewhere in that period. Nonetheless, it was a short path from the appeals for their expulsion to which we have referred, to laws passed by the Polish Seym (Parliament) which expressed these views and tendencies. In 1557, in the reign of Sigismund Augustus, the first law ordering the Gypsies to be expelled was passed by the Warsaw Seym. "Gypsies, or people who are unnecessary, we will drive out from these lands and thereafter they are not to be received back into them." This formulation is fairly generalized, and is really an earnest of measures to be taken in the future. The law was not put into effect, and the resolution simply disappeared into the annals of the Seym. This is indicated by the passing at the Piotrków Seym of 1565 of another resolution, calling for the decrees of banishment to be implemented: "Gypsies, that they may not be in the lands of the Polish Crown. In that much evil is happening in the Kingdom through the Gypsies, we call into execution the Statute of Warsaw of 1557 against this, and order that from this time they are definitely not to be in the Kingdom or in any other of our lands. And when any starost drives them from his starosty, let not one remain there."

The Piotrków statute brought no results either: the Gypsies continued to pour into Poland, and the edicts of banishment were not put into effect, for they were too difficult for the authorities in those days to implement, in view of the way in which the Gypsies were able to hide in the forests, and also in view of the services rendered to the local population by Gypsy craftsmen.

A blind eye was turned to the Gypsy wanderings, and individual municipal judical authorities would mediate cases of disputes between the local population and the Gypsy leaders *(seniores)* who were responsible for the behaviour of their subjects.

In 1578, at the General Warsaw Seym, King Stephen Báthory, in view of the ineffectiveness of the two earlier statutes, pronounced a harsher edict which threatened sanctions against people who harboured Gypsies on their lands – who were to be punished as accomplices of outlaws. This shows that favouring and toleration of the Gypsies, and even deliberate protection of them from banishment were so widespread that special legal sanctions had to be provided against them. Lithuanian legislation was more moderate and did not resort to such harsh measures; it preferred to try to make useful citizens of the Gypsies by means of providing special facilities and reliefs for them. The Second Lithuanian Statute of 1564-66 ordered the settlement under good lords, princes, gentlemen and *hospodars* of those Gypsies who did not wish to submit to exile from the country. The Gypsies were thus offered the alternative of remaining in the Grand Duchy of Lithuania on condition that they gave up their former way of life. This was the first attempt to persuade the Gypsies to abandon their nomadic life-style, and represented a departure from the earlier decrees and banishments which had renounced all sense of responsibility for their fate. The punishments provided for here were intended only for criminals, regardless of whether they were Gypsies or not, and the mere fact of being a Gypsy was not punishable. This tendency, which we might call antidiscriminatory, was reflected in yet other legal regulations. In the Grand Duchy of Lithuania, Gypsy volunteers were accepted in the army: "Whomsoever being willing for military needs, armed and on horseback who can ride, or who goes on foot, including also Gypsies, all shall be worthy of the army. They should go to the hetman to go to war on horseback or on foot."

The above instructions applied only to volunteers in time of war, and not to normal recruitment. The Third Statute of the Grand Duchy of Lithuania, which was ratified in 1588 on the basis of a crown edict, provided for harsher regulations in the matter of the Gypsies; it also superseded all foregoing legislation. The wording of this new statute tells us that there were cases when peasants helped Gypsies, and hid them under their own names. There must have been many well-known cases of this kind since the statute specifically condemns such procedures.

In the Kingdom of Poland, the Gypsies were outlawed. Some of the starosts, who were entrusted with the task of carrying out this decree, turned a blind eye to the wandering Gypsy caravans. The Gypsy way of life, their continual changes of abode, and the vast forests which hid them, made it impossible to banish all of them. These decrees meant that the Gypsies moved into ever more inaccessible regions, into the depths of the forests, or into mountain caves, where the servants of the state could not espy them so readily. Some groups sought refuge on the estates and under the protection of virtually autonomous magnates. There was nothing left to them but passive resistance. There could be no question of protests from the Gypsies, or of appeals to higher authorities.

There was however a protest against the anti-Gypsy laws, which made an impact and achieved some relaxation of the regulations. For in the Podlasie region, the gentry were openly dissatisfied with the increasing number of cases in which landlords were denounced for harbouring Gypsies, on the basis of the statute of 1578. This placed upon all who knew that Gypsies were being hidden the obligation of reporting the fact to the authorities together with the names of those responsible for this breach of the law. This law often provided a pretext for settling personal grievances with neighbours, and offered opportunities for calumny. The gentry of the Podlasie region were not prepared to accept this state of affairs. But it was not only the possibility of hostile calumnies that motivated them, but also the fact that the Gypsies were needed in Podlasie – indeed in some areas were absolutely irreplaceable – as craftsmen. In that period there was an exceptionally large number of Gypsy blacksmiths in the region, and the local population did not wish to lose them. They therefore decided to protest and appeal to the Seyms – as can be seen from the Podlasie mandate to the Seyms of 1601 and 1607. This resulted in new Seym resolutions passed in 1607 at the General Crown Seym in Warsaw, entitled, *On writs of complicum bannitorum* (accomplices of outlaws). This was a more favourable act, which amended the earlier provisions. We learn from this that those who made denunciations had used nominees, in order to protect their identity from the individual who was being denounced. The new act attempted to obviate this danger of false accusations being used as a weapon among the quarrelling gentry. In practice the banishing of the Gypsies from the Podlasie region was restricted to the exile of notorious mischief-makers; responsibility for carrying this out was placed upon the starosts, and no-one else was allowed to assume the duty. In this way, Podlasie ceased to fall within the jurisdiction of the harsh legislation covering the rest of the country, and thus provided a refuge for large numbers of Gypsies who fled here from other areas.

The statute of outlawry did not however prevent the Polish magnates from recruiting members of this currently accursed nation to their private armies, particularly in the first half of the 17th century. Apart from the Hungarians, who were the predominant element in the magnate armed forces, there were also Wallachians, Tartars, Cossacks and Gypsies, particularly in the Przemyśl and Sanok regions. The statute of outlawry was in fact not implemented and it was not even re-issued. None of the measures passed was repealed, but in practice they fell into disuse. And thus when the next stage in Gypsy–state relations developed, marked by the nomination of Gypsy headmen in Poland, this was not carried out on the basis of any new law or decree which annulled the earlier anti-Gypsy legislation. Quite simply, one day the royal Chancery issued a charter to the first official Gypsy headman, giving him power over the Gypsies in the Commonwealth, and over all the Gypsy hordes wandering in the Crown lands and Lithuania. This act represented a return to earlier discontinued practices, known to us from Alexander the Jagiellon's charter of 1501.

The Office of the Gypsy Kingdom

The office of "King of the Gypsies", holders of which were nominated or confirmed by the Royal Chancery, arose somewhere between the passing of the last statute on the Gypsies in 1624, and 1652, when one Matiasz Korolewicz was affirmed in this title. The kings were at first – initially still in the reign of John Casimir – Gypsies, but from the time of the second nomination in the same reign, they were representatives of the Polish gentry.

Matiasz Korolewicz was not, however, the first official Gypsy headman in the Crown lands "after the departure from this world of the late willing Janczy". Was this Janczy a Gypsy, or, like the later nominees, a Polish nobleman who had nothing in common with the Gypsies? The text of the charter tells us nothing on this score, but we may conclude that he was a Gypsy, and indeed bore the same name as the Gypsy piper at the court of King Ladislaus IV. The charter was issued in the hope that it would bring about the situation which Seym legislation had been unable to attain: prevention of lawlessness and criminality, and forcing the Gypsies to pay taxes.

The privilege proved most beneficial to Korolewicz himself, for the nominated ruler took full advantage of the rights he was accorded and the concomitant profits. Moreover, in doing so, he was merely following in the footsteps of his predecessors, as we can see from the words of the charter which appointed him "with all the prerogatives, income and benefits, to this office according to the custom preserved heretofore". As Tadeusz Czacki wrote, "rulers of the Gypsies were nominated from the Royal Chancery in the Crown lands, and these despots – known as Kings of the Gypsies – were Gypsies and retained a kind of police".

The ratification that these rulers received from the state authorities only served effectively to increase their impunity and magnify their malversations. As far as Korolewicz is concerned, there were particular reasons why the collection of taxes from the Gypsies – always a difficult matter in view of their scattered and changing places of abode – was even more complicated than usual.

These were turbulent times, with the Swedish invasion, wars against the Hetman Bohdan Khmielnitski and with Moscow, and Lubomirski's rebellion. At the end of his reign over this war-torn country, King John Casimir issued yet another privilege to a Gypsy headman, but this time there was a difference: for the first time it was not a Gypsy who was nominated, but a Polish nobleman. Probably because this was a difficult, post-war period, the nomination not only fell to a nobleman, which was in itself a novelty, but to a knight who was at the same time a representative of the armies of the Commonwealth. The role of Gypsy headman was later to be restored permanently to civilian hands, but it was never to return to a Gypsy.

On 11 April 1668, the Royal Chancery confirmed the nobleman and warrior Jan Nawrotyński as headman of the Gypsies in the Crown Lands and Lithuania.

The indications of favour shown at that time to the Gypsies, in pleasant contrast to the discriminatory tendencies and practices seen earlier, are interesting and significant. Contemporary documents provide illustrations and proof of wider support of Gypsy citizens whose behaviour was acceptable to the authorities.

The under-starost who was the author and signatory of one such document explains that he was giving the Gypsies a document "by rights of my office and thus according to the duties laid down by the office of starost". This letter of recommendation was not therefore just an act of goodwill on the part of this under-starost, but must have been in accordance with the current regulations, or at least in line with permitted and recognized practice, with common law.

16

The preserved documents date from 1669, and therefore little more than a year later than the charter granted to Jan Nawrotyński. They were almost certainly given to Floryanowicz at his own request and constituted a kind of safe conduct to ease his passage in his wanderings with his caravan, in his visits to towns and settlements and in short halts en route. These "passports" are not only proof of support for the Gypsies on the part of officials and estate owners, but also provide indirect evidence of the difficulties which wandering Gypsy bands must normally have encountered without this kind of pass. These difficulties were not only due to the fears or dislike of the Gypsies on the part of the local population, but also to the old laws, as yet unrepealed, which forbade the reception and harbouring of Gypsies as outlaws. And therefore the document speaks only of free passage and of receiving them merely "for a short time, such as the Crown laws permit". This kind of legal position, even given the interpretation and practice most favourable to the Gypsies, must have encouraged the continuation of a nomadic Gypsy way of life, and could in fact effectively prevent any attempt to settle the travellers. Nevertheless, in the context of the contemporary legal and social conditions, these "certificates" constitute a praiseworthy example of ensuring, if only in part, rights of citizenship even for these people who were tainted with the stain of "strangeness" and a general reputation for being, at the very least, non-beneficial for the country.

We do not know when Jan Nawrotyński, the "follower of the colours", ended his reign over the Gypsies. It is only 32 years after he was granted the office that we can find in the archives another mention of attention being paid by the Royal Chancery to the question of the Gypsy king, this time in the reign of Augustus II. This king issued successively as many as six charters, each granting this strange office to a nobleman who sought the title. All the candidates volunteered for the post, canvassed for the nomination, doubtless tempted by the income and benefits accruing from the office.

Augustus II issued the first of these charters in 1703, nominating Jan Deweltowski headman of the Gypsies in Samogitia and the Grand Duchy of Lithuania. Deweltowski and his successors were to prove ineffectual, or at the worst actually harmful, in their exercise of this office, for a number of reasons. The Gypsies were suspicious, unwilling to make pacts with the *gadjé* (non-Gypsies) and recognize direct "foreign" rule; the Polish noblemen on the other hand despised these nomads, and were ignorant of Gypsy law, customs and social organization; it was also difficult for them to keep in touch with the hordes continually travelling about the country. The Gypsy people, surrounded by mistrust and dislike, discriminated against by the constitution, provided a profitable field for exploitation. Certain magnates – for example Prince Paweł Sanguszko or Karol Radziwiłł – irrespective of royal charters, granted titles of headmen of the Gypsies on their own authority in their own estates.

Apart from these kings or headmen imposed upon the Gypsies, they themselves always maintained their own hierarchies of elders, so that the introduction of gentry headmen into Gypsy affairs could be at best superficial; it in no way broke down the exclusiveness of the Gypsy community, but in fact rather reinforced it.

Augustus II's charter to Jan Deweltowski granted this nobleman "authority over the vagabundorum Ciganorum" for life, and instructed the functionaries of the public administration not to hamper him in the fulfilment of his duties as the elder of the Gypsies. He therefore became the ruler of the travelling Gypsies throughout all Poland, with particular mention of Samogitia and Lithuania.

The Royal Chancery made similar grants in the charters for other noblemen. In 1705, and thus barely two years later, Augustus II nominated Bonawentura Jan Wiera headman of the Gypsies of the whole Commonwealth, although with particular mention of the Lvov, Sanok and Przemyśl region. Although there is no mention of it in the text of the charter, we must accept that this took place after the death or abdication of Deweltowski. The charter granted to Wiera introduced certain new commissions, consisting in charging the new headman with nominating "headmen and judges" who were to act as his deputies. In this way he obtained the right to set up his own administrative apparatus in order more easily to collect the taxes and donations conferred upon him by the charter which added the significant phrase permitting the headman to "maintain and keep up the income". The post of Gypsy headman became increasingly profitable. The next charter of this kind dates from 1729, and was granted to Jakub Trzciński. In the text of this nomination we can find valuable information on two of his predecessors: on one Żulicki, who died, and on Stanisław Godziemba-Niziński who was nominated even earlier and who moved abroad, abandoning his Gypsy subjects and leaving them leaderless. The next charter of nomination therefore deprived him of the right to the office he had abandoned, and also condemned him for "incorrect behaviour".

The introduction of intermediaries between the "king" and the Gypsies in the form of "viceroys" and "substitutes" made the task of the ruler easier while detracting not at all from his authority. One novelty in the charter granted to Trzciński was the highly significant mention of usurpers who exploited and oppressed the Gypsies without any right to do so. The office of ruling over the Gypsies was so attractive that all kinds of miscreants could be found hiding under the skirts of the King of the Gypsies in order to rob and black-mail freely.

Jakub Trzciński resigned from his post after less than two years, giving up his royal title; for we should note that the charter that he was granted for the first time referred to the office as "the office of the Gypsy Kingdom". Probably Trzciński himself when he applied to the Royal Chancery for the office of Gypsy ruler requested that the charter should be provided with various guarantees just to be on the safe side, and therefore he also obtained in the text the right to denounce pretenders to the title – who had perhaps represented a threat to his predecessor and therefore might also trouble him.

He however benefited from his charter for only a very short time, and as early as 3 March 1731 Franciszek Bogusławski was being granted a charter for the "office of the Gypsy Kingdom" after the resignation – "abdication" – of his predecessor. Probably in order to protect himself as effectively as possible against unofficial competitors, Bogusławski proclaimed his charter in various towns, for records of this can be found in the municipal archives of Cracow and Lvov.

Augustus II, who during his reign had nominated a whole series of Gypsy kings, had only two years more to reign when he confirmed the appointment of the last of these, Bogusławski. His successor, Augustus III, almost certainly did not take such a close interest in the Gypsy Kingdom. It was only thirty years after the nomination of Bogusławski, on 10 September 1761, that Augustus III issued a charter – this time for a "regional king" for the Gypsies in the Little Poland region of the country only: "the office of the Gypsy Kingdom conferred on Józef Gozdawa Boczkowski for the districts of Little Poland". This is the only information that we possess about this Gypsy king whose appointment was confirmed by the Royal Chancery.

In 1780, King Stanislaus Augustus Poniatowski nominated Jakub Znamierowski Gypsy headman for the area of the Grand Duchy of Lithuania only; he was granted power over "our faithful Gypsy people". This king of the Gypsies – although he was no longer officially called by this title – is a little better known to us than his predecessors, and the person of this brawling country nobleman, who led a quite extraordinary life, deserves a little attention. He undoubtedly possessed more "qualifications" for the post than those who preceded him, for he had been a horse trader, and therefore had followed a profession close to the Gypsy heart; this had brought him into close contact with Gypsies from his earliest childhood. He is also said to have ᵏⁿown Romany well – or at least the Polish-Lithuanian Romany dialect – and ₒsy customs were familiar to him. If we also take into consideration his black hair and swarthy complexion, we might even come to the conclusion that he had some Gypsy blood running in his veins. In addition, he was a man of great physical strength and outstanding courage, and apparently also of exceptional intelligence. He had attended a monastery school of some kind, after which he had become a horse trader, from which profession he had made considerable profits. However, later his business fell off and he became impoverished; and his last horse was carried off by the Gypsy grouping known as the "Golden Horde", which was one of the wealthiest in Lithuania. It was this act of horse-stealing that eventually brought Znamierowski to power over the Gypsies of Lithuania. Determined to discover the thieves and recover his horse, Znamierowski set off in search of the Golden Horde, together with two Gypsies whom he had recruited as assistants. He came across the horde on the outskirts of a village, in the forest on the borders between the districts of Troki and Lida. There were several hundred members of the horde, but Znamierowski and his two companions managed to subdue them by force of arms. After this victory, Znamierowski bound the leaders of the horde and flogged them soundly, thereafter forcing the entire horde to swear allegiance to him. Within a short space of time, the leaders of other hordes were compelled to submit to him, and recognise him as their new leader, as proof of which they showered him with gifts – or, perhaps, rather allowed him to plunder them without resistance. After this, Znamierowski went to the marshal of Lida, Kazimierz Narbutt, and having obtained from him letters of recommendation, set out for Warsaw, where on 17 August 1780, King Stanislaus Augustus granted him the charter. "So in his eminence," wrote Narbutt in his book on the Gypsies published in 1830 "he judged quarrels that developed amongst the Gypsies, and approached the authorities and citizens on behalf of his people whenever occasion arose, and collected a poll tax of 15 groszys, or half a Polish zloty. He was frequently to be found with the Golden Horde, which usually travelled around the Lida district. But the town of Ejszyszki was usually considered the residence of this headman."

In about 1789, when Znamierowski had already made his authority well felt among his Gypsy subjects by oppressing and exploiting them, the Gypsy hordes rebelled against him, and gathering together in one place, they imprisoned their absolute ruler and condemned him to be flogged. "After which they did not release him.. until they had obtained a general absolution and amnesty. Finally... this noble headman... stayed at his post, but from then on was graciously willing to rule his people fairly and kindly." Znamierowski was mainly linked with the Golden Horde, the richest grouping in Lithuania, and because he had the right to collect taxation for his own use, he must have been in touch mainly with the richest Gypsy tribes, tending to bypass the poorer ones which might not prove so profitable to him. This would be all the more true in that the poorer Gypsies, fearful of officials carrying out royal decrees, hid themselves deep in the forest, and only came out surreptitiously to beg or steal, in order to keep body and soul together. The Lithuanian forests sheltered the very poorest of the Gypsies, who had no real clothes and went out even in winter in torn sheets of cloth: "They live in the Lithuanian forest and even in severe frosts they go out covered only in sheets, carrying their babies in bags hanging from their backs," wrote a contemporary diarist. There were also other groups who hid in the forest in flight from the tax collectors, and made raids from their hiding-places where they were very difficult to track down.

In 1795, Jakub Znamierowski died: his position by now had greatly deteriorated, for he had been impoverished by the mass exodus of the Gypsies from Lithuania after the fall of the Polish Commonwealth. The Gypsies who remained in Lithuania "elected as their headman Miłośnicki, a nobleman of a family from the Lida district", according to an account of the Gypsy authorities written 35 years after the event. This Miłośnicki, who was probably an usurper, did not enjoy a great deal of respect among his Gypsy subjects. He was seen for a few years in the Lida district, where he travelled about together with the Gypsies, but shortly all trace of him vanished. He was last seen at Ejszyszki in 1799, and later two contradictory versions of what had happened to him were in circulation: the first that he had been deprived of his position, and the second that the Gypsy horde had left the region for Turkey. Whatever the case, he was almost certainly the last ruler of the Gypsies in Lithuania.

On the situation meantime in the Crown territories, we can read for example in a newspaper of 1811: "And that the Polish Gypsies, despite the above laws, never left Poland, but might only have fallen in numbers... the King and his Chancery would nominate for them a Ruler, whom they called their king and to whom they had to be in all circumstances obedient, especially in the matter of contributions to his profit. The last king of this kind in Poland was a certain Babiński."

In the same way as the Polish kings, the magnates – as absolute rulers in their extensive estates – also nominated separate Gypsy headmen, and granted them letters of protection on the model of the royal charters. Prince Paweł Sanguszko in 1732, when confirming the appointment of the Gypsy Bartosz Alexandrowicz as scultetus, made him Gypsy headman in the towns of Zasław and Stary Konstantynów. The prince not only enjoined Alexandrowicz to ensure that the Gypsies behaved well and earned their living honestly, but also ordered him to collect the taxes which the prince imposed upon his Gypsy subjects, and to deliver them to the princely treasure house.

We know a little about the life of the Gypsies on magnate estates from later memoirs. These show that only groups of the Gypsy "aristocracy" could successfully make a living there, since the snobbish whims and fancies of the great lords treated these "estate Gypsies" as an exotic embellishment for feasts or hunting expeditions – where the Gypsies provided an attraction which might be compared with that of the jesters and dwarves at the royal court.

This was the case at the court of the Radziwiłłs in Lithuania. The Gypsy headmen appointed by the Radziwiłł family exercised authority over those Gypsies who lived on the Radziwiłł estates. In 1778, we know of the death of one of these Radziwiłł Gypsy kings, named Stefanowicz. In the same year Prince Karol Stanisław Radziwiłł ("M'lord"), who by now had on his estates a large number of Gypsies many of whom were leading a settled life, nominated a Gypsy living at Mir, Jan Marcinkiewicz, as the Gypsy headman. Thus in contrast to other earlier or contemporary nominations, a Gypsy was this time appointed to the function. He was probably the leader of some Gypsy grouping, and Radziwiłł's patent only reinforced his authority and broadened its scope. This Radziwiłł charter placed Marcinkiewicz and his immediate followers in a favoured position, and enjoined him to treat other, wandering groups severely.

Teodor Narbutt observes that these charters of protection placed the Gypsy leaders above the law and led to oppression and exploitation of those over whom they ruled: "The authorities in power over the Gypsies," he wrote, "while they were based on legitimacy and faithfully respected old customs, and until they encounter unshaken compliance, were respected by all and the rightful headmen was feared and if not he was punished by a mutiny, or completely deprived of his office, and therefore in Mir the headmen sought to receive the charter of headman from the prince, so that being under his protection, they could ignore the judgment of the horde and in this way rule more freely."

Marcinkiewicz ruled over the Gypsies at Mir for twelve years, dying in 1790. Czacki refers to the last "ruler" of the Gypsies in the Radziwiłł estates as Ignacy Marcinkiewicz. This was probably the son of the privileged Jan, with whose death, according to Narbutt, "the splendour of the office died, and new national arrangements were not conducive to the liberty of the Gypsies, who therefore in large numbers, in teams and hordes, travelled to territories which at that time were under the Turkish sceptre. Even the Radziwiłłs no longer nominated a headman at Mir, for although admittedly Marcinkiewicz's son received the honour that had been his father's, he set off on his travels and moved to Multan."

In recollections of old people about the 1780s, recorded by a 19th century memoirist, we can find references to Jan Marcinkiewicz, the king of the Gypsies on the Radziwiłł estates: "On his head he had a cap in the shape of a kind of crown;... in it there was struck a short peacock's feather; he wore a long, black, loose robe which came down to his ankles, tied with a black belt, and he wore red boots; round his neck, outside his robe, he wore a chain of broad white beads which hung down over his chest, and from it was suspended a likeness of a bear, with a monkey in a red jacket sitting upon it. In approaching His Highness the Prince as a faithful vassal, the king of the Gypsies had taught several bears to draw a cart in harness, which pleased the prince exceedingly. A Gypsy acted as forerunner for these bear teams, and the outriders were monkeys. When once the king of the Gypsies rode in this way unexpectedly into the courtyard of the Radziwiłł palace at Nieśwież, the Prince was extraordinarily astonished and delighted and treated his guest royally, rushing up and saying; 'M'lord, gracious sovereign! You will be received as no guest is received anywhere in the world. Your visit has done me great honour which should be held in memory through the generations.' And the feast that had been prepared for one day lasted for several days, and the royal Gypsy equipage travelled to Alba, the summer palace, amidst a throng of surrounding courtiers and noblemen who had ridden there, and also a crowd of the people of Nieśwież."

Such were the entertainments of those years – the last years before the fall of the Commonwealth.

Times were soon to come when these patterns would cease, and the approaching period of the partitions of Poland would finally deprive the Gypsies of the remains of their rights of citizenship – which in any case had existed only on paper – and drive them into forest hiding-places.

The partitions took place and the royal and Radziwiłł nominations of Gypsy kings came to an end. In some parts of Poland, for example in Lithuania, Eastern Little Poland and the Sub-Carpathian regions, for a certain time settlements of Gypsies who no longer travelled were to remain. But the majority of the travelling Gypsies now either escaped from the territories of the Polish Commonwealth, making chiefly for the Balkans, or took refuge in the local forests, where they were shortly to become subject to new legislation passed by the partitioning powers.

The idea of electing Gypsy kings from among the local gentry was not a Polish innovation. A century earlier than in Poland, gentry headmen had been appointed for the local Gypsies in Transylvania and Hungary: in Transylvania Queen Isabella appointed Casper Nagy and Francis Balatfi Gypsy headmen, and the two of them sold their Gypsy subjects to one Zuchaky. We can see from this that they behaved with some licence towards their subjects – indeed apparently much more ruthlessly than our Polish noblemen who sat on the Gypsy throne.

After the Fall
of the Polish Commonwealth

The affairs of the "Gypsy Kingdom" in pre-partition Poland are interesting as a curious mode of subjecting the Gypsy people to the state authorities, but in fact this all had little effect on the life of the Gypsies, and indeed certain Gypsy groups did not come into contact with it at all. It was for this reason that towards the end of the 18th century, attention was being paid to the idea of reforming the relations of the state to this national grouping, for we have information that Tadeusz Czacki himself submitted to the Four Year Seym a project for new regulations that he had prepared. And less than eight months after the passing of the 3rd May Constitution, in December 1791, a manifesto on the Gypsies in Poland based on Seym resolutions and the new Constitution was published with the signature of Michał Wandalin Mniszech, the Grand Marshal of the Crown. The contents of this manifesto speak well of those who drew it up, and although the proposals for practical solutions to the problems somewhat over-simplify the issues, this is still a document the like of which it would have been hard to find elsewhere in this period. It is worth citing in full this "Manifesto of the Commission of Both Nations":

"The Commission of Police of Both Nations is known to do what is its task by those whose task it is to know of it. When Providence was pleased in its goodness to accord among the many events favourable to our country, that through the Government Statute of 3 May of the year now ending, it came about that every inhabitant of the countries falling under the Commonwealth received protection, the Commission of Police of Both Nations, which has recorded in its obligations the duty to monitor the effects of this law, realizes the need to extend care to the people to date living in our country under the name of Gypsies. This people, in the severity of the law nowhere having its own home, was forced for ever to wander, and was therefore not only not useful to the country, but was indeed harmful, for it was deprived of a way of making its living by work and service, but was forced to seek ways of meeting its needs to the harm of the society amidst which it found itself. When therefore the Constitution of the 3rd May of the current year, called the 'Government Statute', which ensured all the protection of the government and abrogated all measures in conflict with this statute, it also annulled that law which forbade the taking in for settlement of this people under the name of Gypsies living in our country. Therefore, the Commission of Police of Both Nations, receiving constantly reports from various Civil and Military Commissions and Magistrates, that this species of people is in large numbers known in various places under the name of tramps, sees a need to inform these honourable Civil and Military Commissions and noble Magistrates and every Citizen in particular that this species of people is not excluded from government protection, and that everyone is free to receive a Gypsy to settle or to serve in one of his villages, and that furthermore, the Civil and Military Commissions and the noble Magistrates are not to arrest this species of people as tramps, but are to inform them of the government protection, of their freedom to settle, and are to encourage them to settle in the lands of the Commonwealth. When however through the above-mentioned laws they obtain the blessing of a fixed place of residence, it will be the duty of the Military and Civil Commissions and the Magistrates to take pains to ensure that they do not wander about in bands, but that each, after taking a passport from the Civil and Military Commission or the Magistrate in the district or town where he was surprised by this Manifesto, that he should try within a year at the most to choose a fixed place of abode and a certain livelihood, and if during a period of a year from the date of this Manifesto he does not find a settled place and continues to wander as before, then such shall be held to be a tramp and shall be handed over to a house of labour or gaol in the area determined by the Commission of Police. And that this Manifesto may come to general knowledge, published by the Commission of Police, let it be sent to all Civil and Military Commissions, and from every chartered borough to every town of its respective administrative district immediately, and attempts must be made to have it proclaimed from every pulpit.

"Given in Warsaw at the Economic Session of the Commission of Police of Both Nations, on 29th of the month of December in the Year of Our Lord 1791.

Michał Wandalin Mniszech
Grand Marshal of the Crown"

The significant words of this Manifesto refer to the abrogation by the Constitution of 3rd May of all laws which "forbade the taking in for settlement of this people under the name of Gypsies living in our country". It was therefore only at the end of the existence of the Polish Commonwealth that in 1791 the statutes of 1557, 1565, and 1578 formally ceased to apply – statutes which had ordered the Gypsies to be driven out of the country, and which had forbidden the harbouring of Gypsies on one's lands, on pain of the punishment provided for accomplices of outlaws. In this way the law had prevented the Gypsies from giving up their nomadic way of life. Unfortunately, later experience was to show that it was not only these legal restrictions, and not only a dislike of a settled way of life, that was to keep the Gypsy caravans moving. The concessions granted by the constitution did not necessarily imply that the local population was prepared to receive Gypsies. Even those who wished to give up their wanderings were unable to find a place where they would be allowed to set up a permanent home. The Manifesto permitted the punishment of Gypsies only if they did not take advantage of their new right to settle. And this is where the noble Manifesto began to make mistakes. It allowed the Gypsies too little time to change their way of life: barely a year to find themselves a permanent roof over their heads, and a source of income in their chosen place of settlement: and this after centuries of nomadic existence! Even with the best will in the world from both the Gypsies and the land-owners, who were able to "receive a Gypsy for settlement", this time scale was quite unrealistic. And given mutual dislike and lack of any kind of help from the authorities – well! And therefore on this occasion too, the regulations were a dead letter. The second and third partitions of Poland took place. After the setting up of the Kingdom of Poland under Russian sovereignty after the Congress of Vienna, the process of "implementing" the settlement recommendations was carried out under the watchful eye of the tsarist authorities; in practice this turned into a great "Gypsy hunt". On 11 May 1816, the new authorities issued an "Order of the Government Commission for Internal Affairs and Police", based on the provisions of the Manifesto of 1791, but providing much more detailed instructions for the effecting of particular provisions. Even from the date of this Order alone, we can see that the period of a year designated 25 years earlier as the deadline for settlement had been ineffective. A new deadline was therefore laid down, this time reducing the period allowed for settlement to six months. The local authorities were instructed to proclaim that "the government provides protection for this people and permission to live in the country, on condition that they settle in the villages or towns and employ themselves in agriculture or in some industry, or services or as wage labourers". The local district, municipal and parish authorities were obliged to record the personal particulars of Gypsies on special forms provided for the purpose; these data were to include also information on the place which the Gypsies had chosen for permanent settlement. On receipt of this information, the local authorities were to provide the Gypsies with certificates which would enable them to travel to the place that they had chosen for settlement.

The regulations contained a new point, which had not been included in the Manifesto: "In the case when even some of these people did not declare a place of permanent abode, if only they can prove that they can maintain themselves from their labour or from an honest and useful craft that they practice, their liberty to move from place to place should not be fettered, and they should be given an appropriate certificate, stating where and with what intention they are travelling, with the reservation that the local authorities when they stamp these certificates with visas, should record the time spent in the place and their employment there." However, soon it was only settled Gypsies with a permanent place of residence, and moreover only single men, who were permitted to travel in search of employment. On 16 April 1816, the Prefect of the Radom Department sent a letter to Warsaw with the information that during a round-up carried out on 10 April in the Świętokrzyskie Mountains, a "band of Gypsies consisting of 40 persons of various ages and sexes" was apprehended, placed in gaol and interrogated. The Prefect asked for "communication of the government regulations" on the treatment of Gypsies against whom no offence had been proved, but "from their way of life there is no profit".

In line with the regulations, the authorities of the Mazovia voivodship sent in a list of all Gypsies by name, appending a question as to what they were supposed to do with them. The list contained twenty four names. On 13 July 1819, Warsaw sent instructions that Gypsies "who can show no evidence of permanent employment" were to be given a passport valid for the year to travel to a district that they themselves chose. There they would be permitted, under police supervision "to stay with their bears" for a year at the most, without the right to leave the confines of the voivodship, and that during that time they were to find a permanent abode. If however they failed to comply with this, they would be punished as "breaking the law of the country". It is not difficult to imagine that neither the Gypsies nor their bears were ever taken in to settle, and that they simply made use of these passports to continue to move on from place to place. The authorities decided to punish the village headmen for granting "visas" to Gypsies "who engaged in vagabondage" and imposed a fine for this of six Polish zlotys.

In the face of this fine, the zeal of the local village authorities increased. On 1 July 1820, "the headman of the village of Jabłonna took for lazy vagabondage fifteen families of Gypsies, comprising seventy persons, who had suddenly descended upon the inn at Rzyszew and behaved very noisily".

Gypsies were arrested and immediately placed in gaol; the courts passed sentences ordering the Gypsies to be taken under escort to a place of settlement which they themselves chose, and also ordered the punishment of all officials who had permitted their wandering to continue. The Gypsies would give any name that came into their heads for the places where they wished to settle.

The court verdicts were carried out, and in this way for example wandering blacksmiths were deprived of their living, and minstrels lost the right to play in different towns at weddings or in inns. Finally, a decision of the governor, which was to have dangerous consequences, was published on 3 November 1849: this provided for the payment of a reward of two silver roubles and 85 kopeks for every adult Gypsy apprehended, and of half of this sum for each Gypsy child.

A month after this decision was announced, instructions were issued that "all police officials like presidents and mayors of towns and village headmen" were also liable to punishment for failure to implement the regulations and tolerating the presence of wandering Gypsy caravans, and moreover were themselves to bear the costs of rewarding the policemen for apprehending Gypsies for "vagabondage". The decision of the tsarist governor marked the beginning of persecution of the Gypsies by policemen motivated by chance of gain. A real hunt for Gypsies began.

Thus a dangerous situation, with far-reaching consequences, developed: it did not pay the Gypsies not to steal. If they were to be arrested and imprisoned for travelling alone, then there was no longer anything to lose. Instead of performing an educative role, the regulations forced the Gypsies to commit crimes.

In 1850, 113 Gypsies were arrested in Jarosław gubernya for failure to possess the required identity cards. In 1851, the Jarosław provincial governor demanded that the central authorities should at the earliest opportunity check in which gubernya these Gypsies had been registered, "because these arrested Gypsies have already been in prison for more than a year". The Government Commission sent out an enquiry in the matter to all gubernya authorities, but this brought no result and the matter was dropped. There is no further mention of the 113 prisoners in official correspondence and we do not know what happened to them.

Not only were the Gypsies held responsible for their own opposition to the regulations, but they also suffered from the antipathy towards them of the local authorities and local population. The Lublin gubernya authorities on 5 October 1851 sent a special transport of a group of Gypsies, comprising 30 persons including men, women and children, to Radom gubernya, claiming that these Gypsies came from the town of Głowaczew in that gubernya. When they arrived in that town, it proved that they were not to be found in the municipal registers of inhabitants, and although they were known in Głowaczew, they were not considered to be permanent residents of the town. The Głowaczew townspeople, "probably to avoid the burden which they usually had to bear when bands of Gypsies made their appearance, denied that these people came from the town". In view of this, the gubernya authorities kept them officially "in transit", and because there was no room for them in the town lockup, a building was rented to hold them, where they were imprisoned while further investigations were made. It proved that these Gypsies had stayed at times in the neighbourhood of the town; there were indications that they had been registered in the local population registers, and then later removed from them. "The whole cause of the present confusion... lies in the local police authorities... and the former mayor proved most guilty of all... since he entered and crossed out the Gypsies in the population registers at will." The gubernya authorities ordered the Gypsies to be settled in the territory of Radom district, and that they should be encouraged to earn their living honestly and not allowed to wander. Before this could be put into effect, almost five months had passed since the Gypsies' arrival. The decision of the gubernya authorities was taken in February 1852, but by now it was too late to carry it out. For after nearly five months of imprisonment, on the night of 2/3 March the Gypsies broke out of their temporary prison and disappeared. And there is no evidence in the records that they were ever apprehended. It is therefore possible to conclude that they were once again able to enjoy the freedom of the Gypsy people – which in that period differed very little from the freedom of hunted animals.

They hid in forests and thence made robbing raids before again taking refuge in the forests. From the time when the nomadic way of life became in itself a crime, theft inevitably increased, and law-breaking rose as a logical consequence of the current legislation. Gypsies who were camping somewhere on their wanderings could not safely earn their living honestly, and were therefore pushed over the frontiers of legality. And once they were over that frontier, there was only the possibility of a life of crime left to them. In this hopeless situation, even those Gypsies who wanted to settle were often driven out, for they were treated by the ordinary population as unwelcome settlers.

Robber bands were caught and handed over to the authorities But the same thing happened to those Gypsies who did not steal, but only travelled about from place to place. There was therefore no additional risk in crime; there was only one way to avoid loss of freedom: to hide and to flee. The village headmen apprehended travelling Gypsy caravans in order to have the Gypsies put in gaol. The Gypsies often fled from the convoys. Thus in September 1855, a "band consisting of ten Gypsies" having broken through the guard escaped, on which occasion one of the Gypsies, Wincenty Radomski, hit a guard named August Wójcik on the head with a stick, and wounded him, taking from him the travel warrant and report to the penitentiary court". It later proved that this same "dangerous band" consisted of women and children. The only adult male, the 39-year old Radomski, had been handcuffed together with 16-year old Józef Pran. A search was begun but the escaped prisoners were not found.

And here is another typical case, where the old proverb, "The blacksmith committed the crime and the Gypsy was hanged" was proved true. The owner of the village of Szlubowo near Pułtusk, Aleksander Sędzimir, was travelling from Tuszyn to Piotrków by post coach when it was set upon by unknown highway robbers. A search was begun for the criminals. The deputy headman of the village of Grabica surrounded the local forest which lay near the scene of the attack, and began to search the undergrowth. When he discovered that Gypsies who had been living in the forest had recently moved to a camp elsewhere, he tracked them down into the heart of the forest. A search of their camp revealed nothing: no weapons, no stolen goods, but "they had no signed certificates, and their hiding in the forest and their behaviour gave rise to suspicion, and therefore he arrested them and sent them to the town of Tuszyn together with their horse and carriage". There were twenty-five people in the group, including twelve children. Their leader, Franciszek Paszkowski, claimed in his interrogation that the Gypsies had nothing to do with the attack on the passengers of the post coach, and that two local gamekeepers had carried out the highway robbery. And indeed, when one of these, Celestyn Dłuski, was questioned, he confessed that he had carried out the attack together with his friend, Antoni Kijański. And therefore the Gypsies were not only innocent, but had also helped to find the criminals. And so what happened to the Gypsies? They were arrested, and were sent on to Piotrków district police court together with the arrested gamekeepers. The Gypsies' crime was failure to possess the required identity certificate, and this was why they went off to gaol together with two highwaymen.

As the years passed, the hunt for Gypsies never ceased. The police, tempted by the reward waiting for them for every Gypsy "caught" would arrest settled Gypsies for "vagabondage", or would sometimes only give numbers for those caught, without giving their age, in order to get the higher reward offered for adult Gypsies. Complaints found their way to Warsaw, along with pleas for arbitration, for example to determine who was to receive the reward of 14 silver roubles and 25 kopeks for the capture of the Gypsy Pawłowski and his wife and three children in June 1860: the village headman claimed that this reward should not go to the policeman, since it was he himself who "captured Jan Pawłowski the father, while the police only helped him to detain the wife and children of this Gypsy". There were plenty of complaints and appeals of this kind – although not as many as the financial bargaining amongst the eager catchers. What a long and sad way it was from the aims and intentions of the Manifesto of 1791 to this "implementation" of its provisions in a country no longer free.

Let us give one further example to bring this unhappy chapter to a close.

In 1861 a policeman apprehended a Gypsy woman, Elżbieta Dytlof, near an inn which she had entered with her four little children to buy them bread rolls. This was less than half a verst from her permanent residence. She did not travel, she earned her living as a paid hand, and she lived in the village of Zembrzus. None of this interested the policemen who were greedy for their reward, and they arrested her together with the children. The village headman, Olszewski, who appeared in defence of the Gypsy, wrote: "Finally the High Government Commission should take into account that the mother Elżbieta Dytlof, a widow, when she left her home... took with her her infant children, for two were little more than babies in arms... After the arrest by the police, the babies were also counted as adult persons, so that a greater reward could be obtained."

Months passed and 1862 was drawing to a close. The police repeated their demand for a reward for the apprehension of Elżbieta and her children. The official correspondence went on, and the year 1864 was approaching. Elżbieta Dytlof was now in prison at Chorzele, together with her children. There were now only three of them, "for the fourth, a daughter called Franciszka, died during their time in Chorzele, and is buried in the cemetery there". This explanation was necessary because the officials corresponding about the case could not make the numbers under arrest agree with the numbers originally apprehended. We know nothing more of the tragic history of Elżbieta, which was also the story of hundreds of her kinsmen. After the January Uprising, the autonomy of the Kingdom of Poland was finally abolished and later documents are not available.

The campaign to settle the Gypsies in the Kingdom of Poland was not successful, for it was impossible for it to succeed. There were suggestions that the Gypsies should be settled on government estates, making separate plots for this purpose, and letters reached Warsaw with the timid suggestion that often the Gypsies were unable to settle for the simple reason that no-one wanted to take them in. "The Gypsies for the greater part complain that the landowners, despite the encouragement of the Voivodship Commission... never want to accept them, and no landowner can be forced to do so." But these were simply voices crying in the wilderness.

We should recognize finally that despite all the oppression and injustice, and despite the total bankruptcy of the policy implemented towards the Gypsies in the Kingdom of Poland, the Warsaw central authorities attempted to prevent and counteract the dangerously excessive zeal of some local gubernya authorities, and did not sanction clearly discriminatory undertakings. There were various manifestations of excessive zeal among the provincial authorities. Thus in one paper sent to Warsaw there was a proposal that "Gypsies who are fit for work should be sent to prison, to be used on public works, and the children that are with them should be given to villagers to bring up. Having received recently seven families of Gypsies made up of 37 persons, who have all their lives wandered from place to place, whose wives and children and who even themselves are without shirts to their backs but cover their nakedness only with rags, offending propriety, the Voivodship Commission sent them all to the Central Inquisitional Prison and House of Punishment and Correction with instructions to make use of them daily for public works... Wishing however in addition that the children who are with them should in their young years be adapted to a better way of life, the Commission intends to distribute them about the villages to be brought up. Each village woman taking them should be paid a reward for her service, of eight Polish zloties monthly for each suckling babe and of six Polish zloties monthly for each child that no longer needs its mother's milk, which for a year requires a fund of about 2000 Polish zloties, from a rough estimate of the numbers of Gypsy women and children apprehended." This shameful proposal was firmly rejected by Warsaw.

Another and similarly iniquitous project was sent in by the gubernya authorities of Podlasie in 1844. This gave a list of Gypsies "who qualify for work in the fortress" – that is, who wandered in the forests of the region – and proposed that the Commission should order their compulsory employment in the Novogeorgevsk fortress. The governor provided the information that "Czechowicz, the son of Gypsies, 12 years of age, and the only one in the whole family fit as a recruit... will be qualified if the gubernya government takes the appropriate measures". In an earlier letter, this same governor proposed handing over all men of conscription age without exception to the army, sending all those over 30 to punitive battalions, those over 14 to work houses and the youngest as boy soldiers. The Government Commission expressed the following opinion of this project: "The proposal of the gubernya government is quite unjustified – the Gypsies are not exempt from the protection of the same laws that govern all citizens of the country; they should not therefore be treated as the last rejects of society, who do not even deserve that the laws of the country be applied to them. "Warsaw's reply firmly rejected the project: "It would be unjust to a whole class of people who have as yet committed no crime, to hand them over to the army or punitive battalions," and the women whose husbands have been sent either to the army or to corrective companies, "must from poverty become criminals or a burden on the community".

Thus the acts of cruel discrimination proposed by the provincial governors did not come about: the Gypsies' children were not taken away from them as the miserable provincial administrator had wished, and as was elsewhere practiced by the Empress Maria Theresa.

Nonetheless, the policies of the Kingdom of Poland authorities increased criminal behaviour among the Gypsies, the results of which can be seen to the present day, and also made worse the already considerable poverty of the Gypsy people.

The disappearance of the Gypsy crafts and skills among large groups of the population stems from this period. There still exist hair-raising descriptions of the conditions in which the Gypsies lived, their rags, the holes they inhabited. A German traveller who visited the Kingdom of Poland in c. 1840, wrote: "They mainly go about half naked, wrapped only in linen cloth, usually living in the forests and eating the meat of cattle stolen from pastures. The Gypsy hordes, which usually number more than forty or fifty people, can melt away with as much speed as they again come together. They receive no passports from the authorities, and are not therefore privileged robbers like the others". Only the wealthier ones lived in tents, while the poorer ones lived in holes or shacks in deserted areas. In winter, in regions where they were able to live relatively freely, for example in Lithuania, they split up into small groups and rented for themselves some room in the villages. But where the local law did not permit them to come out of hiding, they hid in winter "in caves, dugouts and underground holes, wherever a fire could be made and some sort of miserable bed be laid out: and in this case they are most dangerous".

The majority disappeared over the frontiers of the Kingdom of Poland, where admittedly the Gypsies did not find any more favourable laws, but where there were more unpopulated or inaccessible areas where it was easier to lead a nomadic existence.

In the territories of the former Polish Commonwealth which were now excluded from the Kingdom of Poland, the Gypsies were treated in accordance with the laws of the partitioning powers. In this period the authorities here used measures of terror against the Gypsies to an exceptional degree.

In 1773, Maria Theresa forbade the Gypsies to bring up children, which were forcibly removed from their parents to be brought up "in a Christian manner"; twice in the night a great general raid was organized, when children were torn away from the Gypsies and distributed among the peasants to be brought up for a fee. In 1782, the Emperor Joseph II, the same man who abolished serfdom and proclaimed an edict of toleration, ordered draconian measures against the Gypsies. As well as religious principles, the imperial orders contained a ban on wearing multi-coloured clothes and on speaking Romany, a ban on owning horses and horse trading, and compulsory employment in agriculture. These laws and methods brought certain immediate consequences. Not many families thus threatened and terrorized, settled down permanently. The remainder was forced into increasingly criminal paths of existence.

In the Grand Duchy of Lithuania, the policy of the Radziwiłł magnate family left certain traces behind in the form of settled groups of Gypsies. The Manifesto of the Commission of Both Nations of 1791 also managed in the last moments of Polish independence to procure certain results. Czacki noted that in the southern regions of Poland and in Lithuania about 150 Gypsy families were settled in villages by 1 June 1792. The Gypsies, "assured by the government that in settling in villages they would not lose their personal freedom and would not become tied peasants, showed their joy in settling even willingly in a few places, and in particular they began to have their permanent abode in ever greater numbers in small towns". But the partitions of Poland baffled the noble intentions of the Manifesto. One tsarist decree followed another, but the Gypsies continued to lead a nomadic existence, moving to those areas where they were less constricted. They were seen ever more rarely in Poland; they either moved outside the frontiers of the Kingdom of Poland, or hid in the depths of the forests. "Poland only relatively recently freed itself of the Gypsies. They used to live in the forests and in some rural settlements," wrote K. W. Wójcicki in 1830.

The Great Migration of the Tinsmiths and Their Throne in Poland

In the 1860s a new wave of Gypsies suddenly began to enter the southern territories of the former Polish Commonwealth. Long, horsedrawn caravans arrived, and new Gypsies appeared, who spoke a dialect completely different from that spoken by the Polish Gypsies, and who were dressed much better and more colourfully.

Leaving aside the smaller groupings, these were mainly two great tribes: the *Kalderari* or Kalderash (tinsmiths) from Romania and Hungary, and the *Lovari* from Transylvania. The former were engaged chiefly in boilermaking and all related trades, while the latter group specialized among other things in horse trading.

With the passage of time, the more vital and expansive Kalderash largely absorbed the remaining groups, with only the Lovari retaining some sort of autonomy to the present day. The tinsmiths were the wealthiest group, and their profession provided them with the opportunity for high earnings; they therefore enjoyed an economic advantage over the other groups which were more scattered, poorer and had no comparable efficient and coherent forms of self-government.

"We have received reports from Cracow," wrote a Warsaw paper on 26 September 1863, "that for several days the Gypsies, wild sons of the Hungarian deserts, have been camping at Błonie. These are not however the usual tramps wandering about our villages and small towns, begging or stealing for their living, but travelling smiths. They are beautiful figures, well-built, with clear features and piercing eyes; these Gypsies, some of whom wear Hungarian dress and others Banat-fashion in skirts. Their leader, who has a great staff bound in silver, like the marshal of the Seym or a doorkeeper at a great house, rules over the whole troop and deals on their behalf with outside authorities. Crowds of the curious have hastened to see the nomadic life of the Gypsies, and many have allowed their fortunes to be told, for if the Gypsy men are smiths, their women are fortune-tellers by trade; it is said that they earn more here than the men."

Events in the Kingdom of Poland – connected with the January Uprising – dissuaded the Gypsy caravans from leaving Galicia, and it was only a few years later that they began to penetrate further North.

"From Hungary they come in dense crowds across the Tatra mountains and scatter through the whole of Galicia in smaller groupings, visiting us as well," wrote the periodical *Kłosy* in 1869. "The men are chiefly employed in repairing tin cooking pots while their women, as always, tell fortunes by reading palms. The richer of them, to show a better face to the world, usually wear the rich Hungarian costume. We saw a group of this kind last year in Warsaw."

Wojciech Gerson left a portrait of a group of Gypsy tinsmiths at Saska Kępa in Warsaw in 1868. This group camped there for several weeks. Gerson appended to his drawing a note with additional information: "Their headman wears a short Hungarian fur coat with silver bosses and a staff with a silver ferrule and long hilt... Married women wear headscarves on their heads, tied at the back, and they have various gewgaws like silver coins, glass studs and pottery beads woven into their plaits; they wear necklaces of talars or often of golden doubloons... The men work as smiths and according to the citizens of the Praga district of Warsaw are skilful in their trade. The women, as is the Gypsy custom, tell the fortunes of passers-by."

The Polish Gypsies treated these newcomers with resentment as intruders. On their part, the new arrivals treated the "local" Gypsies with some contempt, since they were poorer than themselves and did not practice the profitable occupation of tinsmith. The mutual antipathy between the Polish Gypsies and the newcomers increased with time due to various forms of oppression and harassment practiced by the newcomers, either through informing upon the local Gypsies to the authorities, or through forcing them to accept their "tinsmith" royal authorities. This vital, enterprising and mobile grouping shortly overran Europe and before the First World War reached America. It is moreover difficult to say precisely where they came from and what made them undertake this mass migration.

Many factors undoubtedly contributed to the Kalderash invasion. Before 1856, in the Romanian territories Gypsies had been slaves, bought and sold by the boyars. In the 1850s, Gypsy slavery was abolished, and tens of thousands of slaves were restored to liberty. And within a few years, the first great hordes began to move towards the North and West.

The abolition of Gypsy slavery coincided with political changes: in 1859 Moldavia and Wallachia joined in a union, and three years later formed the Grand Duchy of Romania. In Hungary ten years earlier, Lajos Kossuth's uprising had broken out. These changes and upheavals, which disturbed the previously stable state of affairs, must have encouraged the emigration of the Gypsy caravans from their earlier centuries-long homeland.

This entailed a real migration of peoples: they moved westwards from the Caucasus and from the heart of Russia. Many of these groups did not stay in Poland long. However, a few did remain, only to move on further West a few decades later, in the period between 1905 and 1913. It was in this period that the second stage of the tinsmiths' migration took place: the caravans went on to France, England and farther afield, under the leadership of members of a generation that had been born in Poland, Russia or Germany – the generation of the sons of the newcomers to Central Europe from the Balkans in the 1860s and 1870s. In the first years of the 20th century they appeared in the countries of Western Europe, although smaller groups had moved, for example to France, in a somewhat earlier period, in the 1860s. But the real Kalderash invasion of Western Europe did not take place until half a century leater. 1906 was the first year when this migration was noticeably increased, and by 1911 the nomads were already in England.

In Liverpool and further afield, when these arrivals from the Polish territories were asked where they had been born and where they came from, they would mention Poland. Some, for example one Adam Kirpacz, later returned to the land of their birth. When Kirpacz's baby son fell ill, his parents brought him from England to Częstochowa in July 1911, and a month later returned to Birkenhead.

One of the groups which went to England came from Lvov, which they had reached from the Caucasus. One Miłosz Czoron stated that he had been born in 1858 in Cracow and had left Cracow in about 1890, after which he had travelled in the Russian empire for two years, visiting the major cities, before returning to Cracow. He did not stay there long, but travelled on through Silesia to Prague, Vienna and Budapest. He visited Transylvania and Croatia; three of his sons married Hungarian Gypsy women, and the fourth married an Italian Gypsy. Later, having travelled through Austria, Italy, France and Germany, Czoron reached England. His son, Todor, had his photograph taken in 1913 in Nottingham, together with his wife, Liza, and the costumes that they were wearing were also highly typical of those of the Kalderash who were in Poland at that time.

Sequins or talars, either as necklaces or as ornaments woven into their plaits, were very typical parts of Gypsy women's dress. Todor's dress had oval silver studs on the jacket and waistcoat, which are another eye-catching ornament of Kalderash clothes. These studs, which were usually silver, were of various sizes: they might sometimes be the size of a hen's egg, or even larger. Todor's father, Miłosz, had large, heavy studs on his jacket which he had made from gold in Italy and which were decorated with an engraved design. The poorer Gypsies did not wear decorative studs.

The "King" of the Gypsy tinsmiths in Poland, whose photograph was published by a British journal in March 1910, was dressed in a costume with this kind of decoration, which had long been worn by the Gypsies in Transylvania. A Gypsy named Kośmian who was staying in London before the First World War had been born in Warsaw, which he had left at the age of five, and had later travelled in Hungary, Croatia, Serbia, Bulgaria, Romania, Italy, France and Germany. He called the group that he travelled with "mixed" or international, because in his words, it contained various Gypsies, "Hungarians", "Russians", and his family – "Poles".

In 1911 a group appeared in Budapest under the leadership of Wojciech Kwiek – that is, a representative of a family which after the First World War was to provide a dynasty of Gypsy kings in Poland. This Kwiek came from Poland, and had been born in Galicia; according to his own story, he had in 1909 gathered together nine families in Warsaw to form a horde, of which he was the leader, and which later travelled to Paris, Belgium, Germany, Southern France and Trieste. This had been a very wealthy group, and his property amounted to 200,000 crowns.

In all of these groups the men wore jackets with silver studs and some of the elders – the caravan headmen – had the mace as a symbol of authority. Today, after the Second World War, these costumes have more or less completely died out in Poland, but before the war they could still quite frequently be seen. At the beginning of the 20th century, the Kalderash women on holidays wore decorated belts: sometimes these were silver, gilded and studded with gold coins, and with silver pendants hanging from them. Today, there are no traces of these rich ornaments: some may have been lost during the war, while others may have been buried with their owners. For example, Zofia Kirpacz, who together with her husband Adam took her sick son to Częstochowa in 1911, and who died in the same year, was buried in England in a massive, broad belt of silver. Maces and jackets with silver studs disappeared in a similar way into Gypsy graves.

"The Gypsy mace with a silver ball denotes the power of a leader of a whole band," noted I. Piątkowska in the Sieradz district at the end of the 19th century. This headman's insignia has today vanished without trace.

The last decades of the 19th century and first years of the 20th were a period when the Polish Gypsies were able luckily to travel more. It is symptomatic that even settled Gypsies at this time set off on their travels, and it was a period of a return to the nomadic way of life. Even those who had until recently been unable to travel, for example the Romanian slaves, now set off, leaving the country where they had been born, and the permanent roof over their heads to which they had become accustomed.

Like other Gypsy tribes, the Kalderash are also divided into many clans, which are often at enmity with one another. The larger Kalderash clans living in Poland include the Bumbuleshchi, the Butsoni, the Nonokoni, the Chandzhironi, the Gomoya and the Dzhurkoni. The names come from the first names or nicknames of the founders of the clans, or outstanding members. Not many of these are still remembered today: there is for example, Tsandzhiri, the king Janusz Kwiek; the Gypsy Bumbulo, the founder of the Bumbuleshchi clan, who was rumoured to have died at a ripe old age from a surfeit of sweets: according to this humorous legend, Bumbulo's greed was his only claim to fame and to the role of patron of the clan.

There might even be fights – or, rather, battles between individual clans at times. When these were over, the women would dress the wounds of the bruised and injured, and a cloud of feather down would rise up in the air from the eiderdowns and pillows that they tore up to do this. Sometimes a battle would result from the kidnapping of a girl by members of another clan, or sometimes it would be enough to cast a verbal slur on the honour of the clan for the menfolk to range themselves up with staves in their hands.

Within a relatively short space of time, the newcomers established dominion over the local Gypsies in Poland. Not only economic factors were at work here. The newcomers willingly made contact with government bodies in order to obtain a position of privilege among the Gypsies in Poland. The Polish Gypsies, who regarded appeal to the authorities as absolutely inadmissible in any circumstances, regardless of the aim of the exercise, found themselves discriminated against in relation to the Kalderash and Lovari.

The migration of Gypsy groups from the Balkans continued. After the First World War, this again increased, and was further stepped up in the 1930s. This was the peak period of Kalderash domination over the Polish Gypsies, most clearly and notoriously apparent in the usurped power of the Kalderash king, whose authority was kept in the hands of the Kwiek family. This family, eager for power, took the initiative in obtaining the title, but the idea was taken up by the state authorities, who offered them support. Some of the leaders of the clan groupings, known as *vitsa,* applied to the state authorities, sometimes directly to the police, offering their services in return for the recognition of their superior authority over all the Gypsies in Poland. Each of these pretenders to the Gypsy throne acted not only in his own interests, but also to reinforce and strengthen the position of his family group. The state authorities did not disappoint the expectations of these enterprising usurpers, and accepted their services, while at the same time acknowledging their power over the Gypsies. This opened up for these self-styled Kalderash Gypsy kings wide-ranging opportunities for oppression and exploitation of their subjects, while the state security apparatus theoretically obtained the possibility of investigating Gypsy society more thoroughly and of easier control of criminal behaviour. In fact, the services expected from the Kwieks proved somewhat problematic, for the widening of the scope of their power over the Gypsies in this way could not be effectively used in relation to Kalderash from other Gypsy groupings. Moreover, the sharp rivalry amongst competing tinsmiths hampered the exercise of authority by representatives of their families, and led to mutual blackmail, false accusations and settling of personal grievances. The Gypsy throne became extremely profitable, and therefore the dynastic disputes – the struggle for the mace – became exceptionally fierce. Sometimes there were two kings ruling simultaneously, and fighting each other bitterly, giving misleading interviews and making false accusations against their rivals. Some even claimed that they were rulers of all the Gypsies in Europe.

Under the guise of an attempt to emancipate the Gypsies and with public declarations of an alleged attempt to set up a state, the first tinsmith leaders who sought the Gypsy throne appeared in Poland in the 1920s. They made their presence and aspirations felt to the authorities and the public through various spectacular appearances. In 1928 the "King of the Gypsy bands", Jan

Michalak or Michalescu, applied to the Electoral Commission with a Gypsy list of candidates for the Seym and Senate, declaring that the Gypsies wanted to settle. In the same year, the "King of the Polish Gypsies", Dymitr Koszor Kwiek, went to the Government Commissariat to announce that he intended to pay homage to the president of the Republic, and present him with a gold ring; at the same time, he requested permission to purchase five Browning rifles for himself and his bodyguards. Shortly, these pretenders to fame and power were outshone by Michał II Kwiek. In 1930 he was elected "King of the Polish Gypsies" at Piastów near Warsaw, after his father, Grzegorz, had abdicated on account of his advanced age. The election took place under the supervision and protection of the Polish state police, and the new king did not spare reporters colourful details about himself, about his life as a globetrotter, and owner of a boiler-making factory at Poznań. Later at the request of the Polish government, he carried out at Cieszyn an all-Poland census of the Gypsy population, which showed that there were 14,000 Gypsies in the country; in fact this was only about 50% of the real numbers. In this same period, Bazyli Kwiek also proclaimed himself king, and there were often scuffles and battles between the followers of these two rivals. At this point, Matejasz Kwiek appeared on the scene in order, in his own words, to put an end to these quarrels and unrest. A few months later, on the outskirts of Łódź, he presided over a congress of Gypsy headmen, at which Bazyli Kwiek was elected king. Bazyli was a friend of "Baron" Matejasz, who announced: "Bazyli Kwiek has been proclaimed the true king of the Polish Gypsies, and Michał Kwiek is to pay a fine for abrogating to himself the royal title." The dethroned Michał was forced to abase himself by kneeling before Bazyli. And the former tinsmith headman began to exercise power over the headmen who headed the caravans. This however did not prevent another Kalderash, Mikita Kościeniak, from announcing at the same time that he was the true king of the Gypsies in Poland. In 1934, there was bitter fighting at Dąbrowa Górnicza between the caravans led by Mikita and Michał, for the latter, despite his abasement before Bazyli, had by no means given up his claims to the throne. After the battle, which was finally stopped by the police, Michał made an appearance at the Procurator's Office in Sosnowiec with a complaint against his opponent; he was draped with a red and white sash with a golden eagle and stripes of golden coins, and an inscription, "King of the Polish Gypsies".

Nothing more is recorded about Bazyli, while Michał II Kwiek became increasingly active. In October 1934, he set off for Romania where he participated in a Gypsy congress, and gave assurances that he was making attempts to "set up a Gypsy state in Asia on the Ganges, where we have historic claims to territory anyway". He announced that in connection with these plans, he was going from Romania to India. However, ten days later he was to be found in a wood near Łódź, organizing a Gypsy congress and election at which he was chosen king "for a further five years". In his election speech, he announced that the tax on horses was to be abolished. Only a few days later, King Michał II appeard in Czechoslovakia, whence he was expelled by the police; somewhat later he claimed at London's Hyde Park Corner that the Gypsies wished to settle in Africa. And that is our last news of Michał.

In 1935, Bazyli's former confidant, "Baron" Matejasz Kwiek, re-appeared on the scene. In a communiqué issued to the press, he announced that in November 1934 he had been chosen headman of the Gypsy nation, and that he was invalidating the title of Gypsy king, and dethroning Michał, the "tax extortioner". He also announced that the ex-king was abroad and would not dare to return as one who had "long been crossed from the list of honest Gypsies". After delivering this message, the "Headman" set about carrying out a purge. He nominated one Józef Kwiek "President of the Gypsy Council in Poland"; the latter travelled about Poland as a secret agent of the criminal police, blackmailed foreign Gypsies, robbed and stole, and handed over to the police those who resisted him. The headman gave an interview to the press, in which he said for example that "Mr Józef Kwiek is in particular searching for one kinsman who is very onerous to the rest of the Gypsies – Michał Kwiek, who is the chief organizer of many robberies, and recently has pretended to the Gypsy throne and has attempted to communize the Gypsies". Matejasz also stated that he had sent "delegates to the League of Nations to try to obtain part of South Africa" for the Gypsies to settle in. "In the beginning," he added, "we had intended to set up a state in Polesie, but we would have had to wait too long for that." Matejasz Kwiek was however soon to be shot to death in mysterious circumstances smacking of assassination.

In the spring of 1936, the former assistant of Matejasz, Józef Kwiek, announced preparations for the second coronation of the former King Bazyli; this was to have taken place at Równe, but the announced election was never held. It was not until 4 July 1937 that the coronation of Janusz Kwiek took place with great theatrical pomp; he was to be the last ruler of this type before the Second World War. Rudolf Kwiek, Janusz's cousin, announced that "perhaps dozens of hundreds, all from the most wealthy families" would be present at the ceremony. He also stated that the election of the king must take place in accordance with the rules, "for Mussolini, who has promised us Abyssinia, will only take us seriously if we are formally organized, and have orderly relations with the Polish state". After the election of Janusz, Rudolf Kwiek, who was disappointed in his hopes, took the title of dictator, and announced that he would build a palace at Bielany, and impose taxes on all the Gypsies. New quarrels, new denouncements, and new accusations against rivals were born in this atmosphere of hatred. Janusz retained the throne until the outbreak of war, and during the war he disappeared without trace.

After the war Janusz's successor was Rudolf Kwiek, his former rival for the mace of office, who declared himself King of the Gypsies at a congress at Bydgoszcz in 1946. Later he renounced this title, which was inappropriate in the new socio-political situation, and called himself the Gypsy President, and chairman of the "World Gypsy Council", a non-existent organization. However, in June 1947, Rudolf found himself in the dock in the Warsaw District Court. He had been accused by other Gypsies of collaboration with the Nazi occupying authorities, and of working together with the Gestapo in their campaign to wipe out the Polish Gypsies. The evidence of a large number of witnesses proved contradictory, and after some mysterious intervention, he was found not guilty. He died on 25 October 1964, at the age of 87. It was only three months after his death that documents were discovered that provided incontrovertible evidence that he had been a Nazi agent, who had voluntarily and eagerly aided the Nazis in their preparations for the extermination of the Gypsies. This information provided the full picture of this exceptional Gypsy traitor and police agent.

The activities of the tinsmiths' rulers, taking place against an operetta background of police involvement, and ending in a shameful and tragic finale of betrayal as a consequence of opportunistic moves in relation to the authorities, was something that would have been out of the question in the *Polska Roma* communities – communities whose age-old custom had forbidden entering into pacts with non-Gypsies. The hierarchy of Kalderash headmen and even kings could lead only to disaster, to dangerous degeneration, since in attempting to impose their authority over all the Gypsies from all groups, they had to draw their strength and influence from co-operating with the police of the state in which they lived. However, the Kalderash clans, as had been the case for centuries, aimed to make their elders consolidate their power and dominate the remaining clans. The king might be at the same time the protégé and the protector of his clan, and often – apart from acting in his own private interests – acted for its benefit. Therefore the attachment of the clan to its king was great and lasting, and legends formed around his memory. This was the case with, for example, Janusz Kwiek. His father had the Gypsy first name of Dzhura (which came from the Hungarian Gyorgy) and his clan took its name from his: Dzhuron. But after the death of Janusz, who had been nick-named Tsandzhiri, they changed the name to Tsandzhironi, to honour his memory.

After the war, irrespective of the imposed power of Rudolf Kwiek, "honorary power" still rested with the Tsandzhironi family; this was in the hands of Katarzyna Kwiek-Zambiła, the sister of King Janusz. After the death, of all of her six brothers, she was known as "the seventh brother", and until her death in 1961 enjoyed great respect of the kind that Gypsies usually paid only to certain men; she even had the right to take part in the sessions of the Gypsy court, the *Romano Kris*.

Condemned to Extermination

The Nazi plans of genocide placed the Gypsies along with the Jews on the list of those to be completely exterminated. Two years after Hitler's accession to power in Germany the shadow of extermination began to creep upon the Gypsy people. The notorious Nuremberg laws designed to protect "the purity of German blood", classified the Gypsies, together with Jews and Negroes, as an element posing a threat to racial purity.

The first step taken in the direction of extermination of the Gypsies was a statement by Himmler in December 1938, announcing that he intended to deal with the Gypsy question "in the aspect of their racial purity". In the orders then published, he provided for the registration of all Gypsies with the police, forbade the granting of craftsmen's diplomas to people who had no settled abode, and enjoined "racial identification" to determine the presence of "Gypsy blood". A wide-ranging campaign was prepared; the point now was to limit gradually the territory where they lived. After the outbreak of the Second World War and occupation of Poland, the Nazi régime continued consistently to implement its policy of genocide. On 17 October 1939, Himmler sent out regulations to all police and gendarme posts, forbidding Gypsies to leave their place of permanent residence, and ordering the police to supply full lists of the Gypsy population within three days. Six months later, on 27 April 1940, Himmler ordered the organization of the first transports of Gypsies into Polish territory, to what was known as the General Gouvernement, mainly straight to concentration camps, but also to Jewish ghettoes.

In Nazi Germany a *Reichszentrale zur Bekämpfung des Zigeunerungwesens* had been set up attached to the State Criminal Police, and this had for years compiled a detailed file on Gypsies living in Germany, and had effectively limited and controlled the scale of their wanderings and the routes they followed. However, in spite of police methods which were often harsh and extreme, they did not entirely succeed in curbing this intractable people who were not easily made susceptible to confinement to barracks. The Nazis decided to get rid of the Gypsies, bolstering up this decision with the theory that the Gypsies were endogenetically criminal. It was therefore "proved" that the Gypsies were marked by anti-social behaviour and criminality as an inborn racial characteristic that could not be extirpated. The practical consequences were obvious: the complete extermination of the Gypsy race. The small number of available documents makes it impossible to give a full description and analysis of this murderous campaign, but even so they are sufficient to provide indications of the scale and an outline of the bloody course of events. The necessary instructions and orders were given from the top, and the Gypsies became the victims of a slaughter the like of which they had never previously experienced in all their nomadic history.

Thierack, the Reichs Minister of Justice, wrote to Bormann, "With the intention of freeing the German national organism of Poles, Russians, Jews and Gypsies, and of purifying the eastern lands now annexed to the Reich as territory for the settlement of German people, I intend to make the Reichsführer SS responsible for the prosecution of Poles, Russians, Jews and Gypsies. My assumption is that the judicial system can provide for extermination of these nations only to a small extent... Poles and Russians can only be prosecuted by the police if before 1 September 1939 they lived in the area of the former Polish state... However, prosecution proceedings against Jews and Gypsies should be taken without observing these reservations."

The majority of camps for the extermination of Gypsies were located in Polish territory, and Gypsies were brought here from many countries defeated by the Nazis, and from Germany itself. The extermination was preceded by the publication by voivodship and district authorities of regulations limiting the stay of Gypsies in the General Gouvernement; these however only provided for the Gypsies to be confined to Jewish districts, and ordered the confiscation of their property. One of the reasons why the Polish Gypsies were exterminated for the most part outside the camps was apparently that the Nazi authorities feared that they would escape, since they knew the terrain better than the foreigners, they had contacts with the Polish population, and even some links with the partisans. The occupying power therefore speeded up the process of extermination, often giving up the intermediate stage of concentrating the Gypsies together before their final liquidation. This form of extermination without camps was carried out on the greatest scale in Volhynia. There the Gypsies died *en masse* at the hands of both the Nazis and Ukrainian fascists.

The campaign to suppress the Polish Gypsies was carried out with varying degrees of intensity throughout the country, and Gypsies who had previously been citizens of the Reich, but who were now transported to the General Gouvernement, were also affected. At the same time there was a campaign to exterminate Gypsies in the camps, especially the smaller ones. The Nazi extermination apparatus treated Gypsies who had long been settled and assimilated in the same way as nomadic Gypsies. Ethnic origins, and not the way of life, provided sufficient reason for physical liquidation.

The series of murders of Gypsies in the area of the General Gouvernement began in the spring of 1942. In Warsaw voivodship, this was carried out in two ways: some were shut up in the Warsaw ghetto, and from there were taken to Treblinka, while at the same time many were executed all over the territory of the voivodship. The Gypsies had been rounded up and sent to the ghetto from 1941, but the executions on the spot where the Gypsies were tracked down did not begin until 1942, and applied to escapees from the ghetto and camps, and also those who despite the order that they were to move to the ghettoes still lived elsewhere either openly or in hiding.

The whole of the campaign cannot be reconstructed and many aspects are destined to remain for ever unknown. Often, all were killed and there were no witnesses apart from the murderers. Nonetheless, from the accounts of Gypsies who escaped, or from accidental witnesses, a picture of these mass murders begins to take shape.

In 1942 the Germans murdered many Gypsies on the outskirts of Warsaw: 30 in Grochów including men, women and children; and several families in Targówek; in 1943 a great many were shot at Fort Bema; and at Komorów near Warsaw women and children were killed; a Gypsy family was shot in the woods near Żyrardów; in the Bracki and Giżycki forest near Sochaczew, more than a dozen families were killed; the same number were killed at Sochaczew, Końskie and Marki; in Warsaw at Sielce, seven Gypsy families were burnt alive in a wooden shed. At Jadów all the Gypies were herded together in the synagogue, and later all the men were shot. The women and children managed to escape in the night to Karczew, where shortly also the German police started to kill Gypsies, throwing children out of the windows into the street. The Gypsies had fire arms and shot at the gendarmes until all their ammunition was exhausted. Only a few managed to escape. In January 1943 twenty-odd people were shot in a village near Miłosna, including more than a dozen children. In October 1944, near the Kampinos Forest, the Gestapo shot 104 Gypsies, and only one man managed to escape with his life.

There were plenty more murders of this kind. The victims were those who had managed to escape from Treblinka, Majdanek or other camps to which Gypsies were taken from the Jewish ghettoes for extermination. In other parts of Poland, things were similar. In Ostrów Mazowiecka district, and in adjoining areas which were then outside the territory of the General Gouvernement in what was known as the Ostland, only relatively few Gypsies were transported to the nearby extermination camp at Treblinka. The majority were killed in executions outside the camps beginning from the end of 1942. In the Orło forests near Małkinia, there were about 300 Gypsy families in the winter of 1943. After they had been discovered, the Germans murdered mainly the children on the spot, and the rest were herded by bullets and dogs to the Bug river which was then covered with thin ice; the Gypsies were driven onto it, the ice broke, and they drowned. Those who committed this crime were functionaries from the nearby Treblinka camp.

Things were similar in other regions of the occupied country. In 1942 in the southern voivodships, there was a campaign to get rid of those Gypsies who had not been exterminated in the camps at Bełżec and Sobibór. In July, 30 people were killed near Borzęcin and a caravan of several carts was wiped out; in August, 28 men, women and children were killed in the nearby village of Bielcza; in the summer of 1943, 27 Gypsies were killed at Miechów; in 1944, 37 were murdered at Moczydło near the small town of Książ Wielki; 30 people at Krzeszowice, 20 near Zagórzyce, 12 in Wolbrom, 62 in Imbramowice, 47 in Żabno, 98 in Szczurowa, 40 near Pilica in the Olkusz district; 28 in 1944 at Lipiny in the Biłgoraj district. It was the same everywhere: individual families or people who had managed to escape from the transports or from the execution squads were tracked down and killed. Thousands of Gypsies died in the executions, and there would have been far more victims had not many Gypsies been helped by the Polish population, according to the testimony of survivors.

Apart from these executions outside camps, Gypsies were sent to the camps at Auschwitz, Łódź, Chełmno and other centres, and there exterminated; they were also taken to other smaller camps, where they were not separated from representatives of other nationalities. In the labour camp at Zasławie near Nowy Zagórz in the Sanok district there were about 500 to 600 Jews. One day, the gates of the camp opened and in drove six or seven carts drawn by single horses, filled with Gypsy families. In the night, the prisoners were ordered to dig a pit near the camp, on the edge of the forest... The size of the pit suggested that it was for a large number of people. The following morning, a dozen or more Gestapo men came from Sanok, and the Gypsies were divided into three groups: men, women and children. The men, who were beginning to show signs of irritation, which did not escape the Gestapo's attention, were taken into one of the barracks. When a little later these Gypsy men were brought out of the barracks, their hands were tied together with leather thongs. The whole group was then taken out through the gate to the edge of the forest, and there, at the edge of the pit, to the screams of the women, the children were shot first, and then the women and men.

The first, initial stage was, as we have already mentioned, the order of the occupation authorities that the Gypsies were to be put in the Jewish ghettoes. Among others, the starost of Ostrów Mazowiecka, one Valentin, gave an order of this kind, as did the starost of Warsaw district, Rupprecht in May 1942.

In the *Diary* of Adam Czerniakow, the president of the Jewish Council in the Warsaw ghetto, mentions can be found of Gypsies being transported and imprisoned there. Thus for example for 22 April 1942, there is the following entry: "Then Gypsy men and women, headed by their 'king' Kwiek were taken to the Jewish gaol"; on 23 April: "Gypsies were again brought to the Jewish gaol. A larger group is to be delivered tomorrow"; on 9 June: "Recently a transport of 60 Gypsies from Łowicz arrived"; on 11 June: "Tomorrow morning at nine 34 Gypsies from Łowicz are to be delivered to the Jewish gaol"; on 13 June: "Again they have packed some Gypsies into the lockup. There are now more than 1800 prisoners. People are fainting, every day there are deaths because of overcrowding"... "They have ordered Gypsies to be given an armband with the letter 'Z';* on 16 June: "Today on the instructions of the authorities, I released 190 Gypsies from gaol, ordering them according to my commands to wear a white armband with a red letter 'Z'. They have applied to the Service area (Fatigue duties) for armbands, for they had nowhere to go. For humanitarian reasons, I must take care of them, above all the women and children"; on 17 June: "The Gypsies are apparently to be re-settled outside the ghetto".

Dr Edward Reicher's handwritten account also speaks of the Gypsies' stay in the Warsaw ghetto: "One day in August 1942, a beautiful sunny day, a great procession of Jews was brought in. And among the Jews there was a separate group of Gypsies, differing from the Jews in appearance. There might have been 100 or 200 of them. There were men, women and children of various ages. There were some women among them with babes in arms. The majority of the men looked healthy and energetic, and the older ones wore sheepskin coats even though it was hot. The whole group went along Nowolipie Street in the direction of Smocza Street. The Gypsies differed from the Jews in their attitude, and buoyant step, while the Jews rather shuffled along. The Jews must have known for certain that they were going to their death, while the Gypsies obviously did not suspect this... A few days later I had an opportunity to talk about this to members of the Jewish police force, called the Jewish Order Service. They told me that the Gypsies had been sent together with the Jews from the *Umschlagsplatz* to Treblinka. In a few weeks a rumour reached me that the Gypsies had been gassed at Treblinka.

"The Gypsies were brought to the ghetto and locked up in the prison in Gęsia Street in the spring of 1942. During the first phase of the clearing of the ghetto (from 2 July 1942) they were deported to Treblinka together with all the Jewish prisoners. Early in October 1942, the Germans began to bring in new Gypsies from the Aryan side. In November 1942 several dozen Gypsies tied up their guard, took the keys and escaped from the prison, attempting to make for the Aryan side. The Germans noticed them near the ghetto wall and began to shoot, killing many of them. The remainder were taken back to the prison, and were sent on to Treblinka in the January operation of 1943."

The Warsaw ghetto was just a staging post on the way to Treblinka, where together with the Jews they all died in the gas chambers. Michał Chodźko, a former inmate of Treblinka, recounts: "The Germans sent Gypsies to the 'labour camp' at Treblinka with assurances that they would live in a camp especially organized for them in the forest... They arrived in Treblinka to set up their 'camp'. The procession was halted at the edge of the forest which was the place of torment and grave of thousands of people. Trustingly, the crowd sat down upon the grass; they were allowed to make fires on which they cooked themselves hot meals. A few hours later the SS arrived, and the men were sep-

_____
*Z for *Zigeuner,* in German, "Gypsies" – translator's note.

42

arated from the women and children. Their bundles of possessions were piled up in one big heap. The men were led off deeper into the forest... They were forced down into a pit a hundred at a time, and machine-gunned. Those Gypsies who remained were forced to bury those who had been shot – and who were often only wounded – before they themselves were pushed into the pit, and a further hundred people were deprived of their lives in the rattle of machine guns. The bodies were covered with a shallow layer of earth... When the men were taken away, the Gypsy women did not know what had happened to them, but when they heard the constant rattle of gun fire, they began to scream and wail. The Nazis at that point threw off their masks and ceased to dissemble: they no longer spoke of a 'Gypsy camp' and encouraged the soldiers by example to begin the most brutal massacre. They seized babies in front of their mothers and killed them by banging their heads against trees, and then beat the women, who were crazed with the sight, with whips and sticks. The women threw themselves on the soldiers with their nails, trying to tear their babies from them. This scene was only brought to an end by a wave of fire from the SS-men and soldiers surrounding the group. The bodies of the executed women and children were cleared up later by villagers specially brought in for the purpose: they were taken to graves in the forest that had been prepared beforehand."

It is also known that many Gypsies were killed at Bełżec and Majdanek, but we have no precise data, particularly about a camp as hermetically sealed as Bełżec. It is also known that many transports of Gypsies were sent to the death camp at Sobibór. In her written account, B. Stawska speaks of the transportation of Gypsies from Chełm Lubelski to Sobibór:

"In November 1942, the pogrom against the Jews and Gypsies began, and they were shot on a mass scale in street executions. The Gypsies were driven into the square at the fore of the crowd, and after them the Jews. It was cold and the Gypsy women were weeping loudly. They had all their possessions on their backs – including eiderdowns, everything that they had. But all that was taken away from them later. The Jews behaved very calmly. But the Gypsies cried a lot – you could hear one loud sobbing. They were taken to the station and loaded into goods waggons, which were sealed and taken to stations beyond Chełm, to Sobibór, where they were burnt in the ovens. I lived in a railway building near the lines, and so I was able to see these transports. In the end they even forced them to undress and transported them naked, because there were some who would take the risk of jumping off while the train was moving. Sometimes one of these transports would be held up for several hours. They would beg for water through the barred windows, but none could give it to them, for they were guarded by Germans who fired at people."

Łódź was the first centre organized for the mass extermination of Gypsies. Not a great deal of information has been preserved about the history of the Gypsies imprisoned in the "Gypsy camp" in the Łódź ghetto. No outsiders, apart from a handful of Jewish doctors, nurses and grave-diggers, were admitted, and these were almost all murdered later; moreover, the Gypsy area was strictly separated from the rest of the ghetto.

This special part of the Łódź ghetto was prepared for the first transport of Gypsies in the autumn of 1941. It was separated from the adjoining areas of the Jewish ghetto by a double wire fence and a ditch filled with water. All the windows along the border, on both the Jewish and Gypsy sides, were planked over.

Nazi documents show how carefully, indeed pedantically, this programme of genocide was planned. The transports arrived from five transit camps in the territory of occupied Austria to which whole families of Gypsies had been taken earlier. Successive transports were formed in accordance with instructions drawn up personally by Adolf Eichmann.

The first transport arrived from the Hartberg camp on 5 November. 200 families were brought there, including 229 men, 224 women and 547 children – in all, 1000 people. The second transport arrived on 6 November from the Fürstenfeld camp. The prisoners were kept for the whole evening and night in the railway siding locked into cattle trucks. Again, as on the previous day, 1000 people were brought: 147 families, consisting of 186 men, 218 women and 596 children. The third transport, the arrival of which was planned for 7 November, arrived from the Mattersburg camp on the following day, and was unloaded on 9 November. Again the transport brought 1000 people: 167 families, consisting of 263 men, 273 women and 464 children. The fourth transport arrived from the Roten Thurm camp on 9 November, and consisted of 160 families: 227 men, 226 women and 547 children. In all 1000 people. The fifth and last transport arrived on the same day, 9 November, from the Oberwart camp, with 172 families, consisting of 225 men, 247 women, and 535 children. This last transport brought 1007 Gypsies to the Łódź ghetto. According to Nazi reports, the Gypsies' baggage weighed on average 30 kg per head. In all, 4,996 live persons were transported and 11 dead bodies. The majority of the prisoners were children: there were 2,689 of them.

These were all the transports that brought Gypsies to Łódź. Although they arrived from Austria, they were not composed entirely of Austrian Gypsies, but also included – perhaps predominantly – representatives of the Kalderash, Lovari and Sinti Gypsy tribes. In the transit camps where they had been held before being sent to Łódź, the German authorities had taken from them all their money, gold and valuables, as we know from the register of property plundered in this way.

At first the Jews who lived near the boundary with the Gypsies, could hear music on the violin or guitar coming from the *Zigeunerlager*. The Gypsies worked in locksmithing and boilermaking workshops, use having been made of their age-old craft skills in metal working.

Shortly, however, the Germans forbade the Gypsies to play on their instruments which they had brought with them into the camp. There was now silence, broken only by the screams of the tortured and murdered and the bellows of their executioners. The Gypsies were in the final stage of starvation, in poverty, without medicines; they lay on the floor in the dwelling blocks assigned to them. The only thing the doctors were to do was separate the sick from the rest in order to prevent disease spreading. Soon after the Gypsies were brought to the camp, an outbreak of typhus had occurred. The ghetto health department received orders to send medical personnel to the Gypsy camp. Certain doctors and nurses (who were all to catch typhus) were assigned to the task. In the mornings they set off in an ambulance for the Gypsy camp, and they returned in the afternoons at about 2 or 3 o'clock. Dr Vogl told a witness called Kalman that he had been forced to sign death certificates for several dozen hanged or strangled Gypsies, giving the cause of death as "heart failure" (Herzschwachheit).

Abram Rosenberg, who at that time was working as a grave-digger in the Jewish cemetery at Łódź, records that "transports of killed Gypsies began to be brought to our cemetery... I noticed that almost all had been ill treated, and some of them had marks on their necks that showed that they had been hanged. After closer investigation of the matter, I discovered that every day the kripo came to the camp and ordered the Gypsies to hang their nearest and dearest. These hangings took place in the smithy at 84/86 Brzezińska Street, and the Germans from the kripo attended, including Schätter, Schmidt and Neumann...

"One morning in the autumn of 1942, at about 9 or 10 o'clock, a cart arrived, and together with the other workers I helped to take out the box where the corpses were kept, and at that moment we heard a whimpering sound. We automatically jumped back, but a second later I went up and opened the box. Out fell a little Gypsy child, and tumbled to the ground in a fit. With a pair of scissors I cut the rope that she still had round her neck. The child continued to cast around for some time, and finally fully regained consciousness. We couldn't understand a word she said. We workers who were there were trying to decide what to do to hide the child, when up came the cemetery commissar with the head of the prison, and ordered the child to be taken back to the hospital in the ghetto. But they immediately got in touch with the kripo, who took the child from the hospital. The next day the child was brought to the cemetery, by now dead. She had been bestially murdered. It was a little girl of three or four."

The mortality rate among the Gypsies in the camp steadily rose. In December 1942, 400 people from the Gypsy camp were buried, in comparison with 213 in November. In the first period, the great majority of bodies brought from the camp were those of children, with their clothes torn off, and they were buried in a specially marked-off corner of the cemetery.

The Gypsy camp at Łódź lasted for barely two months. Already in early January the final extermination of the Gypsies from the Łódź ghetto was begun. Both the seriously ill and the healthy were loaded into lorries which took them to their death, to Chełm-on-the-Ner, to the death camp, where they were all immediately killed. Not one individual was saved from among the prisoners of the Zigeunerlager-Litzmannstadt. And therefore there is today not a single witness in the Gypsy community who can tell of the events described above.

The experience gained with the Gypsy prisoners at Łódź was intended to help the Nazis in the organization of the largest centre of Gypsy extermination at the Auschwitz-Birkenau concentration camp. In the winter at the end of 1942, the camp authorities began to employ the Birkenau prisoners in the construction of a camp to which the first Gypsy transports were to be brought early in 1943. In order to avoid unrest among the population, the orders provided for the arrest of the Gypsies to be carried out during the course of one day for one Kriminalpolizei district, and on the same day all those arrested were to be transported in a train already prepared for the purpose.

The first groups of Gypsies were placed temporarily in Block 18 in the general Birkenau camp in January 1943. By March, the transports were already being taken to the Gypsy camp, and the Gypsies from the general camp were also transferred there. The organization here differed from that in other parts of the camp. This was what was termed a family camp *(Familienlager)*: in order not to arouse suspicion, families were not divided, and on arrival at the camp the Gypsies' clothes, money and baggage were not taken away, and nor – initially – was their hair shaved off. Black triangles were sewn into their clothing, which marked the Gypsies as an "anti-social" group. And on their arms, the letter Z *(Zigeuner)* was tattooed alongside their number. Long after the main group, numbering some 14,000 had arrived, Gypsy babies aged only three to four months were brought in from various orphanages and children's homes etc. under the "care" of their teachers and criminal police officials.

The Gypsy blocks – a group of 32 barracks – were surrounded in July 1943 by an electrified wire fence, and thus separated from the other parts of the Birkenau camp. Theoretically, the Gypsies were not treated as prisoners, but as "internees". Soon there were c. 20,000 people in the Gypsy camp, the greatest number being Czech and German Gypsies. But there were also Polish Gypsies, and smaller numbers of Russian, Hungarian, Dutch, Norwegian, and Lithuanian Gypsies, and in the last period a small number also arrived from France. The German Gypsies were the wealthiest. They were often circus performers, jugglers, dancers, musicians, and the owners of dance floors. By March 1943 for example, Gypsies were arriving from Germany who had served in the German army as ordinary soldiers or even officers, and some of them had the German military decoration of the Iron Cross. They made applications to the camp authorities, on the basis of their past services. The largest transport of Polish Gypsies came to the camp in the summer of 1943: this consisted of more than a thousand Gypsy men, women and children who had previously been concentrated at Szepietowo in the Wysokie Mazowieckie district, and had been brought from there by rail to Auschwitz. Here they were assigned separate blocks, but the Gypsies from the Wysokie Mazowieckie district remained in the camp for a relatively short time. After two or three weeks they were wiped out in the gas chambers. These Gypsies, just like the others, did not realize what fate awaited them, and expressed pleasure at being able to talk in Polish to the medical personnel about their native parts, and the idea of being able to return to them soon. Among the Gypsies there were a few Polish men who were married to Gypsies who had voluntarily accompanied the transports because they did not wish to be separated from their wives, and chose to stay together with them in the camp.

When this large group of Gypsies was being exterminated even sick Gypsy children were taken from the camp hospital.

Relatively few Polish Gypsies were left in the camp after this and those that remained were mainly from the sub-Carpathian region or Great Poland. These included members of well-known Gypsy clans: the Kwieks, the Paszkowskis, the Sadowskis, the Majewskis etc. There was a canteen for the wealthiest of them, where for very high prices in German marks, it was possible to buy something to eat. The Gypsies also paid in gold and valuables, and the possession of these also made it possible to take advantage of the venality of some of the SS-men and bribe them to supply food from outside the camp. But in May 1943, in an attempt to deprive them of gold, the Gypsies were ordered to put all their reserves of this commodity in deposit.

From time to time, transports of Gypsies were taken off to work. In 1943, several hundred were sent to the stone quarries at the Mauthausen concentration camp.

From May 1943, the health situation in the Gypsy camp became much worse. From the beginning there was no water supply, and water was supplied in barrels; only later was it piped. Medical treatment or surgical operations took place in the chimney conduits that stretched horizontally along the barracks, in view of the lack of the most elementary of hospital equipment. In the second month that the Gipsy camp was in existence, a primitive hospital was organized, but there were practically no medicines. Epidemics broke out. The mortality rate, especially among typhus victims, rose steadily and there were ever more cases of tuberculosis; illnesses spread rapidly. The Gypsy camp hospital came under SS administration. Non-Gypsies served as nurses, along with some Gypsies, although these on the whole played a subordinate role. The patients slept three to a bed, freezing in winter and stifling in summer. Their food rations were smaller than those outside the hospital. And they were completely naked in their hospital beds.

Between March and September 1943, more than 7,000 Gypsies died. In September there were about 2,000 sick Gypsies in the camp. Despite the high mortality rate, the barracks were overcrowded, with c. 500 people living in one block (10 to one bunk).

Mengele, the chief German medical officer, carried out anthropometric research and other "scientific" experiments on the prisoners. He was particularly interested in Gypsy twins as subjects for experiments and he placed these in a special barrack on a special diet. Mengele, the initiator of the extermination of the Gypsies at Auschwitz, ordered twins to be tattooed with the letters ZW (Zwilling). Mengele himself shot a pair of Gypsy twins in order to carry out a post mortem. The Gypsy twins were killed separately at the first crematorium in the presence of Mengele, who then carried out a post mortem before the bodies were burnt. On one occasion he ran into the hospital in annoyance, reviling the prisoner-doctors for failing when they had examined one pair of twins to discover tuberculosis in the lungs, which he himself had now found during the post mortem.

In June 1944, the initial steps were taken to exterminate finally all the Gypsies in the camp. In planning this, the camp authorities feared active resistance on the part of the younger Gypsies, who had indeed gained some inkling of what was afoot. The men had made for themselves long hidden pockets in the lapels of their jackets in which they carried razors and knives. The Germans announced that the Gypsy men were to be sent to work, and a roll-call was held of the Gypsy blocks. Those "fit for work" were separated from the rest, and taken out of the Gypsy camp. In this way three transports in all were sent, with about 1000 people. In fact however, they were not taken out of Auschwitz, but to the main camp, where they were housed in the ninth and tenth blocks. Among them were the former German soldiers and their families.

A rumour spread among the Gypsies remaining behind in the Gypsy camp that those young people who had been taken were to be put to death, or had indeed already been executed. In order to put an end to these rumours, the camp authorities loaded the Gypsies from the main camp into a train, which they then took along the railway siding that ran past the Gypsy camp. The Gypsies, seeing that the young people were still alive and "were going off to work", calmed down; they even shared their bread with those who were setting off on the journey. However, the train only made its way back to the Auschwitz main camp, where the Gypsies were again unloaded. From there, a further small transport was sent on to Ravensbrück and Buchenwald, but the remainder of these Gypsies were sent to the gas chambers and crematoria in July 1944. Only a tiny proportion survived: those who were transferred to other camps, those who had earlier been sent to work, and those who had been imprisoned in the general rather than the Gypsy camp and who were treated as political prisoners. But these were only a small number of individuals.

On 1 August 1944, at a few minutes past eight o'clock in the evening, the Nazis began the extermination of all the inhabitants of the Gypsy camp. All the non-Gypsy personnel had earlier been removed from the camp, which was now closely guarded by the SS. Six lorries were standing by the *Blockführerstube.* Mengele was also among the armed SS-men, wearing a uniform and high boots. The extermination programme was preceded by a sitting of a special commission in which the camp inspector, *Reichsarzt* Lohle, took part.

It was only when the first lorry-load of people turned in the direction of the crematorium that screams and sobs could be heard. There were however only a few cases of desperate self-defence. A German Gypsy woman who had been a *Lagerälteste,* threw herself at an SS-man armed only with her bare hands. Others dashed about the area of the camp, hiding themselves, escaping and shouting for help. The Gypsies were driven into the lorries with sticks. At 11 in the evening, the lorries drove up to the Gypsy hospital where 50–60 patients were loaded into one lorry and taken to the gas chambers. The whole programme was completed at about midnight. The whole Gypsy camp had been taken to death in the gas chambers, after which the bodies were burned in crematoria IV and V.

In the twenty-ninth block in the *Zigeunerlager,* one Gypsy woman and two children had managed to hide themselves. On the following morning they were found and immediately murdered. In the camp, a Gypsy man was also found, who was pretending to be a German. After the camp had been liquidated, he was sent with all the personnel of the former Gypsy camp to a penal battalion. But when on 2 August this battalion set off for work, the camp commandant called him back, checked his papers, and after making certain that he was a Gypsy, sent him off to the gas chamber.

The mass murder was carried through to the very end. More than 20,000 Gypsies died. The oldest victim, Hanna Tomaszewicz from Nowogródek, was 110 years old; the youngest, Wiktoria Ditloff from Szepietów, had enjoyed one month of life.

> *They took us through the gate*
> *They let us out through chimneys*

run the words of a Gypsy song that survived the extermination.

The Post-war Years

After the war there were, according to somewhat imprecise estimates, over 20,000 Gypsies left in Poland, who had managed to evade the camps, gas chambers and executions. Some of them now came out of the depths of the forests where they had managed to survive; others returned from the concentrations camps where they had not yet been exterminated; still others came back from the Soviet Union as repatriated persons. A very few highland Gypsies had managed to survive the war in the mountain fastnesses that their ancestors had inhabited for generations. They went back to their old occupations. The nomads did not give up wandering, and the settled mountain Gypsies again took up stone breaking, making music and smithery. The antagonisms amongst the different groupings had not died out: the Kwieks did not wish to give up the power they had usurped, and other lesser leaders of the tinsmiths even tried to take advantage for their own ends of the government-initiated productivisation campaign.

Initial activities in the campaign designed to settle the Gypsies and make them productive began late in 1949, with the carrying out of a Gypsy population census. By that time about 25% of Gypsies were already leading a settled way of life; the great majority of these lived in the sub-Carpathian region, and were from groups which had given up a nomadic existence long since. The state authorities began their campaign by offering material assistance to settled Gypsies in order to encourage the nomads to change their way of life. However, unfortunately, while intentions were good, there was insufficient awareness of the realities of the situation. The nomadic Gypsies still, as formerly, despised the settled mountain Gypsies as an inferior and foreign people, with whom they maintained no connections. For this reason, material assistance rendered to the Gypsy inhabitants of the sub-Carpathian region could in no way influence the behaviour of the remaining groups or provide an inducement for them.

Something which frequently happened and misled the authorities was that fairly large numbers of Gypsies would report, declaring that they wished to settle down. This usually happened in the autumn, and a few months later, in the spring, it was found that what they had wanted was simply safe winter quarters, always intending to set off again on their travels in the spring when the weather got warmer outside, deserting their place of residence and employment, sometimes disappearing in the night. In 1950 in the Zielona Góra region, a group of nomadic tinsmiths was employed by a co-operative, and to tin the boilers in the town slaughterhouse and the dairy at Skwierzyna. When it was suggested that they settle permanently, the Gypsy headman said that he would discuss the matter with the king, and a few days later the whole caravan disappeared, no-one knew where. In the autumn of 1951, in the Bydgoszcz region, a large group of Gypsies settled down; their children were placed in schools, and kindergarten facilities were made available. Attempts to persuade them to take work however failed, for the Gypsies stated that they did not need to work, since they had resources sufficient to last two years; later, at the end of March 1952, and therefore only a few months later, they disappeared unnoticed. At Świdnica, at an "explanatory consultation" organized by the local authorities for the Gypsies, one of those present stated that "life is too short for a Gypsy to work". This pronouncement was greeted with loud applause. Only a few took up temporary employment as a pre-condition for receiving a flat, and settled down permanently; but they treated their new home as a fixed point of residence, while still leaving it to travel in the summer.

By 1951–52 there was no longer basically serious pressure on the Gypsies to give up their nomadic way of life, and they gradually came to understand that they could continue to travel without too much difficulty. The more successful attempts at that time to employ Gypsies were made with the settled families in the mountains, where the nomadic habit did not have to be broken, for it had long died away. The poverty – often extreme – in which they lived meant that the offer of better-paid work was an inducement that they could not bring themselves to refuse. But here, too, those who were implementing the decisions of the central authorities made many mistakes which might have been avoided. They failed to take into consideration the completely different nature of Gypsy customs, social organization and ethics, and as in the distant past they tried to change at a swift pace all the habits and traditions that were deeply rooted in Gypsy society. Thus for example the employment of the Gypsies from Nowy Targ, who were the blacksmiths of the sub-Tatra region, as agricultural workers in state farms in the Szczecin region was doomed to failure from the beginning. Tempted by the provisions and new clothes with which they were supplied, they agreed to move to the other end of Poland, by the sea, in order to work on the land – which neither they nor their forebears had ever had experience of before. Their reasonably good housing conditions – incomparably better than their previous accommodation – did not help: the group of more than a hundred Gypsies began slowly to melt away; they missed the mountains, they missed their primitive forges, and one after another they returned to their native parts, abandoning the agricultural work that was quite unnatural for them.

An undertaking that seemed to offer greater hope of success was the employment of the Gypsies at the new Nowa Huta steel mill near Cracow. However, in this case too, the venture was only partly successful, where it applied to members of the settled mountain Gypsy groups, while the small groups of nomadic Gypsies – for example a 40-strong caravan from Nysa – after a short stay in the new town disappeared without warning or farewells. In 1952, a group of newly-settled Gypsies shortly before leaving Nowa Huta moved out of their flats into a nearby thicket, and stayed there for a time in shacks knocked together from planks. They explained that in the blocks of flats, they felt as though they were in prison. They too before long "left for freedom", to use the Gypsy expression.

Short-lived bureaucratic campaigns of this kind meant that the productivization could show but few and short-lived successes. Even the most exemplary Gypsy workers, when they had earned a little money, returned to their old mountain cottages; only a few stuck it out for longer.

The concrete effects of the first stage of the settlement campaign were therefore the employment of a certain number of settled Gypsies, and the registration in places of permanent residence of a part of the nomadic Gypsy population, mainly in the cities and towns of the regained Western territories of

Poland. Registration of this kind did not always mean that the Gypsies had settled; more often, the allocation of a roof over their heads simply gave a Gypsy family a permanent point from which they could set out for the travelling season, and to which they would return when winter began to set in. The kind of work that was offered to the Gypsies – unskilled, poorly paid and physically demanding – did not hold much attraction for them. However, employment was a necessary pre-condition for the allocation of a flat. Therefore, frequently, the Gypsies would accept an offer of work, only to give up the job when they had already been allotted a flat. After a short period of sitting out the storm, the caravans again set off. Just as centuries before, government decisions remained largely a dead letter. Opposition to the travelling of the Gypsy craftsmen, who had taken their tinsmithing or blacksmithing crafts into the uttermost corners of the country, began gradually to bring about the disappearance of the traditional Gypsy skills in these professions. The attempt to introduce settlement as an aim in itself, inevitably brought undesired side effects.

In some groups, after the loss of opportunities to practice traditional professions, the main source of livelihood became preying on the rest of society. New experiences brought about the reinforcement and consolidation of pre-existing tendencies and habits in certain Gypsy circles, whose only real contacts with the host society in a situation of mutual distrust and antagonism, were limited to links with the local criminal element and social outcasts. And often even when Gypsies did not turn to definite lawbreaking, tradition forced them to accept this kind of method of earning a living, or at least to acknowledge that it was a necessity and norm sanctioned by Gypsy tradition. The disappearance of most of the crafts that they had previously practiced led to a form of social degeneration of many of the groups, who specialized in more or less criminal ways of making a living. The women, upon whom fell the duty – harshly enforced – of feeding the entire family, which usually had many children, were forced to take up illegal ways of earning a livelihood, in the absence of any other skills with which they could earn an honest living. Anti-Gypsy xenophobia, which still existed in a lively form, and which would generalize and demonize symptoms discerned in ethnically foreign groups, could find confirmation of prejudices in these developments. Once again a vicious circle could be seen: the isolation of the Gypsies fostered and increased the animosity of the host society, and was at the same time reinforced by the behavioural consequences of this isolation: the preying by the Gypsies on those around them. To change this state of affairs requires a very long period and a great deal of effort. And above all it requires an awareness of Gypsy society, Gypsy traditions and psycho-social conditioning, their social hierarchy and behavioural patterns – awareness that at the moment is almost entirely lacking. The Gypsies are totally defenceless against all exploitation on the part of government officials. The shadow of discrimination in opinion, which is so deeply embedded in social prejudices, falls equally often on those groups of Gypsies who never break the law. This gives rise to feelings of difference and being wronged which, if not new, are always painful, and effectively hamper their social emancipation.

A resolution of the Government Presidium of 24 May 1952 on aid to the Gypsy population in entering upon a settled way of life is the basic legislation on further relations with the Gypsy community. This resolution enjoins Presidia of National Councils to undertake a "broadly-based campaign of educational influence", and also obliges particular official bodies to co-operate in providing comprehensive aid to the Gypsy population. The Minister of Education was under this resolution to exercise supervision over "allocating Gypsy children to schools", to provide material assistance, school-books, clothes and shoes, and also to undertake the teaching of all illiterates. The Minister of Health was to pay particular attention to their state of health and sanitation. The Minister of Culture and the Arts was instructed to supervise the artistic and musical work of the Gypsy community, and to send talented young Gypsies to art schools. The Minister of State Farms was to aid the settlement of Gypsies on state farms; the Minister of Agriculture was to begin a campaign to facilitate agricultural training for Gypsies, and to provide credit for those who wished to settle on private farms. The Minister for Small-Scale Industry and Handicrafts was obliged to support Gypsy manufacturing co-operatives and to help in setting them up. Finally, the Minister for Social Security was to provide care for those who were not able to work.

The implementation of this resolution was hindered by the complete ignorance of Gypsy society demonstrated by the greater part of the executive. Moreover, both those who drew up the resolution and those who were to put it into effect seem to have assumed that its provisions would be eagerly seized upon by the Gypsies themselves as a blessing, while in fact it was simply a plan thought up by the authorities which the Gypsy population bitterly opposed. At the lowest, local levels of administration, the provisions of the resolution often merely gave rise to formal review activities, and sometimes even led to irregularities. With hindsight, it is now clear many years later that these plans led only in a minute degree to observable changes in Gypsy society, and entailed additional difficulties and hindrances as side-effects. On the surface, the changes that have been produced are obvious, indeed conspicuous; the Gypsies no longer lead a nomadic life, and the number of illiterates among them had considerably fallen. It would however be worth looking a little more closely at these two examples of change among the Gypsies.

In 1964, without the passing of any special resolution or orders, the Polish Gypsies were forbidden to travel in caravans; and in practice this meant that nomadic travelling was made almost completely impossible. This did not however mean that social changes in the desired direction had taken place. Admittedly, the horse-drawn Gypsy carts disappeared from the scene, but after all, there are trains and motor cars, and Gypsy fortune-tellers are still ubiquitous, to the same, or perhaps even to a greater extent than in the past. Thirty years on, while illiteracy is of course somewhat less universal than used to be the case, it still exists, and the schools have been able only to teach the bare elements of reading and writing to a few. A Gypsy girl of twelve or thirteen is ready to marry and have children. And therefore elementary education has to end early – much too early to give the younger generation an opportunity to obtain a proper education. In the very few cases where individuals are properly educated, they usually leave the Gypsy community. And yet it is only effective and universal education that could provide the basis for the emancipation of the Gypsies. And this has proved a far from simple matter.

In fact, it is only their music-making, their playing of instruments, their dancing and singing, that has really received proper recognition, offering these self-taught artists the possibility of following their favoured traditional profession and offering them an adequate livelihood. But even this field of Gypsy activity operates without control or organization – it has become commercialized and receives none of the care and protection provided for in the 1952 resolution.

Many Gypsies emigrated from Poland in the post-war years. Among those who remained, the same divisions still remain, and the same legal system is still in force. The effects of the settlement campaign – known as the Great Halt – do not apparently go very deep. Children who have been born within four walls listen to the tales of their elders, and are waiting until the Great Halt comes to an end and the Era of Travels can begin again – an era which in their view is synonymous with Freedom. Twenty years after the ending of the Travels, here and there one can again see as before, Gypsy tents on the edge of the forest or in the suburbs of towns, although now there are no colourful horse-drawn carts. These have been replaced by cars or the railways.

A cottage beyond the village – a Gypsy headquarters that was somewhat isolated form the rest of the community – usually had no other contacts with the remainder of the inhabitants of the towns and villages, apart from this positioning. Relations between the Gypsies and their non-Gypsy neighbours are often poor. The old antagonisms grow and strengthen in new circumstances, and the fact that the old nomads now have a permanent residence rarely leads to integration, but more often to conflicts. In its most extreme form this could be seen in 1981 at Konin where there was an attempt at an anti-Gypsy pogrom. Sharp economic differences which sometimes occur between the "natives" who live in modest circumstances and the comfortably-off Kalderash Gypsies, who often receive considerable assistance from their relations abroad, additionally sharpen the animosities which develop, leading to quarrels and increasing the Gypsies' feeling of isolation. There were fewer opportunities for confrontations of this kind – that is, for obvious symptoms of these animosities to be seen – during the age-long nomadic period when the Gypsies were only passing visitors, who came from nowhere and disappeared into the unknown.

What lies ahead for the Gypsy community? What chances does it have? Has a beginning already been made? Are the present trends irreversible? Only the future can tell. And the answer that the future gives to these questions may be surprising, since history has provided us with much evidence of the exceptional resilience of this people, which itself has no historical memory, against all attempts at change, which are always treated as millstones tied around the Gypsies' necks. And if their path is to lead in the end to a non-nomadic resting place, then many generations will still have to pass before this goal is attained.

Despite the changes imposed from without, the eternal core of Gypsy custom has remained untouched, and guards the identity of this unique people, preventing them from melting without trace into the surrounding world. Let us now look, even if somewhat superficially, at the forms of Gypsy folk culture, both those which were observed formerly and which have already died out, and above all, those forms which have been preserved down to the present day.

The Four Gypsy Tribes

The Gypsies in Poland can basically be divided into four tribes, which differ in the dialect of Romany that they speak, in their way of life and in their customs. These are the lowland Gypsies, the highland Gypsies, the Kalderash and the Lovari. The Polish lowland Gypsies, the *Polska Roma,* were until recently nomads who had travelled in Polish territory for many generations, and whose travel routes did not usually cross Polish frontiers. They are therefore natives of Polish soil and treat the Kalderash and Lovari as foreigners. Their language contains a great many German borrowings, which appears to suggest that the forebears of these Gypsies came to Poland from Germany.

The Polska Roma have Polish surnames, usually ending in –ski. In 18th century documents these names do not yet appear, and the names used by the Gypsies were usually patronymics like Aleksandrowicz, Marcinkiewicz, Stefanowicz, and some of these have been preserved among the Gypsies of Lithuania. However, by the early 19th century the names that are still in use today began to appear: Majewski, Brzeziński, Dębicki, Krzyżanowski, Pawłowski, Piotrowski, Grabowski, Czarnecki, Cybulski, Dąbrowski, Głowacki, Rutkowski etc. The first stereotypical question asked by one Gypsy of another when they meet for the first time, is *"Savey Romendyr san?"* (Which Gypsies are you from?) This is not a question about surname or about tribe, for the surname is not a fundamental method of differentiation, and members of different tribes recognize this fact without asking questions. The question concerns the name of the clan or group, which is distinguished territorially: the Warmians, the Jaglanians, the Bosakians, the Tonakians, the Bernikians, the Plunakians, the Servians and so on. These groups are sub-divisions of clans, or result from the different times when the groups arrived in Poland, or later local inter-Gypsy patterns of relationships and territorial distribution of groups.

The Polish lowland Gypsies called the Russian Gypsies who travelled in Poland *Tsharnobyltsy,* and Galician Gypsies, *Galitsyaki.* These are also groups of Polish lowland Gypsies, but are distinguished from those which lived in the former Kingdom of Poland. One fundamental unifying factor is the preservation of tribal solidarity within the framework of Polish lowland Gypsies, and their acceptance of the customary law, and the authority of the *Baro Shero* (The Great Head). This has often in practice played the role of defender of the interests of "better and more influential" groups and individuals, making Gypsies lower in the social hierarchy dependent upon them. All quarrels and conflicts are usually settled within the Gypsy community, without recourse to outside authorities.

The majority of Gypsy men do not have any profession, and the whole burden of maintaining the family falls on the Gypsy women, who win their livelihood above all by means of fortune-telling. The relations between the *Polska Roma* and other Gypsy groups in Poland are marked by strong awareness of difference and can even be antagonistic. It sometimes however happens that a man will take a wife from a Kalderash tribe, for these women are supposed to be exceptionally good fortune-tellers and therefore can sometimes make a lot of money with their skills. Marriages of this kind are made by kidnapping the girl.

The Kalderash also like to kidnap girls from the Polish lowland tribe, for they are considered thriftier than the Kalderash women. However, in the main part, the Kalderash treat the lowland Gypsies with a good deal of contempt and some feeling of their own superiority. One element in this is the fact that the Kalderash, as an exceptionally mobile and enterprising tribe, who set out on their Great Travel less than a century and a half ago, feel entitled to look down upon Gypsies who have always wandered within the frontiers of one state; it is like the contempt felt by the free bird for household chickens.

Moreover, the Kalderash, even within the confines of their own tribe or even sub-sections of it, are not particularly loyal and often make complaints to the Polish authorities with false witness against their kinsmen with whom they are quarrelling. The name of this tribe – the *Kalderash* or *Kalderari* – comes from the Romanian language, *calderar,* which means a tinsmith. Since this is an exceptionally wealthy, resourceful and enterprising group, which has tried to keep "royal" power over all the Gypsies in Poland in its hands, the Kalderash have swallowed up smaller Gypsy groupings which arrived in Poland at the same time as they did. They are divided into many clans, whose names are usually taken from the first names of the original clan leaders. After the Second World War the Kalderash and the related Lovari began to follow a similar style of nomadic life to that of the Polish lowland Gypsies, of necessity confining their travels to Polish territory. It was difficult for Gypsies who were Polish citizens to emigrate, and their travels could not therefore continue on the earlier basis. However, the desire for long-distance wanderings did not die out in many of the groups, and this inevitably led to sporadic attempts to cross the Polish frontiers illegally.

The Lovari, who also now often work in tinsmithing, and the organization of song and dance groups, are today undoubtedly closer to the Kalderash than was the case a few decades ago, although they probably do not have such rich folklore. The name of their tribe comes from the Hungarian word for horse, *(ló)* but horse trading is dying out and can no longer provide them with a living. Nonetheless, their trading skills and abilities have not deserted the Lovari. They are not a uniform group: as well as the groups which arrived in Poland many years ago and whose present members were born in the country, there are also groups which arrived in Poland after the Second World War from the Soviet Union. The Michaj, Łakatosz and Kopacz clans, who live mainly in the Lublin, Wrocław, Poznań, Szczecin and Cracow regions, are the most important Lovari groupings in Poland. They, like the Kalderash, have their clan hierarchies, power structures and occasionally leaders who pretend to authority over a larger number of clans. Their leaders call themselves headmen or even kings. One of these kings, after the Second World War, was Jeluszka Łakatosz, and after his death his widow Zerfi exercised "royal authority" until her death in 1980. The Lovari consider themselves the Gypsy aristocracy, being on the whole wealthier than the other groups, and they like to surround themselves with their property – also after death. The tombs of their leaders are outstandingly magnificent, built of the finest marble, and sometimes crowned with a cupola; the tomb of "king" Moro Łakatosz in Wrocław is like this, as is that of Wasyl Michaj in the Bródno cemetery in Warsaw.

The fourth group, the Polish highland Gypsies, who are almost certainly descendants of the first Gypsies to inhabit Poland, do not maintain any contact with the tribes discussed above. Because of their way of life, and because some of the age-old Gypsy skills, for example fortune-telling, have largely died out among them, they are not taken very seriously by the other Gypsies, or are even regarded with contempt. They have for centuries lived a settled life, and live in the sub-Carpathian belt or in the Tatra mountains, in the area which is called the "Wallachian route". The districts of Nowy Targ and Nowy Sącz are the places where they mainly live. In earlier periods they eked out an existence only in dug-outs and sheds, while now they mainly live in wooden cottages, chiefly in Nowy Targ, Harklowa, Maniowy, Zakopane, Rabka, Biała Woda, Krościenko, Jurgów, Czorsztyn, Bukowina Tatrzańska, Czarna Wieś and Szaflary. These are the poorest Gypsies in Poland. They have replaced fortune-telling with begging, to which they are accustomed from earliest childhood, and their main occupation, which is totally unskilled, is stone-breaking for roadworks and more rarely, black-smithery – which a few decades ago was still in greater demand and provided a livelihood for some of these groups. The surnames of the highland Gypsies are either of Hungarian origin, like for example Gabor, or, unlike the "gentrified" names of the lowland Gypsies, are highland peasant names like Gil, Szczerba, Czyszczoń, Siwak, Dunka, Mirga, Oraczko, or Kacica. These are the Gypsy proletariat and it was people from this tribe that were employed in the building of the Nowa Huta steel works. Their language is a dialect which differs considerably from that of the lowland Gypsies, and has none of the German borrowings to be found among the *Polska Roma,* whereas there are many traces of Hungarian influence. In spite of their settled way of life, they have not assimilated into the host society, marrying mainly among themselves – although the number of mixed marriages has been rising over the last few decades – and have on the whole retained their Gypsy characteristics, like black hair, and eyes, and a sallow complexion.

This then, in very abbreviated form, is a picture of the four main Gypsy groupings in Poland, with a summary of the most important features that divide them. The Gypsy leaders who decide on conflicts and quarrels are separate for the different tribes. Thus the *Baro-Shero* (The Great Head) has authority only over the Polish Roma, while the *Kris* (court of elders) has jurisdiction only over the Kalderash. The dialects spoken by these four main groupings sometimes differ radically. In view of these differences and deep divisions among the Gypsies in Poland, the attempt by the Kalderash in the inter-war period to usurp royal powers over all the Gypsies in Poland was a self-evident nonsense.

Housing, Clothing and Cuisine

The traditional home – *kher* – of the nomadic Gypsy is three-fold: the waggon, the tent, and an ordinary roof over the head in the period when travelling is broken off, in the winter. Until recently, the Polish lowland Gypsies mainly travelled in canvas-covered carts, the roof stretched over arched struts. This sort of cart, which they called a *verden satrasa* (cart with a cabin) and which the Kalderash called *harnevo,* was basically only for travelling, and did not serve for living quarters in camp. But the cart with a canvas cabin disappeared among the *Polska Roma;* the richer among them later travelled in habitable vans, with a roof and windows, and usually richly decorated.

When they are travelling the Gypsies maintain contact amongst the caravans of the same clan, travelling by separate routes. This communication is maintained through leaving Gypsy patterns at crossroads and at camping sites. These patterns are called *shpera* by the lowland Gypsies, and consist of bunches of straw tied up in a certain way, thrown into the road at junctions, indicating the direction taken and even further particulars about the caravan that has passed that way; they may also consist of broken twigs, tied branches, a rag tied to a branch, or sometimes a notched bone. The Gypsies leave these patterns at places where they have pitched their tents, and these *shpera* are on the whole not touched by the local people, who fear "the devil's spawn" and spells.

The Kalderash carts are usually not *harnevo* any longer, but are similar to those adopted by the lowland Gypsies: something like circus waggons, but lighter and much smaller, known as *amvago.* They are at the same time a means of transport and a dwelling for the summer travelling period. The great circus-type waggons are only used as a dwelling for the winter period and do not travel with the caravans. If they have to be moved they are usually transported for longer distances by rail, or are towed over shorter distances. They are usually old waggons which the Gypsies have purchased from travelling circuses, while their *amvaga* are specially made for them in workshops that specialize in their production. The richer Gypsies, who wish to demonstrate their wealth in their carts, have the outside walls painted in multi-coloured patterns, and in the corners under the roof there are decorative griffins or dragons carved in wood.

These Gypsy dwellings on wheels are laid out inside like a one-roomed flat: there is a place to sleep, and sometimes a table and stove. This does not mean that the inhabitants always cook indoors on that stove: while they are on the road they cook over an open fire and a tent often replaces the cart as a sleeping place.

The Gypsy tent, which the lowland Gypsies call a *shatra,* and the Kalderash a *tserha,* is constructed in various ways and is of differing shape. It is however always made of long, broad strips of canvas, with poles and little pegs that hold the canvas down to the ground on both sides.

The Polish lowland Gypsies' tents are usually lower than those of the Kalderash. They are held up at the front, at the entrance, by one vertical pole with a fork at the top, in which another horizontal pole is fitted, which stretches along the top of the tent to fit into a fork in the top of a second vertical pole at the back of the tent. Each of the tent poles is called a *berand* or *sokh.* The tent is high enough to accommodate seated figures; the Polish Gypsies' tents are not usually high enough to allow them to stand up. The typical Kalderash tent can be higher, and is more pointed in shape. The angle formed by the tent walls where they meet at the top is an acute angle, rather than a right angle, as in the case of the tents of the lowland Gypsies. Each of the main poles has a name of its own: the front horizontal pole (or two crossed poles) is the *kovyetka;* the top pole is the *byerand* and is placed at an angle to the ground at the back. The tent provides only a summer home for the Gypsies, for they never travel all the year round.

According to contemporary accounts, at the beginning of the 19th century only the wealthier Gypsies had canvas tents, while the poor nomadic Gypsies built themselves shelters from branches and moss in deserted places.

The owners of the large circus waggons live in them during the winter. Other Gypsies return in the autumn to their permanent residences, or, if they do not have them, rent themselves rooms in villages in which they can live until the spring. Things were much the same more than a century ago:

"During the winter, where they are not persecuted, they look for shelter in country cottages, divided into small family groups; where however they are unable to find winter quarters safely, they hide in caves, dug-outs and pits."

The highland Gypsies, who have for generations been settled in the sub-Carpathian region, no longer use either travelling carts or tents. They live in wooden cottages, and until relatively recently – even after the Second World War – they also lived in dug-outs. The difference between these and the tents of the nomadic Gypsies lay mainly in the fact that these were not movable dwellings, but in their primitiveness and poverty of equipment they did not differ from a tent.

The Gypsy dress, especially of the women, which has been preserved to the present day, is generally considered to be their age-old costume. This, however, is not the case. Male dress has already almost completely lost its traditional characteristics, and that of the women has also changed considerably over the centuries. Only certain features of the female costume can be considered characteristic, and have been preserved in basic outline despite changes occurring over the years. These are the long, gathered skirts, the shawl over one shoulder, and the decorativeness of the costume resulting from their love of things that shine, and bright colours. Depending on whether the Gypsies are poor or rich, their costume will be more or less magnificent: the ornaments can be of gold, silver or copper, or even coloured glass beads.

According to a mid-19th century description, the dress at that time of Gypsies from poorer groups in the Kingdom of Poland, was as follows: "The Gypsies dress in sheets... in which two holes are made, through which the naked arms protrude to the armpit. The ends are tied at the neck, and this circular rag then falls in the shape of a Carbonari coat, light and flowing; the better to hold it, a belt is tied round under the hips, and this is the basic point. The belt and sash are decorative and on them are stitched hanging costume ornaments: glass spangles, gewgaws of metal, fragments of pottery, and all manner of other peacock feathers of human pride and vanity... Their hair falls in ringlets and is never cut... shining ornaments... on a belt of willow bark..."

In those days the Gypsies did not cut their hair short. The men wore it long, falling generously onto their backs and shoulders. Cut hair was in those days one of the signs distinguishing a non-Gypsy from a Gipsy. It is therefore not surprising that the Gypsies called the Poles *chin do bawo* (short hair), as Czacki noted. As we could see, even in the costume of the poor Gypsies described above, they made sure that there were ornaments, and that their dress was brightened up with spangles. This love of decoration was not to die out among the richer Gypsies: the ornaments became greater in number, more magnificent, and were made sometimes mainly of gold. It is extremely difficult to trace the metamorphosis to which Gypsy dress in Poland was subjected, because there is no iconographic material in this field from earlier periods. The earliest drawings that we know of showing Gypsies date from the mid-19th century. It is only on the basis of various fragments of drawings and descriptions that are not particularly accurate that an impression can be built up of Gypsy costumes in earlier periods – and then not earlier than the beginning of the last century.

"A poor Gypsy will turn and patch his coat to eternity, after it has lost – and several times at that – its colour and original shape, in order not to have to put on a rustic's russet coat. Those who are better off insist that anything that they wear must be so mottled and so strangely made that at the first glance it is possible to tell that the man is a Gypsy," wrote a contemporary chronicler.

Even in the same period, Gypsies from different groups dressed in different ways. A description of the splendour and magnificence of the retinue of the Gypsy king in Lithuania in the 18th century has little in common with the dress of the "coated Gypsies" dressed in sheets with holes, who were living in the same period and same region as the Gypsy king Marcinkiewicz. According to evidence compiled by Narbutt in the first half of the 19th century, the dress of the richer Gypsies from those parts was much more grand than that of the Gypsy poor: "He who can get for himself a padded wrapper made of chintz with as much red in the design as possible, considers himself the most fortunate. From thongs on his back or at his waist must hang his tinsmiths' tools, a leather bag sewed with brass fastenings, a tobacco pouch, a pipe, and a Gypsy whip... The women dress in what they can find, and a flighty plait, long and ebony-coloured, hangs down over their backs and shoulders. But in order to maintain a national flavour in their dress, they wrap themselves in sheets which are not sewn, but worn on the model of a Roman toga, draped over their arms so that their right arm, over which the sheet is fastened, is free and uncovered."

Another, rather detailed description of the Lithuanian Gypsies dating from a somewhat later period, differs considerably from the foregoing account. This description is of costumes which according to the author were "already gradually dying out" in the 1880s. At that time, the Gypsy costume consisted of a long, black coat, similar to a Jewish gaberdine, decorated with two rows of silver buttons about the size of pigeons' eggs. On their heads the Gypsy men wore black felt hats with a round brim and tied with red strings under their chin. There was black kerchief round their necks, tied at the back. On the right side, a large leather pouch hung from their belts, and on the left side, a whip. Their black trousers were decorated with a red thread, sewn down the legs. Unmarried Gypsy girls wore little black caps decorated with flowers and ribbons, and in their ears they had long silver earrings. Married women wore red kerchiefs on their heads.

Until recently the Kalderash were distinguishable by virtue of their more magnificent costumes, which were much more splendid than those of the Polish Gypsies. They had necklaces of gold and silver coins, decorative earrings, coins woven into their plaits, and wide silver or even gold belts went to make up the clothing of their women. The men had embroidered jackets and waistcoats, with great oval silver bosses, ornamental maces sometimes decorated with silver – but all this has now disappeared, although in part it lasted until the Second World War. To the present day, the Gypsy women have retained their earrings and the custom of plaiting their hair in two plaits on each side which are joined beneath the ears in one thicker plait. And finally the Gypsy women's long gathered skirts have survived, along with the colourful headscarves and shawls over their shoulders. The present fashion in Gypsy clothing was brought by the Kalderash from the Balkans in the 19th century, and caught on in Poland.

Some of the richer groups which are settled in the towns, especially the Lovari, have completely abandoned their different style of dress; they have however retained an exaggerated fondness for a lot of jewellery and shiny ornaments.

It is interesting that the Polish highland Gypsies who are completely settled and do not practice the traditional Gypsy professions, have retained specifically Gypsy characteristics in the dress of their women. Here and there, there are cases where a *Polska Roma* Gypsy woman who had abandoned the traditional costume has met with condemnation and antagonism from Gypsy public opinion, while the men are no longer obliged to wear any dress that separates them from the rest of society.

There are certain specific characteristics of Gypsy cuisine. The Kalderash like especially spicy dishes, and many of their favourite foods have been borrowed from the peoples of the Balkans. Horse and dog meat are forbidden, and this applies to most of the Gypsies in Poland. The most frequent meat dish for the wandering caravans is stewed chicken *(kakhni)* and chicken broth, since it is chickens that are the main loot of the Gypsy women who go about fortune-telling. A peculiarly Gypsy delicacy – considered one of the most tasty dishes – is hedgehog: *yezho* or *kanralo.* According to the Gypsies, not every hedgehog is edible. If a hedgehog that is caught (usually with the help of a Gypsy dog) has a "dog's muzzle", they let it go, for to eat a "prickly dog" of this kind is forbidden, just like the eating of dogs. They only take hedgehogs for baking or boiling that have "a pig's snout", that is, are "prickly pigs". The oldest and most primitive way of preparing hedgehog is to bake it in clay. The Gypsies cover the dead hedgehog and its prickles with clay, and place the resulting ball in the embers of their fire. The clay hardens as it is fired, and inside the hedgehog roasts; when the clay shell cracks, the Gypsies break it open and there is the roast hedgehog, with its prickles removed, left behind in the lump of clay. Gypsies also sometimes bake chicken or goose in this way, without plucking them first, and the feathers are left behind in the clay after baking.

Other typical Gypsy dishes apart from hedgehog are nettle soup, sour cherry borsch made with meat stock, and borsch made with formic acid. Nature does not begrudge the raw materials provided by wild cherries, anthills and weeds for typical Gypsy dishes of this kind.

It has, according to various sources, happened on occasion that when Gypsies have obtained a large amount of meat – a whole sheep, calf or pig –

which they were unable to eat at once, they have made stocks for themselves. Their method of conservation was fire, and their larder, a hollow tree. The meat was "roasted dry... and then buried in the trunk of a tree, filling up any cracks and sticking in twigs and brambles".

Gypsies like to eat mushrooms, of which the forests provide them with plentiful supplies. Many Gypsies consider one particular mushroom that grows on tree trunks an especial delicacy. Apparently, it is the Kalderash and Lovari who know and like it best. They call it *gelva* (from the Hungarian) or *prostavo*. It grows on deciduous trees like maple or willow, and unlike touchwood has no tough fibrous tissues, but is soft and curly. Gypsies are prepared to climb even tall forest trees to get it. They prepare this mushroom by cutting it into narrow strips, soaking it in water, simmering it and then frying it with onion, or they make a kind of soup, or sometimes add it to gulash. Dishes made with the *gelva* taste a little like tripe, and it is a delicacy not frequently eaten, since it is not easy to find this mushroom which ripens in the autumn, when the travelling season is already over.

Gypsy women are exceptionally careful about cleanliness and hygiene when they prepare dishes. This is all the more astonishing and noteworthy in that they do not usually pay the same attention to personal hygiene in the matter of bodily cleanliness or freshness of clothing. There is a special dish for washing chicken meat and other foodstuffs; the cooking pots are cleaned until they shine, and for example a plucked and dressed chicken is rinsed carefully several times inch by inch, the water being changed each time. When you watch this cleaning process you have the impression that these are procedures that are somewhat exaggerated, with almost a religious, ritual significance. The Gypsies like to drink beer (*wovina*), vodka (*bravinta, hachkirdy, tzhard-zhimow*) and wine (*mow*). It is above all the men who drink, and there is no small proportion of alcoholics among the Polish Gypsies. The Kalderash make themselves fruit cordials based on pure spirit, and the root of the herb known as "vag" (*Alpina galanga L.*) is also a favourite flavouring for vodka. This is also sometimes used by Gypsies as a medicine for stomach complaints. Herbal medicine is traditionally practiced among some groups of Gypsies, and they have a rich fund of folk knowledge and quack medical practice in this field. Gypsy food used to be cooked in pots hung over the fire, or on tripods. Now, the pots are placed directly onto the fire, sometimes on specially arranged stones, or small iron grids.

Only the women cook, but they are not allowed to sit down to eat together with the men. They eat separately, usually only after their husbands and brothers have already eaten their fill.

These observations on Gypsy cooking were made shortly after the Second World War, and it is difficult to establish how Gypsies cooked their food in earlier periods. Only descriptions of baking hedgehogs in clay, or drying meat and storing it in hollow trees are known – and these are culinary practices no longer employed today, although they may have survived in forest hiding places during the Nazi occupation.

In a description of Gypsies dating from the first decades of the 19th century, we can read: "Travelling and staying in forests, they often prepare meals in their own way; they bake vegetables and meat in gaps between hot

stones, and make pancakes from flour, which they cook on the live embers."
But since the time when bread has been easily available in shops, pancakes
have disappeared from Gypsy cooking, although the ancient name for them
has been preserved in the Polish Romany dialect: *bokheli* (probably derived
from the word *bokh* – hunger), which today means bread rolls.

Pollution and Oaths

The unwritten code of customary prohibitions, the breaking of which brings
the threat of pollution *(mageripen)*, provides the basis for respecting and over-
seeing the intrasocial order of groups of Polish lowland Gypsies *(Polska
Roma)*. This code, which is based on the specific Gypsy concept of law, is traditional and has evolved from centuries-old social experience; it is a collection
not so much of instructions for conduct as of lists of things that are forbidden
to Gypsies. In the absence of elements ensuring coherence in the Gypsy community to preserve its identity and separate character, like for example a re-
ligion of its own, this code defines for the use of the Gypsies the major models
for behaviour, norms for living in society, and leads to the preservation of
social cohesion within the framework of a group bound by unified customs,
and makes possible, or indeed enjoins, self-sufficiency and autonomy in laws
and customs, without reference to foreign, non-Gypsy authorities. Of course,
the *mageripen* code applies only to offences committed within the *Polska
Roma*, which are their own internal concern. It does not apply to conflicts with
the non-Gypsy world, nor to crimes committed against foreigners *(gadjé)*; it
regulates matters within the Gypsy community, and restricts the power and
scope of its prohibitions exclusively to this community. The prohibitions are
divided by the Gypsies themselves hierarchically into two categories: major
pollutions *(barey mageripena)* and minor pollutions *(tykney mageripena)*. They
can only be dealt with by Gypsy jurisdiction, for outwith this framework they
would have no implication of breaking the law. Fear of pollution of this kind is
still a vital force among Gypsies, and the practical observation of the
prohibitions, and the punishment of offences remains the unchanged domain of
Gypsy judges. The category of taboo pollutions which in the nature of things
cannot be the object of any kind of interest outside the Gypsy community, is still
solved by the *Shero-Rom* (The Head Gypsy), known at the *Baro-Shero* (Great
Head), who is the chief judge of the Polish lowland Gypsies.

The older Gypsies can remember only fragmentary details, of little significance, and stretching back only a few generations: at least during the period of three generations back that they are able to recall, this office was
inherited on a dynastic basis, although formally each time the Gypsies
elected a Great Head at a special electoral congress known a *Romano
Tselo*. The *Shero-Roma* that are remembered were until recently grand-father,
father and son, and it was only recently that this principle of *de facto* inher-
itance was broken. The first of the trio mentioned was according to the
Gypsies, a *Shero-Rom* called Basho, who acted as judge at the end the 19th
century and in the first decades of the 20th, and died before the First World
War, or just after it. According to the accounts of the older Gypsies, he had

five wives and five horse-drawn vans. Basho himself travelled in the first van together with his senior wife and her children; then after him, in order of seniority, came the other four wives, each with her own children. "He was a wise Gypsy," say the old people. "He was very rich, for each of his wives was a good fortune-teller, and brought him money. Today Gypsies know almost nothing at all about all this and it sounds like a fairy tale to them." Basho's successor was his son Daderusho, of whom, apart from the general opinion that he ruled and judged fairly, no further details have been preserved in the Gypsies' memories. Following his death after the Second World War, his son named Felush became the Great Head. He was also nick-named *Kororo* (blind, quite blind) because of the glasses that he always wore, and he was called respectfully *Kak Felush* (Uncle Felush). There were plenty of complications during his life-long term of office as judge.

Both Felush and the Great Head called Zoga or Dzhoga, who stood in for him for a certain period of time, and also the present Great Head, Wochi, were in office in peculiar circumstances – against the new background of the People's Poland, and thus in a period of exceptional difficulty for traditional Gypsy society. There were many new problems for the Gypsy authorities to cope with. It would however seem that the office of *Shero-Rom* or *Baro-Shero* is by no means on the way out, and that external circumstances which seem to threaten the Gypsies with gradual loss of their national identity have currently strengthened the role of the Great Head as a form of self-defence, which integrates the community of Polish lowland Gypsies and protects them from loss of identity.

The province of the Great Head covers the principles governing the taboo categories of the code of *mageripen* pollution, the ability to apply them in practice, and also appropriate interpretation, not to mention the accompanying rituals. The endurance of this unwritten code, which favours the maintenance of Gypsy ethnic isolation, largely results from the ages-long existence of the executive body consisting of the *Shero-Rom* and his deputies known as *Yonkary*. The regulations of the *mageripen* code, preserved only in oral tradition, have continued to exist as a social pragmatism obligatory for Gypsies, even though it contains no commandments or positive precepts, but is limited exlusively to matters concerning prohibitions. The worst offences against Gypsy law are beyond the category of ordinary pollution, and are particularly strongly condemned, and basically cannot be punished by penal sanctions limited in time, nor are they subject to a Gypsy amnesty. They entail for the culprit, known as *famuso* (infamous, villain, covered in shame) total life-long exclusion from the Gypsy community, and sometimes even lead to the mysterious disappearance of the culprit from the face of the earth. This category of unforgiveable sins against Gypsy society is sub-divided into two categories; those who commit these two categories of crime are known as *Phukaney Romengrey* (Gypsy traitors) and *Chorachaney Romengrey* (Gypsy thieves, Gypsy killers etc.). The first category includes all those who tell tales about Gypsies to outside authorities, Gypsy informers, police agents working against the Gypsies etc. "Gypsy thieves" and "Gypsy killers" are those who steal from, cheat or kill their own kinsmen, and in this way commit a crime against social solidarity.

Major and minor pollutions come only after these offences in the hierarchy of crimes. A decision on major pollutions, and also on their "removal" from the culprit, is taken only by the *Shero-Rom*. Minor pollutions do not necessarily require his personal participation in decisions and the attendant ceremonies – a *Yonkary*, the assistant of the Great Head, and at the same time a kind of deputy judge with lesser authority, is enough in this case.

We should begin a review of the various kinds of pollution with the major pollutions – *barey mageripena*. One of these is *dzhuvlitko mageripen* (woman pollution) and the closely associated derivative *oden podzhitko, terakhitko* and *mamitko* or *mamiakro mageripen* (skirt, slipper or childbirth pollution). All these apply to female "uncleanness", and the polluting power of parts of female clothing (from the waist down) like a skirt or a slipper.

The *dzhuvlitko mageripen* (from the Romany *dzhuvli* – a woman) protects the strict moral code which rules the Polish lowland Gypsies. "Uncleanness" does not apply to old Gypsy women, or to young girls before puberty. All departures from the normal pattern of sexual relations, as the Gypsies understand this – including for example kissing one's wife in a particularly "unclean" place – are punished according to the prohibitions of the *dzhuvlitko mageripen*. The danger of such pollution is not too great, in that the prohibitions deal with that area of human life which is most hidden from the eyes of outsiders. It would only be if someone happened to spy on such behaviour, or if the wife told another Gypsy about it, that the Gypsy concerned could be recognized as polluted.

The taboos associated with certain parts of female clothing are related to female pollution. One of these is the *podzhitko mageripen* (from the word *podzha* – skirt). This is one of the most highly unclean items of clothing, and has considerable powers of pollution. It represents a kind of weapon for a woman, and as such may be used in a special way in special circumstances for self-defence – which is of some importance in Gypsy communities where a woman is not a fully enfranchised, indeed is an oppressed, member of society. If, for example, a Gypsy has seduced a woman but does not want to live with her as his wife, then she can pollute him by throwing her skirt over his head. Then, in order to cleanse himself, the Gypsy must obey the orders of the Great Head to recognise the woman in question as his wife, or at least pay her an appropriate sum in compensation. A Gypsy woman is entitled to throw her skirt over a Gypsy man's head in defence of her own rightful interests as recognised by Gypsy law.

The role of the skirt can also be played by a slipper or shoe. This is called *terakhitko mageripen* (from the word *terakh* – slipper). A Gypsy man who is hit on the head with a slipper becomes polluted *(magerdo)*, and can only cleanse himself by righting the wrong that he has committed. Undoubtedly, this kind of slipper or skirt self-defence constitutes a brake on Gypsy men from committing acts of lawlessness against women.

The skirt and slipper female taboos have not disappeared in modern times in settled conditions of living, which have created hitherto unknown difficulties and complications in observing the customary prohibitions. Cases are known where Polish lowland Gypsies who had opted for a settled way of life, refused the flats that they were offered in multi-storey apartment blocks, and if they did accept a flat in a block, then it could only be on the top floor. The reason for this is simple, and is linked with the system of taboos. Gypsy men do not want to accept a situation in which women live over their heads, on higher floors in the block: if this were to happen, the man would be lower than a woman, in a way beneath her, and could therefore not avoid pollution. Basically it is the Gypsy woman, and not a *gadji* (foreign woman), who is unclean, for the concept of uncleanness does not apply outside Gypsy society, but, as the Gypsies say, "it isn't pleasant to be under any woman". There were no problems of this kind during the nomadic period, living in tents, although even then, during the winter, similar housing difficulties occurred though in those days they were easier to settle. In the autumn, as winter approached, the Gypsies would break off their travels and rent a room where they could have a roof over their heads until the spring. They had then to be very careful about the danger of "female pollution", which came with living in a house, and not in tents. For even if the house or cottage where they spent the winter was only one storey high, there was always an attic over their heads, and usually a cellar underneath. Therefore the Gypsy women were forbidden to go into the attic for chickens, or harness or parts of the tents, or to hang out washing to dry, since this entailed the danger of pollution for the men folk in the room beneath. The mere hanging out of female underclothes in the attic was not – and is not – allowed.

For these same reasons, foodstuffs, like for example potatoes, cannot be kept in the cellar in houses that Gypsies live in: they would be under the floor of a room where Gypsy women were living and would therefore become "uneatable". Therefore always in Gypsy homes you can see stocks of food kept in the living room or kitchen, or sometimes on the balcony, or in a cellar in the garden, or in a cellar in the building which is not situated underneath a Gypsy home.

Changes in their way of life, the general and indeed compulsory change to a settled existence, and also all kinds of surprises brought by civilization which could not have been foreseen and provided for by the age-old norms of behaviour, have sometimes produced helpless amazement among those who try to observe the Gypsy laws. In the early 1960s, a certain Gypsy woman flew by aeroplane to Cracow. When the plane was over the town, the Gypsy elders, informed of what had happened, fell into a rage and sent up curses to the heavens: "Hadn't she anything better to do than fly about over our heads? May God strike her dead!" A Gypsy who owns a motorcar will, if the car breaks down by the roadside and he needs to look underneath it, order the Gypsy women inside to get out before he does so, to avoid the risk of pollution.

The *mamitko* or *mamiakro mageripen* referred to above, applies to the increased and particularly polluting uncleanness of women during menstruation, and above all during childbirth and for a certain time afterwards. Irrespective of sex, no Gypsy is allowed to help a woman in childbirth, touch her or the baby, or eat or sleep with her. The woman is separated from the rest of the family because of this maternal uncleanness for three weeks after the birth of a baby, or in exceptional cases justified by financial and family circumstances, for at least two weeks. Today it is increasingly common for Gypsy women to have babies in hospital, but if the birth takes place at home, and the woman needs assistance, a midwife *(mami)* must be called, or at the least a *gadjo* (non-Gypsy) who would agree to deliver the baby. It is forbidden to shake hands with or to eat together with the midwife, other woman or doctor who has delivered the baby. The *mamitko* is usually strictly observed.

However, in some Polish lowland clans, the matters are not treated so strictly, and it sometimes happens that one may help a woman in childbirth in an emergency. During the period of puerperal uncleanness, a Gypsy woman is not allowed to touch kitchen pots, and has to eat alone from specially reserved utensils, which only regain cleanliness after three weeks, together with the woman.

Here, as with the other Gypsy taboos, the rational motivation for the prohibition *(mamitko mageripen)* on hygienic and health grounds is not known, although it undoubtedly originally existed, and the "uncleanness" is understood as a quasi-magical form, not requiring any practical justification, based only on emotional reactions of fear or repugnance.

Kushfawytko mageripen (from the word *kushfawo* – dogcatcher, butcher) is another of the major pollutions. It is forbidden to eat dog or horsemeat. Gypsies do not explain to themselves in any way the reasons why these dishes are harmful, or the reasons for the inviolability of these animals, although the original motive for the taboo would seem to be that these are the two species of animals that are most necessary in the nomadic way of life that the Gypsies have followed for centuries. Today, the Gypsies will simply say that this is "dreadful" meat and that no right-thinking Gypsy would let it pass his lips. A dogcatcher, or a horsebutcher, or someone who sells horsemeat, is also possessed of polluting powers, and it is forbidden under threat of pollution to shake hands with one of these, or to sit down to eat in their company.

Minor pollutions include *wubnitko mageripen* (from *wubni* – a prostitute, a woman of loose morals) and refers to the prohibition on Gypsy men having relations with prostitutes, and this applies also to "loose" Gypsy women – that is those who lead an immoral way of life. Anyone who seduces the wife of a Gypsy while he is in gaol is polluted, and the unfaithful wife of the prisoner is also herself polluted. These matters are covered by the *shtaribnitko mageripen* (from *shtariben* – prison). It sometimes happens that an innocent man goes to prison while the guilty man manages to escape detection. But the prisoner is not allowed to tell the court who is the real criminal, and he must therefore serve his sentence for him. He is however entitled to compensation from the Gypsy whose prison term he has served. If the latter evades this responsibility, the *Shero-Rom* will condemn him to isolation until he has fulfilled his obligation. *Chkhuritko, tovorytko, sasterytko mageripen* (from the words *chkhuri* – knife, *tovor* – axe, and *saster* – iron) are among the minor pollutions, which means that they are less shameful transgressions and carry a lesser punishment. During a fight, it is forbidden to use a knife, an axe or anything made of iron – this of course only applies to fights amongst Gypsies. This prohibition is only lifted in cases of self-defence, if a Gypsy is attacked by at least two assailants. It is also forbidden to wound, or even hit, a dog or horse with anything made of iron. It has sometimes been the case that even to threaten an opponent with iron has been enough to entail iron pollution.

There are many more other kinds of pollution, of which no few have already lost their Gypsy names. Sexual contacts with those suffering from venereal diseases are forbidden; sharpening a knife used to cut food on the doorstep is forbidden; it is forbidden to wash foodstuffs in a bowl that has been used to do washing or for washing oneself. For this reason, every family must have at least three bowls; one to wash meat, potatoes etc.; the second for washing the men and the men's clothes; and the third for washing the women and the women's clothes, for it is also forbidden to wash men's and women's clothes in the same bowl. It is forbidden to use standing water from a pond for drinking or for cooking, since human beings, and cattle bathe in it; this prohibition does not apply to river water. It is forbidden to cover oneself with an eiderdown which is upside down – that is, which has the bottom end for the feet at the top near the face. For this purpose, the Gypsies mark the end of the eiderdown that is supposed to be at the top by the head. The *mageripen* taboos are often used as a prophylactic to prevent undesirable events and excesses. There is a danger at Gypsy weddings or other special feasts that quarrels and fights will break out among the participants. In order to prevent this, at the beginning of the meal, the host will say to his guests, *"Kon hadewa mariben, dava khawa..."* (Whoever starts a fight will eat... and here he enumerates a great many polluting items). In this way, possible troubles are covered in advance by the curse of pollution and the risk of these undesirable consequences is an effective restraint.

In a fairly superficial summary, this therefore is the outline of the *mageripen* code in the field of specific Gypsy taboos.

In addition to this, the activities and duties of the *Shero-Rom* include the judging of disputes among Gypsies of a most universal nature – that is, disputes which do not arise from matters of Gypsy lore, but all problematic questions, family conflicts, injustices, wrongs or violence, which can in this way be dealt with by Gypsy authorities without recourse to "foreign" jurisdiction. This requires that the *Shero-Rom* should be a man of great experience in this area, with a sound knowledge of the complex nature of Gypsy affairs. The successive *Shere-Roma* who as sons of the Great Head had the opportunity from childhood to take part in cases of this kind therefore fulfilled this condition well: they had been able to hear the two sides of a case, and learn in this way to take over their fathers' duties in the future, taking over the traditional knowledge and skills that had been passed down from generation to generation.

One essential aid which constitutes a true support for the *Shero-Rom* in his adjudging of cases, and determining the innocence or guilt of a particular Gypsy, is the institution of the *sovwakha,* or ritual oath which verifies the accusation, and is a kind of appeal to God, or to Divine Justice. The Gypsies tell the truth when they are subjected to an oath of this kind, because of their profound belief that a lie told in the majesty of this ritual would inevitably bring down upon them divine retribution for perjury. Thus a Gypsy who is truly innocent and accused without due cause, does not avoid taking the oath for he is sure of divine justice. On the other hand, a Gypsy who denies guilt and does not want to admit that he committed the crime, is prepared to try all kinds of tricks in order to avoid having to take the oath. It has even been the case that a Gypsy who did not want God's punitive hand turned against him in this way, and not seeing any way of escaping from taking the oath, has tried to efface his own guilt by planting the stolen object on another Gypsy.

The *Baro-Shero (Shero-Rom)* demands that an oath should be taken if there is no evidence of guilt, and the accused claims that he is innocent and his accuser guilty of calumny. In these circumstances, the oath is intended to decide the issue. In some cases, with certain types of oaths, various ecclesiastical properties are necessary to reinforce the results and magical effectiveness of the oaths: a church building, a crucifix or holy water; other oaths require a human skull as a symbol of death. Depending on the gravity of the case and the importance of deciding it, either grave *(pkharey)* or light *(wokkhey)* oaths are used.

One of the most solemn is the *sovwakh kkhangeriakri* – the church oath (from the word *kkhangeri* – a church). Here the links with the externals of Roman Catholic religious ritual are more apparent than in the case of other oaths. This oath is taken in a church building while mass is being said. Sometimes, in order to increase the effectiveness of the oath, the person taking it approaches closer to the priest when he is sprinkling drops of holy water, so that the drops fall upon him. In a church oath, as in the other forms, the wording of the incantation contains a demand that God should punish a liar with death. It was through a *sovwakh kkhangeriakri* that the *Shero-Rom* Felush, who had been deprived of his power, cleansed himself in 1949 of the *mageripen* which had fallen upon him as a result of accusations made by his wife. A Gypsy witness of this ceremony recounted: "The church was full of Gypsies. The priest sprinkled Felush with holy water. All the Gypsies who had gone there were very moved, and some wept."

A human skull is another magical property used in "heavy" oaths. The *sovwakh moolikaney sherstyr* – "the oath on a skull" – was probably a fairly rare event, but it has occurred occasionally in recent decades. Gypsies buy skulls from grave-diggers or cemetery guards. They fill the skull with water, and having drunk it, declaim the following words: "I take this water from the skull into my mouth and drink it (as a proof) that I am not a liar. And if I am a liar, then may God break me."

The *sovwakh grobostyr* – "Oath from the grave" – is also based on graveyard scenery. A hole, known as the grave and symbolizing a tomb for the oath-taker, is usually specially dug for the swearing of this oath. The man taking the oath must be naked, wrapped only in a sheet. He enters the "grave" beside which a crucifix or holy picture is placed. The Gypsies taking part in the ceremony check that the accused has not hidden in the sheet or in his hair any pins, safety pins, earrings or any other metal objects, since metal "absorbs" the oath, and extinguishes its power, and thus also its consequences. It is not only at the "grave oath" but at all the others, that the Gypsies carefully check that the man swearing the oath has not smuggled in any metal, which would make it possible for him to lie with impunity. When he has entered the hole, the Gypsy lies down in the bottom and recites the incantation:

"God, you see my truth, that I did not do this. And if I did do it, then show me, O God, a miracle in three days, three months, three years, break me, dry me out, so that I lie in this grave." In addition to these oaths, there is also a "light oath", the *sovwakh momelatyr* – "with candles" – which does not require so many accessories as the one described above, and is probably taken most often.

68

The accused lights as many candles as there are persons involved in the conflict, and he gets undressed and recites the wording of the oath, after which the lighted candles are broken in half and thrown to the ground.

Gypsy oaths, a form of divine judgment, when they are taken either in exceptionaly serious matters, or involve some eminent individual, are sometimes taken in the presence of the *Shero-Rom* himself, who by his dignity and authority raises the gravity and significance of the ceremony; in general however, they take place without his participation. *Sovwakha* are means of unravelling the mystery of guilt, and in many cases make it possible to establish the culprit without using other means of investigation, or in other words, physical force.

A polluted Gypsy is expelled from the community, isolated even from his closest family, and he is not allowed to "eat and drink with Gypsies". In this way he is deprived of his rights to participate in society, and in view of the antagonistic foreignness of non-Gypsy society, he is in fact condemned to living in a social vacuum, to loneliness, which for a Gypsy who is used to living communally, is particularly hard to bear. Even if the *magerdo* (polluted) does not leave his caravan or flat, he has to live in a separate tent or room by himself, and he is not allowed to eat at a common table with the rest of the family. In order to free himself of the pollution, he has to go to the *Shero-Rom* or *Yonkary,* who will lay down the conditions for cleansing, and a date for the ceremony of restoring the polluted Gypsy to rights of Gypsy citizenship. When the Great Head condemns a man to pollution, he does so by striking him across the face, and when he removes the pollution, he pronounces the words, "You may now eat and drink with Gypsies". Then the ex-polluted member organizes a feast *(piben)* at his own expense, and he is the first to propose a toast of thanks and to drink vodka, then giving it to all present. This is one of the forms of reward for the *Shero-Rom.*

Felush, the grandson of Basho and the son of Daderush, the first post-war *Shero-Rom,* lived in the 1940s in the suburbs of Warsaw. In 1947 at a great congress, a *Romano Tselo,* the Gypsies deprived him of power, because he was polluted, since in a desire for revenge, his wife accused him of "forbidden caresses". In his place they elected a Gypsy who was aged almost eighty, Zoga or Dzoga. He came from the *Bareforytka Roma* (big-city Gypsies) clan, and initially lived at Służewiec in Warsaw, but later fairly often changed his place of residence, moving in 1948 to Silesia, near Legnica, and then to Pomerania, where he lived in Koszalin. Not all the Gypsies accepted his takeover of the function of the *Shero-Rom,* and in a way he exercised power as a sort of stand-in, since the case of Felush was not entirely settled. The latter did not give up his claims and in 1949 took a ritual "church oath", and having in this way cleared himself of suspicion, he was restored to his previous office by a further Gypsy congress called in May 1950. But on this occasion also, he did not remain in power long: a faction of the Gypsies, which had not been adequately represented at the congress which had rehabilitated him, now refused to recognize him, and renewed the complaints and former accusations. It was therefore decided again to summon a congress, which took place near Warsaw on 24 June 1952, in meadows near the clay pits at Szczęśliwice, a site which had often been visited by travelling caravans for many years. Many Gypsies came from various parts of the country, and there were quite a lot of Gypsy women representing their husbands, who because of some kind of employment (the "productivization campaign" on the part of the authorities had just been initiated) were unable to take part personally in the elections. This turbulent meeting again deprived Felush of his office and power. The Gypsies accused him of "liking various women too much", and they again ratified the appointment the venerable Zoga as the *Shero-Rom*. In 1961, nine years later, he died near Szczecin and at the congress to choose his successor, Felush was again elected to office, which this time he was to retain for life.

Every *Shero-Rom* is elected at a congress, the *Romano Tselo*. The participants speak out, nominating their candidates and speaking in their support. Finally the *Yonkarey* decide who has spoken "most wisely" whose choice was "correct", but taking into account as a deciding factor the views held by the majority. Despite the gaps in his exercise of power, Felush held this office to the end of his long life, and left behind him a reputation as a wise defender of the Gypsy community. As a result of circumstances of which we know no details, both his deputies, the *Yonkarey* Nyny and Rupuno were deprived of their former office and concomitant power. Felush himself, as an old man of ninety, became the hero of dramatic events which led to ill-health and his death within a year.

In 1974, in the street in Kutno where he lived in his final years, and where he adjudged Gypsy conflicts and pronounced verdicts in questions of pollution, he was suddenly attacked by a Gypsy woman, who hit him several hard blows with a stone wrapped in a scarf, and ran away.

Apparently the motive for this attack was a desire for revenge following a judgment by Felush on a member of her family. The fact alone that the chief judge of the Polish Gypsies was attacked by a member of his own community is something quite unheard of, and undoubtedly indicates the dissolution of the strict observance of traditional Gypsy customs; it is a symptom, if admittedly an isolated one, of the shaking of the centuries old hierarchy and weakening of the authority of the Gypsy system of self-government.

The Gypsy woman was beaten for her attack on the Great Head, but this was not the only direct consequence of this incident. Immediately after he had recovered, Felush summoned a public court known as a *Tsachipen* (truth, law) at Łódź on 2 August 1974. Here the *Shero-Rom* appeared in a three-fold role: as the injured party, as the prosecutor and as the chief judge. His attacker and all her family were punished, according to rumour, by pollution – *mageripen* – for life in the category of *famooso,* or infamy.

At this Łódź congress, Felush did not content himself with judging the question of this assault of which he himself had been the victim, but also announced publicly a series of particular prohibitions designed to protect tradition from innovations stemming from outside developments. He therefore warned against – on pain of pollution – the wearing of the tight trousers which were currently so fashionable, and forbade Gypsy men to wear them; he forbade Gypsy women to wear trousers or mini-skirts, to cut their hair short or to dye or bleach it, or to paint their finger-nails. He treated these apparently minor and superficial matters as dangerous steps in the direction of more profound and undesirable change, which would lead to the disappearance of separate identity in customs, and to social anarchy which would entail a threat to the very existence of Gipsy society. The "last words" of the venerable Felush, pronounced on his death-bed, also made a strong impression upon the Gypsy community. This spiritual testament of the Gypsy leader was tape-recorded by the Gypsy elders who had been invited for this solemn occasion, and testifies to the feeling of responsibility for the fate of his people that this Gypsy leader had as he was departing this life – responsibility for a people that was currently passing through a period of exceptionally grave threat to its continued existence as a separate community.

In his last speech, Felush did not refer to personal matters, but only to the problems of the Gypsy community. He appealed to clan representatives who had been summoned, to ensure the preservation of native traditions and to oppose external threats, which were growing in strength and becoming a real danger.

Kak Felush-Kororo died at Opole in July 1975, having, according to the Gypsies, reached the age of 92. The Polish lowland Gypsies thronged to his funeral, with the Pluniak clan, from which Felush came, represented in the greatest numbers. His last instructions, precepts and decisions were regarded as binding both upon his successor and upon the whole of the Gypsy community. In his last words, he again called for the strict observation of the *mage-ripen* (pollution) taboos, and the rejection of all innovations that went against the traditional customs. Of course, the ideas that he held about this tradition were relative, since for example Felush forbade Gypsy men to grow their hair long – in line with the current universal non-Gypsy fashion – unaware that his forebears had always had long hair. In his last words, Felush raised the question of the duty of Gypsy self-government, but also allowed for acknowledging the necessity in exceptional cases of certain departures from the general principles, if these were departures which were in the interests of the Gypsy community. For example, he announced that the prohibition on make-up, dying hair or inappropriate clothing ceased to apply in the event that a change of this kind was necessary and of practical benefit in connection with a job, or with particular forms of employment of Gypsy women. This mainly applied to the dancers and singers appearing in professional ensembles. Gypsy fortune-tellers in the nature of things still retain the traditional costume and appearance.

In his last speech, the *Shero-Rom* Felush also pronounced a general amnesty, removing all the pollutions currently in force against Gypsies and annulling all other Gypsy judgments currently in operation. He only exempted from this amnesty matters connected with debt, and two – or really three – categories of the most severe offences: *phukkaney romengrey* (tale-telling, betrayal of Gypsy affairs to outsiders, collaboration with the police against Gypsy interests etc.), and *zora-chaney romengrey* (Gypsy stealing and Gypsy murder, i.e., crimes committed against Gypsy kinsmen). This second category also includes the concept of *chochaney romengrey,* referring to cheating – that is, Gypsies who cheat their fellow-Gypsies. The Gypsies compared this general amnesty because of its wide-ranging scope and significance, with that declared immediately after the war, when the *Shero-Rom* lifted all the pollutions which had been incurred during the war, during the period of mass extermination of the Gypsies by the Nazis. In these exceptionally difficult circumstances, they must in their forest hiding-places have been forced to commit polluting acts against the *mageripen* taboos: for example eating the meat of dead horses to save their lives when they were starving.

A year's mourning was declared after the death of Felush. It was only when this had passed, in 1976, that the Gypsies gathered at Radom for a *Romano-Tselo* where they elected the next *Shero-Rom,* Felush's cousin, Wochi. Thus on this occasion also, power remained in more or less the same family, although the succession passed over Felush's son Lidko, the direct heir, since at the time of the initial debates on the choice of a successor he was in prison, serving a sentence passed by the courts.

Wochi has remained in power. Fragmentary information available on the way he has exercised his office as *Shero-Rom* seems to indicate that he has tried to dissuade the Gypsies from taking quarrels amongst themselves to the state courts for settlement. A Gypsy singer called Randia had taken to the state court in the 1960s a young Gypsy who had kidnapped her and attempted to keep her with him. This however had been a case where a member of a different tribe was involved. Gypsies who got married in state registry offices have now to apply for divorce to the state courts, whereas earlier contacts between the Polish Gypsies and the judicial system had not taken place on the initiatives of the Gypsies, but only when the Polish police had uncovered some law-breaking on their part. This process of gradual emergence of the Gypsies from their ethnic enclave was bound to disturb the Gypsy elders, and lead them to take various steps to counteract the developments. The *Shero-Rom,* like his predecessors, is *ex officio* called upon to restrain all disintegrative and assimilational tendencies of this kind.

The *Shero-Rom* and those close to him constitute the only authorities accepted by the Gypsies who are subject to them. These authentically Gypsy authorities not only do not attempt to gain wider renown in the outside world (unlike the self-styled "Gypsy kings" from the Kalderash tribe, who ceaselessly attempted to publicize themselves), but on the contrary deliberately conceal themselves in the shadows of Gypsy society, are unknown to the uninitiated and have been to date unnoticed by outsiders.

The danger for these authorities and the state of affairs which they defend, lies not in inexpertly-organized campaigns and other a-legal activities of the Polish administration. Of the many elements which make up the whole of broadly-conceived Gypsy folk culture – in conditions of exceptional oppression, and in moments of particular danger – the most lasting and most resistant, or even advancing, factor has proved to be self-defensive vital elements of a criminal nature. Other components of the Gypsy lore, specific characteristics of Gypsy customs, are more or less in decline, weakening and on the defensive, in view of the pressure from various forms of technological and civilizational change, like motorization, television etc. One exception here, which has also undergone some circumstantial change, is the art of music and dancing, which has been made use of by the State Song and Dance Performance Enterprise, and has provided a small number of Gypsies with a way of earning an honest living. The Gypsies practice unlicensed trading in Poland illegally, and there is no possibility of further expansion in this field; craft skills have almost completely died away among them. In this situation, criminality, all forms of social parasitism which are a part of Gypsy tradition, are flourishing while the rest of the aspects of custom and culture, even in the linguistic sphere, are gradually but noticeably regressing.

The defensive action undertaken by Gypsy groups, represented and symbolized by the *Shero-Rom,* is a struggle for the very existence of the Gypsy community, which after being deprived of the age-old right to lead a nomadic life, wished to retain its right to exist for as long as possible.

The polluting taboos of *mageripen,* the power of the *Shero-Rom* and the *Sovwakha* in the form described here, are binding only upon the Polish lowland Gypsies, the *Polska Roma.* The Kalderash, the representatives of the Gypsy tinsmiths, also have their taboos and oaths, but they do not have individual power of the kind enjoyed by the *Baro-Shero.* Most of the prohibitions have lost their names in this community, and some of the taboos observed by the lowland Gypsies have no significance for them. Thus for example they have no "iron pollution", and as a consequence, the use of knives in a fight is not basically forbidden for them. The prohibition on eating horsemeat is also not rigorously observed as a pollution, although the Kalderash also tend not to eat it. But the prohibition on using one bowl for ablutions, laundry and washing meat which forces the lowland Gypsies to use three separate bowls for these purposes, is even more strictly observed by the Kalderash. They have to have even as many as five or six bowls of which one is for washing the feet, the floor, trousers and men's underwear; the second is for washing table-cloths, shirts and aprons; the third is for washing children's clothes; the fourth is for preparing food, washing meat etc.; and the fifth for washing themselves. The tinsmiths have two terms to denote the uncleanness resulting from taboo: *pikilimiyey,* which means a polluted person, uncleanness as a result of pollution, and *mahrimiyey,* which denotes the polluting object (uncleanness of women, a skirt, slipper), and the act of pollution itself. The family of the polluted person informs a representative of the clans about a case of pollution and the place where the case will be heard and decided. The elders of the clan take personal part in a case of this kind – the *Romano Kris.* Here too, as with the lowland Gypsies, the ceremony of oath-taking *(sowakh)* is practiced to confirm that someone is telling the truth. The polluted person is isolated from the rest of the Gypsies, and if he has a family and children, they are all placed in isolation along with him. Only the Gypsy council of elders, called the *Kris,* can revoke a pollution, and a hearing takes place at the request of the polluted Gypsy. The council of elders is made up of from a dozen to several dozen Gypsies. Every senior man who is respected in his clan and among his kinsmen, can be a member of this council. It is a kind of Gypsy court, a collegiate body, which plays the same role as the *Baro-Shero* among the lowland Gypsies. The *Kris* lays down a date when someone is to be cleansed of his pollution. One of the members of the council presides over the meeting and the trial, and his voice is held to be deciding.

Apart from decisions to expel the culprit from the Gypsy community, fines are also imposed, which are mainly paid in gold, and the level of which is computed in "ducats" *(gawby)* – that is, in gold dollars or roubles which constitute the main currency in circulation among the Kalderash for intra-Gypsy transactions. The man upon whom the fine is imposed need not pay it in gold coins but must pay the equivalent in Polish currency. Fines of this kind are imposed for crimes committed against kinsmen, and the sum is paid to the victim, part of which he then spends on a feast for the members of the *Kris*. Over the years since the war, and in particular during the past decade many Kalderash families have emigrated, and for example in Sweden have formed large groups of Gypsies newly arrived from Poland. They include no small number of "great Gypsies" who played an important role in the Kalderash community in Poland and were respected members of the council of elders. Thus the calling together of the *Romano Kris* court in Poland among those Gypsies who have remained has become ever more difficult; Gypsy authority has become ever more problematic and the continuing of traditional customs has become increasingly undermined. The Lovari tribe Gypsies, who mainly live in Wrocław and Szczecin and the surrounding areas, have still retained relatively strong ties, based on the observation of the traditional prohibitions and rules.

Women are the chief source of pollution for the Kalderash, just as for other groups of Gypsies. Every "clean" thing which a Gypsy woman steps over, becomes polluted, and touching it brings the threat of pollution. A woman is particularly unclean during childbirth, and this lasts for a period of six weeks after the baby is born – that is, twice as long as with the Polish lowland Gypsies.

Unlike the lowland Gypsies, however, the Kalderash do not consider mature girls as unclean and with powers to pollute. A *Shey bari* (big girl), that is a nubile virgin, is not yet unclean. She may, for example, dance on the table, and this does not pollute the food. It is only when she marries that she becomes unclean, and this lasts until the change of life. *Podzhi* (menstruation) does not increase the uncleanness.

As with the lowland Gypsies, the Kalderash divide pollution into two categories: major and minor, which in their dialect is rendered as *bare mahrimota* and *tsyganye mahrimota.* Here too, skirts and slippers carry exceptional powers of pollution, as also does a broom, as an object which most often comes into contact with unclean things. A Gypsy woman who wishes to cast a pollution does not need to hit a Gypsy over the head with her shoe or skirt, but it is enough for her to throw her skirt, called a *rocha,* onto the roof of the house where the Gypsy lives, or onto his tent. This means that all the Gypsies who are "under her skirts" are polluted. Sometimes those who have been polluted have taken revenge on the perpetrator of their pollution and then the *Kris* has had to decide on the basis of oaths what are the rights and wrongs of the case between two polluted families at loggerheads. It is interesting that for the Kalderash a woman's apron does not carry pollution. It can be used in the forest as a table-cloth, food can be spread out on it, and a Gypsy can dry himself on an apron after washing without fear of unpleasant consequences.

The Kalderash attach great importance to the uncleanness of *mahrimos* – faeces or urine, especially human excrement. They therefore do not like toilets that are installed in flats and houses, and there have been cases where, when they have agreed to have one provided, the entrance has been from the outside, and not from within the house. One Gypsy family near Warsaw bought themselves "a house" cheaply – an old circus waggon. Some other Gypsies claimed that this had been used in the circus as a toilet for the workers, and that therefore the Gypsies now living in it were polluted. After a great deal of trouble, a *Kris* was called, where it was proved that the Gypsies who had made the accusation had been wrong, and the waggon was clean.

A polluted Gypsy pollutes everything that he touches. He should therefore avoid public places, like restaurants, in order not to pollute the plates and cutlery that he uses there, which will then be given to other clients, who may include Gypsies. Although tableware is washed, pollution cannot be washed off, even with soap. Once, recently, a polluted Gypsy drank beer from a glass in a restaurant. Other Gypsies were therefore quickly informed that the restaurant had been polluted, and all were warned against using it. From that moment on, no Gypsy dared to enter the "Bar Krakowski" in Gliwice, for it had become *mahrimdzhe*.

As we can see, the *mageripen* and *mahrimos* codes contain many similarities, but also certain differences. But the *sovwakha* and *sovwakha* oaths take place in a like manner in both cases. The Kalderash also use oaths with a skull, a grave and icon. Other oaths are also used, without properties. The basic difference from the practice of the lowland Gypsies lies in the fact that it is not the person who is swearing the oath who recites the formula but someone else, and the polluted Gypsy only confirms the words with the Gypsy "Amen", which is *bateh*. The text of the oath also consists of the enumeration of threats and curses, for example, "that you may wear a black scarf for your children and husband, that hospitals may rot from your disease, that your eyes may fall out onto your breast" etc.

Just as the Great Head of the lowland Gypsies deals, apart from cases of pollution, also with other disputes among Gypsies, so the Kalderash *Kris* also settles what are termed *gwaba*, covering all kinds of calumny and offence, spreading false rumours or questions arising from fights. Offences of this kind are punished by fines imposed by the council of elders. Similar punishments can also be imposed for damaging the good name of persons already dead.

In the light of all these Gypsy customary laws, it is obvious that the popular idea that this is a people that recognises no laws, and that lives in chaotic anarchy, without taking any responsibility for its actions, is highly unjustified. Nothing could be more false! Gypsy laws are very harsh, and obtain for absolutely all members of the society. It is these that for example make it so difficult to emancipate individual members of Gypsy society. The legal order, which forms an all-important conservative factor, does not permit individual attempts at emancipation. The Gypsies are aware that every advancement of that kind leads to the rejection of the Gypsy community, and they do not wish this to come about. The institutions of the *Baro-Shero* and the *Kris* maintain the old traditions and form a dam against loss of national identity, but at the same time a barrier against civilization and education.

The Polish highland Gypsies who are settled in the villages of the sub-Carpathian region not only do not recognize the *Baro-Shero* but are not acquainted with an institution or ruler of this kind. The expression *mageripen* or *mahrimos* is completely unknown to them and quite incomprehensible. However there are residual signs of observance of taboos among this group also. A polluted Gypsy is here called *wabants*. For about two months after childbirth, a highland Gypsy woman is not allowed to cook, peel potatoes etc. She is not even allowed to come close to pots containing food for other people. For this period of two months, other members of her family have to do the "women's work". If a woman does cook during this period, and her husband allows her to do so, then they are both called *wabantsa* by others, meaning unclean, or *phooy manoosa,* meaning "dreadful people". Gypsies who eat dog or cat-meat are also called *wabantsa,* and "decent Gypsies" *(wakhe Roma)* maintain no contacts with them. The highland Gypsies do not shake hands with them in greeting, and they do not sit down to eat with them at table. They have fewer taboo prohibitions and these are weaker than elsewhere, not entailing serious punishment for breaking them, for there is no authority here from a central power, and no sanctions of any kind to exact observance.

The more Gypsies have been assimilated into the host society, the less obvious are relics of the old customs in the forms of pollutions, oaths etc. Undoubtedly they are gradually dying out, but even if in this residual form they will last as long as the Gypsies remain a closed social and ethnic group isolated from the rest of the society.

Birth and Childhood

The arrival of a baby is a festival, bringing joy in the caravan but at the same time, childbirth is considered one of the most "unclean" aspects of life, entailing most pollution. Pleasure at the appearance of a new member of the caravan – especially if the new member is a boy – is accompanied by the separation of the mother and child from the rest of the members in fear of the pollution which would affect anyone coming into contact with the puerperal woman.

The birth takes place in a separate tent. A midwife can take direct part in the proceedings, and an old Gypsy woman may help. But the separation of the woman giving birth is essential. In the first half of the 19th century in the Kingdom of Poland, events were as follows:

"Gypsy women often hide themselves for the birth, or at any event do not admit anyone to themselves... For the woman in labour they make a bed of bullrushes behind the shed belonging to their caravan, in some place under a birch or oak tree whose branches can be pulled down all round to the ground, thus forming a little hut for the woman giving birth. When however there are births in winter, they give up a corner of the shed for the woman in labour, screening it off with branches of pine or larch, or of anything else that is green, such as moss or periwinkle or some such. The women in the meantime all run off round the neighbouring villages to beg rags and nappies, while the husbands light fires in the cottage, although they make quite sure that the first flames do not leap up until after the baby is born."

In some Gypsy groups in Poland there was a custom that as soon as the birth was over, a young girl from the same caravan as the mother would take water into a jug and from twigs prepare something like an aspergillum. Then she would go round all the tents in turn, and sprinkle water from the jug,

76

wishing the inhabitants luck (*Tye avyen bakhtaley* – that you may be happy). Gypsies knew that this was a sign that a new member of the caravan had arrived, and they wished the baby good fortune in life.

There are lots of children in a Gypsy family, and parents want them to be as many as possible. "Lots of children, lots of luck," says a Gypsy proverb. The Gypsy woman's motherlove is proverbial, and it is not only mothers who are obliged to love their children, not only fathers and elder brothers and sisters, but also "the guardian spirit". Belief in guardian spirits, the augurers of fate, is alive today among the Kalderash and Lovari.

These are three sisters, like the Greek Fates, who are known as the *Suwbotara*. They appear at the bedside of a child on the third night, or third evening, after its birth. In former days, the family would leave for them in expectation of their coming, a bowl with something to eat, with three spoons. In Poland, before the Second World War, this custom of providing food and drink for the Three Sisters was still kept up. This ritual meal, prepared on the third night after the birth of a child, consisted of salt, water and a bread roll or pancake baked on the fire, which was called a *kovrygo*. By now, a meal for the Three Sisters is no longer prepared, but it is still believed that they pay a visit. They are invisible, but sometimes in the night they can be heard foretelling the future to the baby. It is forbidden to repeat to anyone what is heard in this eavesdropping. The sisters see the baby's future: one foretells health and happiness for it, and speaks of the success with which it is going to meet in life; the second sister foretells fortunate circumstances that are to happen to the child, kind turns of fate; and the third sister tells of the evils that await it.

The Polish Kalderash tell the story of how once upon a time an older Gypsy woman sat by a fire at the entrance to the tent and when the augurers of fate visited the baby at midnight, she overheard their soft conversation over the mother and child asleep inside the tent. The most important words of the prophecy were, "The child will live just as long as there is a fire in this fireplace." The Gypsy woman, frightened by the prophecy, put brushwood on the fire, in order that it should not go out, but then the Fates disappeared, the old Gypsy woman fell asleep and the fire did go out. In the morning it was found that according to the prophecy, the baby was dead.

The *Suwbotara* never make mistakes. Their final prophecy before they leave always comes true, although sometimes misfortune can be avoided. Other groups of Kalderash call them *Vorzitori,* but they have the same powers and fulfil the same function.

The Polish lowland Gypsies no longer believe in the Three Sisters. However, this belief has persisted in vestigial form among them, for they claim that on the third night after a birth, the tent of the mother is visited by a "spirit" which decides on the future of the new-born infant, and foretells its future to the day of death. There is a custom connected with this visit that during the third night the mother and child should be kept company in their tent by an old Gypsy woman "because it would be too frightening for the mother to wait alone for a visit from the other world".

Amulets and talismans constitute one of the methods of ensuring happiness and warding off ill-fortune. These are especially useful to a child, who is particularly at risk from the "evil eye" which casts a spell.

The ceremony of christening takes place in various ways with various groups of Gypsies. The highland Gypsies settled in the sub-Carpathian region usually christen the child two months after birth. Sometimes, if the child is ill, it is christened before, but in that case, no reception is organized for guests, since the mother is still "unclean". For a christening reception, a Gypsy woman will bake cake, meat and buy vodka and beer. Among the somewhat richer Gypsies these are generous feasts, with music and dancing, and they can sometimes last several days. If the host is not rich and has already spent all the money he had, then the guests will collect money among themselves for further supplies of food and drink.

Among the Polish lowland Gypsies, Kalderash and Lovari, christenings take place later, when the child is already a few years old. When the god-parents come to a Kalderash child to take it to church, they throw a handful of coins into the place from which they have taken it, to ensure that it will be rich. The Polish lowland Gypsies put money under the child's pillow. Before a child is baptized it is forbidden for it to go to church or into a cemetery. After the christening there is a reception, at which the god-parents are the guests of honour. Two festivals are celebrated annually for the christened child: *Patradzhi* (Easter, the festival of spring) and *Kruchuno* (Christmas, the festival of winter). While the child is small, its parents organize these celebrations, and do so also in honour of the god-parents who have taken all the sins of the child upon their shoulders. There are therefore festivals in honour of the god-parents. The Kalderash call the second day of these holidays (that is, Easter Monday or Boxing Day) *Odzhesle Tsirvengo* – the day of the god-parents. Twice a year for the whole of their lives the god-parents receive the thanks of their god-children and presents.

Sometimes until recently, Gypsies would christen a child several times, inviting "great lords" to be god-parents, and these agreed from a desire for exotic experience, and did not neglect to provide gifts for their god-children.

Children are given Christian names which will be entered in their birth certificates – in their "papers" – (*liwa*) but irrespective of their official names, all Gypsies also have a Gypsy nickname, which is given to them by their parents in childhood.

Gypsy surnames are temporary affairs, frequently changed, whereas the nicknames, which exist only in unwritten tradition, remain with the bearer for the whole of his life-time. The following names are for example used by the lowland Gypsies: *Kawo* (Male Black), *Kali* (Female Black), *Nango* (Naked), *Dando* (from the word *dand* – tooth), *Pkhabooy* (Apple), *Bakro* (Ram), *Wowodzhi* (Flower), *Mura* (Blueberry), *Parno* (White), *Koro* (Blind), *Cirikwo* (Bird). Among the Kalderash one can find Gypsy personal names *sensu stricto*: *Wuwudzhi* (Flower), *Masho* (Fish), *Bango* (Crooked), and personal names taken mainly from Romanian and Hungarian, like *Papusa, Lajos, Djurka*, and *Sandor*.

There used to be a custom of holding a "Gypsy christening", something which survives in places in the Balkans, and which at one time was also practiced in Poland. "When a baby is born, they say, they bathe it in cold water which is poured into a hole dug in the earth, but it is impossible to discover anything about this from our Gypsies," wrote Narbutt of the Gypsies in

78

Lithuania in the first decades of the 19th century. There is evidence that this ritual bath of new babies is still practiced among the Gypsies of the countries of the South East of Europe. The Gypsy child was usually bathed in running water in a river, the significance of which in many Gypsy rituals is enormous.

Gypsies, especially the Kalderash, believe that a child is born "shackled", and that if these invisible fetters are not removed at the moment when it tries to take its first steps, it may remain "shackled in walking" to the end of its life: crippled, clumsy, liable to spills and tumbles. This magical removal of the fetters from a child who is beginning to walk is carried out – although in recent years ever more rarely – by an old Gypsy woman "good hands". She takes a bird's feather, as a symbol of graceful lightness, and with this draws a circle around the child's legs, reciting the formula of the spell: *Tye pkhires vushoro sar o porori* – that you might walk lightly as a feather.

This age-old ritual of removing the fetters (in the Kalderash dialect, *Tye sineyw o wumpyns* – cutting the bonds), which until recently was practiced among the Kalderash, has begun to disappear among many clans along with other manifestations of traditional Gypsy customs.

From earliest childhood, boys are more privileged in the family than girls, and much greather care is taken of them. If a mother ties a ribbon in a boy's hair, the Gypsies say that when he grows up he will keep falling off his horse. Children are breast-fed a long time and you can often see a five or six year-old child who after eating dinner along with the adults receives its mother's breast "for desert". Sometimes you can see big, seven year-old boys, who have already successfully tried smoking a pipe, but have not yet given up their mother's milk. If a Gypsy woman wants to take her child off the breast earlier, she uses a procedure that the Kalderash call *tsyrkosar*. This consists in sprinkling the nipple with salt, paprika or pepper in order to put the child off sucking.

From the earliest years of childhood, the child learns almost simultaneously his native Romany language and Polish. The Gypsies are bi-lingual from the very beginning of their lives. Childhood does not last for long. A twelve or thirteen year-old girl is considered capable of house-work, fortune-telling and even ready for marriage. Children brought up in tents in the forest observe the adults and try to copy their behaviour, and many of the children's games are an imitation of occupations of adult Gypsies.

Little girls begin to learn to tell fortunes from their first years, by watching and imitating their mothers, and little boys soon begin to follow in the footsteps of their fathers.

Little girls often and willingly look after their younger brothers and sisters, changing their nappies, rocking them to sleep and singing them lullabies. If a Gypsy woman has no-one with whom to leave her baby, she will take it with her to the forest, or to the city park where she tells fortunes. The baby is always carried in a shawl tied on her back, like a little bundle, carefully fastened to the waist and shoulders of the mother. In this way, the child is already taking part in its mother's fortune-telling expeditions, and a dozen or so years later will set off herself for the same purpose with her own baby on her back. If a baby is seriously ill, the Gypsies take an oath that if the child gets well again, they will every year celebrate a special festival called *prazneeko* with great ceremony as a thanks offering. This usually takes place at

Whitsun, on the feast day of the Assumption of the Blessed Virgin Mary, or on the feast day of St. Peter and St. Paul. While the child is small, its parents organize this festival for it, but later the cured man himself takes over the responsibility, remembering this duty to the end of his days; this festival indeed is the greatest personal holiday for him, for Gypsies do not celebrate name-days or birthdays, since usually they do not use the name they were given at their baptism, and not many of them remember the date of their birthday.

Gypsies try in two ways to ward off the ill fortune that makes children fail to "grow up properly". If a child is born after a previous child has died, the parents pierce one of its ears, in which it may wear an earring. Until recently, you could still see Gypsy men wearing one earring, but now the piercing alone is considered to be enough. This operation is designed to ensure health for the child, and avoidance of the fate of its dead brother or sister. Another custom believed to prevent the death of a child is the "sale" of a baby. The mother is convinced that death results from some evil fate hanging over her, which is inherited by the child. In order to ward off the influence of this evil she carries out a symbolic "sale" of the child: she hands it over to another Gypsy woman for a payment of "a few groschen" although not parting with it at all. She believes that in this way she is freeing the child from the powers of evil that are passed on from her to her offspring. The new mother who has "bought" the child shares her luck with it, protecting it from the evil fortune that its real mother carries. There are also sometimes cases when after a child has recovered from an illness, its parents change its name, as though in a way to change its identity, so that the illness that had troubled it under its previous name would not return.

Nuptials

"To love", in Romany is *te kameyw*. But the meaning of this expression is much broader, for it also means to want, to desire. The derived noun for "love", *kamlipen* or *kamanipel* also means therefore desire, passion etc. There is no word in Romany which would mean exactly the same thing as love: "I love you" and "I want you" mean the same thing.

Gypsies however often use words and phrases which are quite their own to express their feelings, replacing the word "love" with various metaphors or roundabout phrases. Something of this kind can be found in a song sung by the Polish highland Gypsies: *charav tri vodzhori,* which really means "I love you", but is literally translated as "I lick your little heart". The Polish lowland Gypsies use the phrase *me havtre yakha* (I eat your eyes) or *pyav tro muyoro* (I drink your face) in the same sense.

Erotic life is a matter of shame among the Gypsies, something unclean. This attitude to sexual matters, enshrined in the Gypsy customary law, leads in general to absolute primitivism in these areas of life. A Gypsy woman compensates for the inadequacy of her sex life by having large numbers of children, thus finding her fulfilment in her very strong maternal instincts. The strictness of custom in this field is dictated by the code of taboo pollutions, which closely regulates even this most intimate area of life. Admittedly there are cases of professional Gypsy prostitutes in Poland as elsewhere, but these concern only isolated individuals who together with their families have been excluded from Gypsy society, or have themselves withdrawn from it. Today, the Polish Gypsies are basically strictly monogamous, although they can still remember the times when they claim that polygamy was permitted.

The lowland Gypsies only rarely marry in church: "Gypsies consider marriage as a purely civil matter, and if they do marry at the altar this is only in order to enlist support for the wedding feast," wrote Narbutt. In general, Gypsies content themselves with a Gypsy wedding, a *biyav*. Just as among the Polish peasantry, matchmakers are sent and after agreement has been reached the wedding takes place; during this ceremony, an old Gypsy man ties the hands of the young couple together with a kerchief, and asks the bride whether she has agreed to the wedding of her own free will, without pressure. After tying the pair's hands, the Gypsy recites the form of words, which is usually as follows: "I throw the key into the water, so that none shall find it and nothing shall be opened with it, and so nothing shall divide you." After the couple's hands have been untied, the wedding feast begins, which is as sumptuous as can be managed. The custom of testing the virginity of the bride is dying out, but can still be met with here and there. After the wedding the older women place clean bed linen in a tent for the newly-married couple, and the state of this is checked in the morning. If the result of this inspection is favourable, in-dicating that the bride had retained her virginity until the wedding, then there is a joyful beginning to the second half of the wedding feast, and a red kerchief or ribbon is tied to the top of the wedding tent. If however there were to be lack of evidence that the new bride had retained her maiden virtue, then she would be the butt of jokes and insults and the second half of the feast would not take place.

Sometimes a "loose girl" would be stigmatized by the hanging of a holed cooking pot, a symbol of her lack of virtue, on the top of her tent. But this custom is by today exceptionally rare. Especially the Second World War and the years immediately following were not conducive to the maintenance of such age-old customs.

Marital fidelity of women is very strictly observed. Sometimes in the past a married Gypsy woman caught in adultery or in flight with her lover would be branded by her husband with some permanent mutilation like a slit cheek or ear etc. Sometimes only the hair was cut off. Men on the other hand can usually commit adultery with impunity, as long as it is not with prostitutes.

The "buying" of wives is an old Gypsy custom, which the Kalderash and Lovari continued to practice until the Second World War, when it quickly died out and is by today a thing of the past. The purchase of a girl was not a simple commercial transaction, but required many customary initial approaches and ritual ceremonies. First there was a betrothal, or rather an attempt at betrothal, for the outcome was never known beforehand.

The parents or other representatives of the prospective bridegroom would come without official warning, to the family of the girl who was being con-sidered as a fiancée. The guests behaved as though they were in their own home: they spread a table cloth, layed the table and served food. Although they said nothing of a betrothal, the parents of the girl, who took no part at all in these preparations, began to demur, and cast doubt on the sense of all this: "Nothing will come of it; it's a waste of all your trouble and money." The guests did not give up, taking no notice of these warnings or expressions of disapprobation. Meanwhile, the hosts refused to sit down to the table, drew things out, made objections, and by all this delay raised the value of their daughter. Sometimes as long as three days were taken in this kind of drawn-out banquet.

Finally, the *pwoska* appeared on the scene, brought by the representatives of the boy's family. The initial betrothal rituals had not settled anything, and so now a new ritual was to begin. The *pwoska* is a bottle of wine or vodka, wrapped in a red foulard by the boy's mother or father, and decorated with some valuables: a gold brooch, earrings or a necklace of talars. When the *pwoska* was standing on the table-cloth, the boy's family started to try to persuade the girl's father to drink. If he did so, this meant that he had agreed, and negotiations could begin to establish the price which would have to be paid for the fiancée. When this happened the father pronounced the sacramental words, *Tyavel bakhtali o terno hai ternyi* (May the young man and young woman be happy). Then the girl's father turned to the matchmakers *(khanamicha)* and named the sum that he demanded for his daughter, and the sum to cover the costs of the wedding. Then the bargaining began, and if the two sides did not reach an agreement, and the girl's father abandoned the idea of betrothing her, then he had to return the costs of the betrothal feast. If however things did reach an agreement, then the day for the betrothal and the wedding was immediately fixed; the organization and funding of these was the duty of the bridegroom's family.

This custom of wife-buying apparently disappeared in Poland in about 1950. Sometimes 300 or even 500 ducats (gold roubles or dollars) were paid for a fiancée, and in earlier times higher prices were occasionally known, in each case determined by the beauty and intelligence of the girl. In 1908 in the forest near Piotrków, a Gypsy wedding took place between a dazzlingly beautiful Gypsy girl and a Gypsy man whose father had paid 3000 roubles for his daughter-in-law. This price had been demanded because of the exceptional beauty of the girl, by the current head of the large Kalderash grouping at Piotrków, the "ataman" Kamiński. In 1910, 10,000 gold roubles were paid for a wife at a Kalderash camp near Cracow. The custom of buying a wife – which is quite unknown among the Polish lowland Gypsies – has been replaced by the practice of kidnapping the girl, which was known earlier but was much rarer than today. In most cases this is not a "kidnapping" by force, but rather an agreed flight by a young couple, usually for a short time. When they return to their families, sometimes after only twenty-four hours, they claim that they have spent the night together, which in Gypsy custom is the same as marrying. The parents of each must, whether they like it or not, accept this *fait accompli,* and agree to recognize the marriage, irrespective of whether the girl herself was a party to the plans or whether she was kidnapped by force. Kidnappings used to take place against the backdrop of the forest, on horses foaming at the mouth. In the changed circumstances of today, they are sometimes organized by taxi, and the driver has been bribed by the Gypsy kidnapper.

Water, which is so important in Gypsy rituals connected with death, birth etc., is also necessary for the wedding ceremony. When the young bridesmaids take the girl to her husband's home or tent, they pour water over her. The young woman is then called *bakri* (sheep). This name, which is applied to her before she is united with her husband, is not offensive but honourable. After the night, from the following day, she is called *bori* (daughter-in-law), and as a sign that she has given up her maiden state, she puts on her head the brightest possible kerchief, usually red. This custom, which is similar to the Polish ceremony of capping the bride, is still observed among the Kalderash and Lovari to the present day. From the moment when she puts on this headscarf, the Gypsy woman has to wear it for the rest of her life.

Marriages take place at a very early age. Sometimes the husband is sixteen and the wife thirteen or fourteen. Therefore often the young couple are not able to live completely independently immediately after the wedding, but for a certain time have to live with the husband's parents. Depending on circumstances, sooner or later however the couple will set up house on their own – a few days or a few years after the wedding. This turning point in the lives of young married people is called *dabeshka*. *Dzhinye piye dabeshka* (They're going to *dabeshka*) means that a young couple are starting their independent life, away from the old people. When the young people set out on their new way of life, they are wished luck and success. One of the proverbial expressions of good wishes is: *Che gretson toomiye le devleske hai le manooshenge atoonchee, kana gretsowa piye o wont hai manro* (that you may disgust God and man when salt and bread are disgusting). Gypsy marriages, which are now concluded among the Kalderash often by the kidnapping method, can be short-lived, and it is not difficult to bring them to an end. Thus for example one sixteen year-old boy managed to get rid of his first wife and also part from his fourteen year-old second wife who was taken away from him by his father-in-law. A Gypsy has the right to get rid of his wife if she is proved unfaithful to him. But often the "divorce", or more correctly the driving out of a wife by her husband, is not motivated by anything the wife has done, but simply takes place on this pretext. Another similarly invented reason may be that the wife did not look after her husband properly or that she was a poor housewife; the wife's infertility can also be a reason for getting rid of her.

Usually the Gypsy woman who is treated in this way does not insist on her rights, and makes the best of her lot, for Gypsy opinion holds that any attempt to oppose a husband's verdict in these matters would be shameful and humiliating. Basically, a divorced woman, or one who has been thrown out by her husband, only has a chance to marry again a divorced man or a widower.

This short-lived nature of Gypsy marriages is something new, and was unknown to the same extent among the older generation of Gypsies when, even if there were no other restraints, the fact that a wife had been bought and a considerable sum paid for her, made a man think twice before getting rid of such a valuable acquisition, and was therefore a real guarantee of marital stability.

The only factor encouraging lasting marriage at the moment is if a state civil ceremony is concluded, but this takes place only rarely. If there are already children of a marriage, then in order for them to have the right to take their father's name in law, a marriage will be concluded in a Registry Office. The consequent necessity of obtaining a divorce if the couple wish to part makes the break-up of the marriage more difficult – but not impossible. Sometimes marital partners part without going through the formalities of a divorce, and if one of them gets married again, it has to be without state legal sanctions.

From the day of the marriage, the young couple's life together results in a large number of offspring – the more the better. The burden of the majority of family duties, both in housekeeping and in the financial maintenance of the family, falls upon the wife. This does not however bring her any parallel rights. Since she is in the nature of things unclean and of lower value than a man, she has to accept her subordinate and under-privileged situation in the family, although in old age she will live to reap her reward in the respect and equal rights accorded to a matron, a *phuri day*.

Death and Mourning

There are Gypsy funeral and mourning rites that are practiced by all the Gypsy communities in Poland, but the greatest number are observed among the Kalderash and Lovari. The Polish lowland and highland Gypsies have kept them up in a somewhat residual form and indeed occasionally they are rather "Polonized"; they no longer have the coherent characteristics of strict observance of ritual practice that can be observed among the former groupings. The Polish lowland Gypsies also feed the spirit of the dead, for example offering them the first fruits of the year, which they throw behind them over their heads for the ghosts; before they start drinking, they sprinkle the first drops of vodka upon the ground – *paw moowengre dzhi* – for the soul of the departed etc. However, it is Kalderash and Lovari lore that is richest in this area. Probably many of the elements are of Balkan origin, from Moldavia; some however seem to indicate that they have a pedigree stretching back to the much more distant past.

A Gypsy dies. His soul leaves this world for the world of the dead, and the memory of those who are left alive is what protects him in that world from dying of hunger and thirst. While he was among the living, he had to obey Gypsy rules and prohibitions, but now his life, and all that has gone to make it up, has ceased to count and has no bearing on his fate after death. He will receive no reward and no punishment, for these are purely temporal matters. His spirit goes off into the unknown. Until recently there was still the custom – even among the *Polska Roma* – of burning the dead man's possessions, and this may still take place here and there until the present day; this fire was intended to warm his spirit in its journey through the cold regions of the other world. Ethnographic documents referring to the Gypsies of the Balkans mention also remains of Gypsy folk beliefs about the difficulties and barriers to be met with by the spirit during its posthumous wanderings; they speak there of freezing winds and of areas of desert heat. These particular beliefs are not encountered among the Polish Gypsies, but water, which is to quench the thirst of those leaving for the world of the dead, still plays a major role in funeral ceremonies.

A Gypsy dies. If he is able to speak, his last words should be a blessing, wishing happiness to his family and those close to him, who have gathered around his bedside, full of pain and sorrow. This last blessing is regarded as exceptionally important and valuable, and if it is not given, this is regarded as a bad omen. It is the only custom connected with dying.

The family dress the deceased for his coffin, measuring the length of the body with a tape measure called a *mesoora,* and tie up his jaw with a kerchief. Both the *mesoora* and the kerchief are afterwards carefully preserved as amulets that bring luck. Especially the *mesoora* has power to protect from danger, and above all from the police. Just as the fairy-tale cap of invisibility makes everyone who puts it on invisible, so the *mesoora* makes it impossible for stolen goods to be discovered by the authorities in the event of a search.

The family place the deceased in the coffin, together with certain objects which belonged to him and which may be of use to him in the next world. These are usually a cigarette case with some cigarettes in it, or a pipe with tobacco, a comb, a mirror, a watch or a ring. It is however forbidden to put matches in the coffin, since the dead man's soul wanders for six weeks around his family and home, or forest caravan, and he might therefore start a fire.

Then begins a three-day vigil over the dead man. Three days must always pass between the death and burial, for during this time the soul might change its mind and return to the body. In order to make this possible return easier, the face of the dead man is always covered with a kerchief or veil which is torn in the middle. The tear is to show the soul the way by which it can return to the body that it has left. The last breath of the dying in fact represents the flight of the spirit, which leaves through the mouth and nostrils. It can only return by the same route.

The family and friends of the dead man gather, and everyone places some money in his pocket, so that he can buy himself something with it and have nothing to hold against those who are still alive. They all sit down in the room where the dead man is lying. Only married couples who have been married for less than a year are not allowed in to the vigil. This vigil lasts for three days and three nights. Candles are lit – always an uneven number; vodka, wine and beer are drunk, but there must always be an uneven number of bottles too. They sit by the coffin and lament, telling each other fairy stories all night, eating and drinking. The men do not shave and the women do not comb their hair, but for three days accompany the dead man, while his spirit in the meantime remains nearby: they feel his presence. In these first days of mourning it is forbidden to comb one's hair with a comb or wash with soap, while – *aven le spoomi pa o moowo* – a foam comes from the dead man, which is something like the transparent fabric of his soul, which filled him like air. Sometimes, as a symbol of exceptionally deep mourning, the family of the deceased do not wash with soap or comb their hair for a period of nine days. Those who have gathered for the vigil leave the room and re-enter, in order once more to sit beside the coffin, but all may not leave at once, for someone must always remain with the deceased. The Gypsies carefully gather up the ends of burnt-out candles and the wax that has fallen from them, for during the funeral this is thrown into the grave before it is covered with earth. The mourners speak to each other in lowered voices for they are not allowed to disturb the peace of the dead even by singing. There are no requiems: they are forbidden because music of any kind is held to be in contravention of the very principle of mourning. The dead man is still near, his soul has not yet left, and the rituals of mourning must be exceptionally rigorously observed, both for the good of the departed soul and in order to prevent the spirit from disturbing the peace of the living. Any small event can bring with it dangerous consequences in this period, if these are not averted at the right moment. For example, if someone sneezes during the vigil, he must immediately tear some part of his clothing in order to avoid ill fortune. After three days, the funeral takes place. The family carry the coffin, and pour out water from buckets and other vessels, in order to prevent his thirsty soul from returning wanting to drink it. For the first thing that is known about souls is that they suffer from thirst. They want to drink, they long for water. Fear of the return of a ghost is the motive for removing water from the home, but at the same time certain ritual steps are taken, intended to quench the thirst of the soul.

The day after the funeral, the ritual of giving the spirit something to drink begins. For this purpose, the Gypsy family chooses some Gypsy boy and buys for him a jug and glass. If the dead person is a woman, then the jug and a glass are given to a girl. The chosen person every day fills the jug with clean water, pours it into the glass and offers it to all the Gypsies he or she meets to drink. This is continued until the day when the soul of the departed leaves the neighbourhood for the more distant realms of the other world, which occurs six weeks after death. The boy or girl has a stick on which each day a notch is made with a knife, in order to ensure that the ritual is performed for the required number of days. When six weeks have passed after the death, the young person goes down to the river, and counts the notches on the stick for the last time, before breaking it into two, tying the two pieces together in the shape of a cross, and fixing on this five little candles – one in the middle and the others on the four ends. This cross, with lighted candles, is floated on the water, water is again taken from the river and the glass filled, whereupon the contents are poured back into the river. This is repeated as many times as there were notches on the stick. After the water has been poured out of the glass for the last time, both the jug and glass are filled and sunk in the river. The ritual is ended, but the departed has not yet had access to the water that has been passed around, and is not yet able to drink it. It is only when his family pays the person who has been distributing the water, either in cash or in the form of some present, that the soul may begin to quench its thirst, and all the water that has been handed round day after day is then his to drink. At the same time that the "water ritual" begins, the family starts a complicated mourning ritual known as *pomana* (the wake). The first wake takes place immediately after the funeral, that is, three days after the death: *treene dzhesenghi pomana*. This is held at an inn or restaurant near to a cemetery. In Warsaw, there was a restaurant in the Bródno district, next to the cemetery, where the first *pomana* was held after every Gypsy funeral. All those who attend the funeral take part in this ceremony.

The mourning is still going on. For a whole year, the family of the departed is not allowed to have parties, sing, or even listen to the radio. Longer mourning than a year is not recommended for it can lead to the death of the mourner. Every day of mourning over a year is in a way a pre-payment for the next occasion for mourning, and therefore attracts death. The Gypsy woman Jordana Kwiek, in deep despair after the death of her daughter, stayed in mourning for eighteen months. Friends in the Gypsy community advised her to break off what was in their view a dangerous practice, suggesting that she should dress in colourful clothes, but Jordana did not want to heed their advice: she hid the radio, turned off the lights, sat about in the dark – and died. The Gypsies say that she brought death upon herself by prolonging the mourning.

Nine days after the death, there is the second funeral ceremony – the *enya dzhesenghi pomana*. A feast is prepared in the home of the departed for his friends and family. The mourners at the feast eat and drink for the soul of the departed, for by sitting and eating and drinking they in this way also feed and give drink to the departed spirit. Here too there are special rules of behaviour and ritual prohibitions. No-one can get up from the table by himself: everyone at the feast should leave the table at the same moment. But if someone does get up, then he is not allowed to come back and eat. All the left-overs must be taken out of the house of the departed before sunset and thrown into running water, into the river, or given away to someone. Nothing edible can stay in the house overnight. Nor is it permitted to give the left-overs to a dog, cat or to throw them out for the birds.

The undoubted rationale behind these prohibitions is the belief that the soul of the departed might be tempted by the food to return to the house to eat. The Gypsies do not wish to allow this to come about for fear of undesired contact with the ghost, for their own safety. It is only they themselves as stand-ins by eating and drinking that can feed and give drink to the departed. Before eating, they repeat the words, *tye avyel angwa leshche* (may it be before him, i. e. may this food be for the departed). The belief held by the Balkan Gypsies that a soul can be reincarnated in the body of an animal may be the reason why it is forbidden to give the left-overs from the *pomana* ceremony to an animal. The third *pomana* takes place six weeks after the death; this, the *shoviye koorkenghi pomana,* is the most ceremonious. On this day the jug and glass used for the "water ritual" are sunk and the cross with the candles floats off down river. The Gypsies choose someone – a woman after the death of a woman, a man after the death of a man – in a way to play the role of the deceased, and everything that is entrusted to this person is at the same time the property of the deceased. Various things are given: objects for personal use like a comb, razor, tableware for one person and a complete set of clothes. If the person chosen is a man, a new suit is purchased for him; if the person is a woman, then material has to be bought in the morning and quickly sewn into a skirt, blouse, vest etc. so that the garments are ready by the afternoon. Sometimes the material is bought on the previous day, so that the sewing can be started early in the morning on the following day. But then the material has to stay in the shop, or be stored overnight with non-Gypsies, for it is not permitted to keep it overnight in a Gypsy house.

Noon arrives. The table is generously covered with dishes, and the clothing for the chosen person is ready. Some older person who is close to the deceased – his mother, wife, or father – kisses the table and the dishes given to the chosen person, and with every kiss offers the wish: *Tye avyel angwa leshche*. Near the table, incense is burning on hot embers. With the help of the members of the household, the chosen person changes into the clothes prepared. The host or hostess brings a bowl of water and personally washes the feet of the chosen person and dresses his or her hair with the comb that has been presented.

After these initial preparations have been made, the feast begins, at which when each dish is begun, the stereotyped phrase, *Tye avyel angwa leshche* is repeated. When everyone gets up from the table, the chosen person buys vodka or beer for the rest of the company with his own money. Everyone drinks, wishing him that his clothes may be "worn healthily".

The chosen person must be an adult. And therefore this ceremony with chosen people is not organized when someone very young dies. In 1952, a Gypsy teenager called Puyo was killed when he fell from a roundabout in a Warsaw fairground. At the mourning ceremonies, the family could not suggest to the deceased's friend who had come to the *pomana* that he should take part in the dressing-up ceremony. But wanting to carry out this ritual at least to a small extent, they gave him a suit of clothing, although without any rituals of dressing in it.

Though the deceased is now already far away, his "ways are still open" and his return is not impossible. Therefore the mourning ceremonies do not yet cease, and six months after the death, a fourth wake is held: the *dopash-bersheski pomana*. Until the day of this wake, the person to whom the suit of clothing was given at the previous six-week wake can wear it. But on the day of the six-month celebrations, this should be thrown into running water, into the river. On this occasion, too, someone is chosen who is dressed in new clothes and the whole ceremony is repeated. This time the person chosen can wear the clothes until the final mourning ceremony which takes place on the last day of mourning, a year after the death. This fifth wake, the *bersheski pomana,* ends the mourning ceremonies. Here for the third and last time, someone is chosen who is given clothing and other objects and whose feet are washed. This time the clothing presented can be worn for an unlimited time, until it wears out.

Every adult Gypsy man and woman can be chosen in this way at the most three times in their lives; it is prohibited to choose the same person for a fourth time. During the three successive *pomanas,* a different person is chosen on each occasion. Finally the mourning comes to an end. The *pomana* on the first anniversary of the death ends on a cheerful note. One of the old Gypsies says: "The ways are already closed for him. May that be the case for him! Now we shall sing, and dance. Mourning is over!" The way is now closed for the deceased and his departure is now irreversible. His ghost can no longer appear to haunt those left behind in the form of a mist, as he had been able to do previously, particularly in the first six weeks after death. A Gypsy ghost never appears in a clear form, but usually only its activity can be detected, and if it does appear before someone, it is usually in the form of a mist or a veil. Gypsies say that all this is because the face of the deceased is covered in the coffin with a kerchief, and that therefore what lies behind the kerchief cannot be seen when he appears in the form of a ghost. But after a year there is no longer the slightest danger that the deceased will haunt his former friends and family. The *pomana* ceremonies have cut off his path for return to the world. Nonetheless, memory of the dead is kept green, and this is made clear in various ways and at various seasons. When for example in spring the first vegetables are bought, and later the first fruit, and when in summer the first ice-cream makes its appearance, or the first flowers are bought, when a Gypsy woman bakes the first hedgehog of the year, memory of the dead and concern about their further fate after death, can be detected. Before a Gypsy tries the first spring vegetables, he gives some to somebody else, "gives it to him from his hand" – *dzheyw anda vast* – and in this way gives it to the dead. Sometimes, before offering someone for instance an apple, a Gypsy will kiss it, saying *tye avyel anda leshche* (may this be for the dead, may the dead eat it). The dead are therefore supplied with the necessary food through this kind of *anda vast* gift, and are the first to taste anything new in season. The Gypsies do this not only for their own dead, but also for all the Gypsy dead in general. In this way, the dead whose families are already not living and are therefore unable to watch over their affairs on the other side of the grave, can also obtain some food.

On 1 November, All Saints' Day, the Gypsies visit their family graves. At the cemetery at Bródno in Warsaw, where many Gypsy dead are buried, every year the Gypsies lay out cloths on the graves, sit down on them, eat, drink, and offer food to chance passers-by. They repeat to everyone the incantation, "may it be for him!" and "give from their hand". Finally, they pour water, orangeade or beer that they have brought with them over the grave to refresh the dead man. This custom, like all those discussed above in this connection, is still alive to the present day.

During the period of mourning, in the time when the ghost of the departed may still return and show itself to the living, the best time for him to do so is night. And therefore one must be particularly on guard against his visits at night time. To protect themselves from this, Gypsies repeat the incantation, *Tye avyen leskey droma phandadzhe, ay chohara pooterdey* (May in the night his ways be closed and may they only be open again tomorrow). It sometimes happens that a family ends the period of mourning before a year is up. This is frowned upon by the rest of the Gypsy community. There may be varied reasons for shortening the length of mourning to six months, or even to a mere six weeks. Sometimes, a close relative of the deceased may simply forget the ban and begin to sing, thereby breaking the rules of mourning. Also, for example, a few years ago the panic buying of foodstaffs in Poland led the Gypsies to fear that there was "going to be a war", which led those in mourning to break it off prematurely.

Curtailing the period of mourning requires a special ceremony. The mourner takes off the outward signs of mourning – for example a black shirt – and pours water or beer over it. This is called *shordzhas* (wetting) and signifies the end of the mourning period. If the mourning is broken off in accordance with the ritual, the ghost – *chohano* – should not return to trouble the living. It is characteristic that the Gypsies, who so much like valuables in the form of gold and money, should not stint these earthly goods when they are furnishing the deceased to lie in his coffin. This is in no way a sign that they do not attach real value to money, but stems from the conviction that these things will be necessary to the deceased in his life in the future world, and that it is not permissible to take them away from him, for otherwise he will return as a ghost to demand his dues, and to avenge himself for the wrongs done to him. The expression *pomana* is known in the Balkans, and is used by the Romanians in a sense similar to that employed by the Gypsies. Almost certainly, other forms of mourning ritual were also adopted by the Kalderash from other peoples. However, it is also undoubtedly the case that one cannot find in the Balkans the whole range of specifically Gypsy rituals connected with death which have been retained until the present day among the Polish Kalderash Gypsies.

Occupations and Professions

Music-making is one of the age-old Gypsy professions. While this was most widespread in Hungary, it has been practiced over a long period in Poland, and Gypsy bands played not only at weddings and in inns, but also at the courts of the Polish kings.

While the later King Sigismund (I) the Old was still a boy, he loved music, and at the turn of the 15th and 16th centuries he kept many singers and players at his court. These included Gypsy musicians of whom he was very fond. In *Młode lata Zygmunta Starego* (The youth of Sigismund the Old), 1893, A. Pawiński writes: "When a travelling harpist from the country of the minnesängers played a love song, or when the court lutanist, Czuryło, an old singer, sang a Ruthenian song about Lithuania, or when the Gypsies hit the sad strings of their zithers, then Zygmunt [Sigismund] dissolved in pleasure." Things were much the same during the reigns of other kings. The Gypsy Janczy was Ladislaus IV's court bagpiper, and the family of the Gypsy poetess Papusza kept until the Second World War a document that showed that one of their ancestors was a musician to Queen Marysieńka Sobieska. And Gypsy musicians were in demand not only among monarchs. Albrecht Stanisław Radziwiłł wrote that when the 17th century rabble-rouser and outlaw Łaszcz lay on his death-bed, and "some creditors arrived, demanding the repayment of debts, he told them that he wished from the bottom of his heart to comply, but since he possessed nothing, he ordered the Gypsy whom he kept by him to play on his violin; and when he did this his spirit departed."

There is a centuries-old tradition of Gypsy musicians in Poland, although it is not so well-established as in the Balkans or in particular Hungary. The Gypsy musicians were driven out of Poland at the beginning of the 19th century. The partitions of Poland meant that it was becoming harder to travel, and also that there was a growing shortage of wealthy patrons, who kept Gypsy bands at their courts. The majority of the later Gypsy musicians in Poland come from groups which arrived in Poland in the second half of the 19th century or the first decades of the 20th.

The Gypsies from the Cyntura group, which came from Hungary, are the professional violinists who have been musicians for generations. They live in the southern regions of Poland and have continued to work as musicians to the present day. The Gypsies usually play in groups, and the Gypsy musical ensembles are usually made up of members of the same family. It is only rarely that individual musicians appear in public, and Gypsies are very unwilling to accept the emancipation of any members of their circle in this way. An outstanding blind Gypsy violinist from the Cyntura group turned down a tempting offer from the Polish radio orchestra which wanted to engage him. He preferred to continue to make the rounds of the restaurants with his brothers, and earn his living as a wandering musician.

However, this kind of unwillingness to co-operate with undertakings from outside the closed Gypsy world is by now not entirely the rule. The first clear indication of the changes that were taking place in this sphere came with the career of a young Gypsy of the Lovari tribe, Michaj Burano, who in 1963 won great popularity as a singer in Polish pop groups. He did not however sing original Gypsy songs, but stylized pieces composed specially for him with the lyrics in Romany.

In the late 1960s, a young Kalderash Gypsy, Sylwester Masio-Kwiek became a popular singer, with songs based on original Gypsy song themes.

The singer Randia, previously a soloist with the professional Gypsy ensemble "Terno" (Young) which is recruited from among the Polish lowland Gypsies, received a commendation at the Song Festival in Opole, for a song which she performed with a non-Gypsy group. However, she sang mainly in Romany, together with her kinspeople – old folk songs which were collected for the group and arranged by its director, Edward Dębicki.

The Gypsy bands play music that is called Gypsy music. But it is a moot point whether there is really anything that can be called Gypsy folk music, or whether this is made up exclusively of elements taken from other peoples and then "Gypsified". This is a great riddle, as is the case in many other areas of Gypsy history and lore.

There is a variable, highly contrastive rhythm and specific tonality in Gypsy music; it is difficult to find a notation that can clearly and faithfully render the original. This music is written in what is called the Gypsy scale, a minor scale: A, B, D sharp, E, G sharp, or G, A flat, B, C, D, E flat, F sharp, G, and also G, A, B, C sharp, D, E flat, F sharp, G. Basically, this is monophonic music. The rhythm is emphasized by the double bass, and is also kept up by heel-tapping and hand-clapping. There is oriental rhythmics mixed with melodics in which the West is dominant. However, the way in which Gypsy bands conduct their melodic variations is also known to the peoples of the East.

Unfortunately, we have no knowledge of earlier Gypsy music. As a means of earning a living, it had to pander to rich patrons and later to the customers of inns, and therefore must have undergone deformation. And in any case, the very fact that the Gypsies were dispersed among foreign ethnic groups, and wandered for hundreds of years, must have influenced their music. Just as the Romany language absorbed in its many dialects large numbers of foreign elements, so Gypsy music has also built up layers of foreign influence over the centuries.

With the passage of time, the ancient Gypsy instruments disappeared – for example the zither or the Jew's harp. From time to time you can still see small Gypsy boys imitating the music made on these primitive forgotten instruments, by interlacing their fingers and holding them to their chin, and making them tremble, as a result of this, their wordless song, their vocalization, becomes a vibrating sound which somewhat resembles that made by a Jew's harp.

The dances of the women differ from those of the men. A Gypsy woman moves her feet little, her body is held straight and her head is almost motionless, held high. Like the dancers of the East, they mainly move their arms, shoulders and hands. The hands are raised above their heads and fall down, held together and separate. Gypsy dancers pay great attention to the play of hands and fingers. They open and close them as do the dancers of India.

The men's dances are more violent, faster, with more movement and turning. The dancer beats the rhythm with his heel and a swift beating of his hand on his breast, thigh, shin or sole. Those gathered around watching Gypsy men dance, shout, and rhythmically beat their palms together, in this way aiding the musicians and providing an improvised percussion section for the Gypsy band.

The history of Gypsy music-making stretches back a very long way, although we know little about it. The Persian poet Firdusi in c. 1000 A. D. tells how the King of Persia Bahram (430–443) asked his Mobed priests about the condition of his people. Each Mobed praised the king's government in reply, assuring him that under his rule no-one was wronged in any way. They added, however, that the only worry of the poor was that they were unable like the rich to feast with music and wine. Therefore the King Bahram bought from the King of India some musicians called "Luri", who played on zithers. "O most gracious King," Bahram wrote to the King of India, according to Firdusi, "vouchsafe to select ten thousand Luris, men and women, who are skilled in playing the zithers." And there is a hypothesis that these Luri were in fact the Gypsies. There are also theories that the violin, zither and cymbals came to Europe from the East with the Gypsies.

Apart from the age-old music-making, another traditional Gypsy profession, now fast disappearing, is that of blacksmith. It is now possible to find only the very last Gypsy blacksmiths among the highland Gypsies, although in former years, Gypsy blacksmiths were widespread in many countries as well as all over Poland. The presence of the "Gypsy voivode" Polgar in Poland in 1501 together with a group of Gypsy blacksmiths from Hungary, is the first evidence of the appearance of this group in Poland; in 1513, the Gypsy "pixidarius Wanko de Oppavia", was working in the royal service.

For centuries it was the Gypsies who were the blacksmiths in Poland. Their portable smithies were made up of extremely primitive tools, and usually they made use of a stone instead of an anvil. The axes, knives, nails and metal ornaments that they made began to disappear when factory production began: it no longer paid to produce them by hand, for their market had disappeared. Nonetheless, until the Second World War, there was still a group of Gypsy blacksmiths in Poland that lived by their trade. In the depths of the provinces, where it was difficult to purchase anything at all, or to arrange repairs of agricultural implements, the Gypsy blacksmith was still needed. The Gypsy would appear in villages, especially in Southern Poland, in the summer, and produce and sell primitive jewellery: chains, earrings, rings etc.

92

It is thought that the Gypsies brought with them from India or Asia Minor their trades of music-making, blacksmithery and horse-trading. Whatever the case, these are certainly their oldest professions, along with fortune-telling and charming. In the 19th century the Gypsy blacksmiths, like other door-to-door craftsmen, would make their appearance from time to time in larger cities. "What a crowd of the curious would collect in the streets of Warsaw when they arrived! The old Gypsy women told fortunes... and the Gypsy men sold metal goods – of the locksmith's or blacksmith's art," wrote K.W. Wóycicki in 1840.

"Their main ways of earning money are by blacksmithery and theft. Everywhere they set up small anvils, and make nails and horse-shoes, which is very useful for the highlanders," wrote Father Serwatowski in 1851. Other Gypsy trades have, like that of blacksmith, also disappeared in Poland: for example, rushwork and comb-making. The Gypsies, who are very resistant to taking up any kind of new profession, have either taken up other Gypsy professions which have so far not ceased to be profitable like, for example, tinning copperware, or have begun to earn their living by singing and dancing. Or, deprived of their age-old skills and trade, have sometimes become exclusively parasites on the body of society, living by theft. Thus some criminal groups have developed, who have no profession apart from that of burglar. The third chief Gypsy profession was traditionally horse-dealing, which was actually closely linked with the skills of farrier and horse-stealing. In fact, the trade of farrier has already long ceased to exist, although from time to time in recent years there have been cases when a Gypsy farrier has lifted en evil spell which had caused a horse to fall sick.

Horse-stealing continued among some groups until relatively recently, and in the Gypsy hierarchy, the title of *Baro Grengrochor* (The Great Horse Thief) is one of respect – *sit venia verbo*. This age-old Gypsy profession has left many traces in court records. Today, in a period when agricultural work is being swiftly mechanized, and the number of horses is in consequence falling sharply, horse trading is also in decline in comparison with previous periods. But it is still practiced in the Podlasie district by the Polska Roma and the Russian Gypsies – the *Khawaditka Roma*. Once upon a time the Gypsies would buy horses where they were cheaper and take them to areas where the price was higher. They often doctored sick horses, and used all kinds of tricks and remedies to make the horses they were selling look better. For example, the method of "rejuvenating" an old horse by filing down the grooves that appear in its teeth and filling them in with tar, was universally practiced. Skill in suggestively praising the horse offered, and ridiculing the one clients intended to buy, was also an important part of the Gypsy skill in horse-trading. Sometimes the Gypsies even changed the colour of the horses that they sold in case someone realized that he was examining his own horse which had been stolen.

Horse-stealing is considered the most skilled and dignified form of theft. There are many other kinds of theft practiced, down to the everlasting, proverbial theft of a chicken for the Gypsy dinner – *romano khaben*. Wandering Gypsies treat this as something absolutely normal. The Soviet Gypsy expert, A.P. Barannikov, has written: "In order to understand this psychological feature of the nomadic Gypsies, one must remember that the Gypsy psychology is a product stretching right back to the Indian caste system." We might add that the later, European history of the Gypsies also to the highest degree favoured the continuance of these bad habits and the permanent rooting of this Gypsy view of the world.

At the moment, when many Gypsy skills are already things of the past, the most popular current Gypsy trade is tinning copperware. It was above all the Kalderash who have been for generations involved in this, but with the passage of time the Lovari also began to take it up, and some of the remnants of the Churar group, who were formerly comb-makers, and even certain individual Polish lowland Gypsies.

Formerly, the Kalderash also made copper pots, copper boilers and frying pans. But from the time when factory-produced goods deprived them of their market in this area, they have contented themselves with tinning copper boilers, butchers' cambrels and other pots which require the same treatment. The tin *(archichi)* which the Gypsies use for this is prepared in a special way, which is not generally known, and processed into a powder called *kolis.* Thanks to this secret formula which makes their work easier, to the present day the Gypsies are practically indispensable in the field of tinning, and still have plenty of orders. In the post-war years in fact some boiler-makers' co-operatives have been formed which employ only Gypsies. The Gypsies know how to tin *(tiye khanow)* very effectively and fast; according to employers, it is only a Gypsy who can do the work so precisely and in such a short space of time.

Even forty or fifty years ago, the Kalderash still made pots from copper, and repaired holes in boilers; patching holes with copper by a cold welding technique was one of their secret specialities. For this they used an anvil known as a *dopo* which was an iron crowbar, flattened at the top, and at the bottom sharpened and knocked into the earth at an angle. On the top end of the *dopo,* which formed a broadened semi-circular "head", the Gypsies would flatten the copper with hammers and shape the boilers, or carry out all the other necessary metal-work. Wojciech Gerson saw them working like this in Saska Kępa in Warsaw in 1868; he drew them, and described them as follows: "We can see here a completely original way of setting up an anvil. These are long and broad iron bars which are sharpened at one end, and broadened at the other, like an ordinary anvil. They are knocked into the earth at an angle, and therefore offer good resistance to the hammers."

Bear-leading, taking around trained bears, was a very popular Gypsy occupation in the Balkans, and also in the Polish territories, although mainly restricted to Lithuania. The Gypsies who owned bears were usually blacksmiths, and they themselves made the chains and the iron ring for the bear's nose. In the beginning, in times of old, when our forests were full of bears, any Gypsy who wanted could find himself one of these animals to train and lead about. Later, because bears were fast disappearing, it was only the richer Gypsies who could lead bears, or new arrivals from the Balkans, known as Ursari.

We know of the existence of Gypsy bear-leaders mainly from nineteenth century accounts which refer to the 1850s. Prince Karol (Mi'lord) Radziwiłł, took an interest in some groups of Gypsies who travelled on his estates in Lithuania. Many of them had settled on the Radziwiłł estates in the 18th

94

century or earlier, in permanent settlements near the town of Smorgonie which was famous for its Bears' Academy. At that time, Smorgonie consisted of small villages, scattered in the forest, and it was here that the majority of the Gypsies had chosen to settle. They were employed in various crafts – as blacksmiths, in making chains, locks etc.; others made spoons, troughs, spindles, spinning wheels, etc; still others plaited bast shoes, mats or doormats. Under the rule of the Gypsy kings confirmed by the Radziwiłłs, Smorgonie developed and expanded considerably. The duties of one of the Gypsy headmen included the founding of an Academy for Bears at Smorgonie, and the selection of talented Gypsies who would teach these animals to dance and perform other tricks, and arrange suitable accommodation for the four-legged pupils. Young bears caught for the purpose in the prince's forests were brought to the academy at Smorgonie, and sometimes there were as many as several dozen animals there at one time. Radziwiłł also sent monkeys there to be trained. The establishment was open every day and a dozen or more Gypsies were permanently employed in looking after the animals and training them. With royal permission, the Gypsy bear-leaders set off into the world with the graduates of the academy when they had completed their training, "to amuse people with their arts, to collect groats from the spectators, both for the upkeep of themselves and their animals, and also for the payment to the Smorgonie treasury".

In the first decades of the 19th century, because of an official ban and the policies of the partitioning powers, it was increasingly rare to come across Gypsy bear-leaders. There were ever fewer of them to be found in the villages, and they only very rarely reached the towns and cities. "It is as yet less than forty years since bands of Gypsies travelled in large numbers not only through our villages and small towns, but also through Warsaw itself, bringing with them bears that had been taught to dance," wrote K.W. Wóycicki in 1861. "They would be found in the larger courtyards of the houses of the capital of the kingdom, in the squares of the towns, and a gaping crowd of the curious would soon collect to look at our Gypsies, the bears and their gambols."

Another interesting occupation practiced by certain groups of Gypsies was rat-catching, a profession which for centuries has featured prominently in legends and fairy-tales.

There is no way of saying who was the "father" of rat-catching, just as we cannot tell who began the pattern of bear-leading. The Gypsies may have adopted these things from other peoples. It is typical for the Gypsies to borrow some foreign professions and customs and then adapt them to the Gypsy fashion. Sometimes, customs which have died out among the people with whom they originated can still be found in vestigial form among the Gypsies who had at one time borrowed them, made them their own, and subsequently preserved them.

Gypsy rat-catchers appeared in Poland after the last war. After the destruction of war, there was a veritable plague of rats in the ruins of abandoned houses. In 1946 a Kalderash Gypsy appeared in Warsaw who led rats out of the ruins. On 27 May 1946, the daily *Dziennik Ludowy* published an article entitled "The rat-charmer in Pańska Street, a strange procession in the centre of town":

"Last night, late by-passers in Pańska Street were able to witness a strange sight. An elderly man in a hat, the broad brim of which concealed most of his face, was walking down the middle of the street, and beside him walked two small boys wearing the same kind of headgear. The older man was playing on a pipe, and the two little boys were beating on little drums, hitting them lightly with thin drumsticks. Not far behind this strange orchestra ran a band of rats. There may have been several hundred of them. At the corner of Pańska and Chłodna Streets there was a small lorry with a ramp leading up to it from the ground. The musicians went up this ramp into the lorry, and then sat on the roof of the cab, playing all the time. The band of rats stopped at first in hesitation on the pavement, but lured on by the never-ceasing tones of the strange and rhythmical melody, which reminded one of the humming of enormous hornets, began at first singly and then in a group to enter the lorry. When all the rats were in the lorry, several men standing nearby slammed the door shut, and covered the top with a wooden lid. Our correspondent, intrigued by all this, fell into conversation with the elderly leader of the group. He proved to be a 74-year-old Gypsy, Józef Bek, the cousin of Kwiek, the king of the Gypsies who had died in a concentration camp. During the occupation, he also had been in a camp with his whole family, and it had only been thanks to his skill in 'charming' the rats that infested the SS barracks that he had escaped death in the gas chambers along with the other Gypsies. At present he works full time as a rat-catcher, and from rat skins after tanning he makes small items like wallets and cigarette holders etc. Bek has been employed in this profession for forty years. He inherited his skills from his father, who was a famous rat-charmer in Romania, and who had hired himself out as such to travelling circuses, or who had been engaged by various Romanian cities troubled by a plague of rats. He received many commendations and distinctions from institutions for his services in the struggle against rats. His son, who until the war displayed his skills abroad, has only recently taken up the idea of using the rat skins to make various products and has set up a firm to do this. The old man is very mysterious. He did not want to reveal where he lived or the address of the place where he made his rat-skin products. He claimed that it is very easy to hypnotize rats with music, and that you only need to know the secret tones to which the rat's ear is especially sensitive."

Gypsy bear-leading has completely died out in Poland, although it can still be found extremely rarely in the Balkans: in Yugoslavia, Romania or Bulgaria. Rat-catching has also disappeared, and perhaps Józef Bek was the last Gypsy rat-charmer to operate in Poland.

Fortune-telling is another of the most highly typical Gypsy occupations. For centuries it has been Gypsy women who have practiced this art, and they regard it as almost a Gypsy national profession, which was probably brought from Greece, the first "European homeland" of the Gypsies. For many years now Gypsy women have told fortunes mainly from cards, and have only much more rarely read palms.

In fortune-telling, Gypsy women observe certain rules on the whole, but they are never slaves to them, for the main role in fortune-telling is played by improvization. The Gypsy notices the reactions of her clients and in accordance with the clients' semi-unconscious reactions, and the expression on their faces, she gradually realizes what fortune they require, and what they most want to hear. While speaking without break, almost without pause, the

Gypsy woman carries out a careful psychological analysis of her clients. One Gypsy fortune-teller told me the following secrets of her profession: "If a Gypsy women is clever, she can tell fortunes better, and if she's stupid then she can't do it so well, not well enough to get something for it and earn money. In my case, for example, I tell fortunes psychologically: I notice when someone's in a bad mood, or when they're in love, and from their brow I can tell what sort of people they are – good or bad, clever or stupid, strong-willed or weak. That's how I tell fortunes, and as for other Gypsy women I don't know how they do it. When I lay out the cards, I put on a serious face and tell fortunes seriously. That's how people tell fortunes if they know how to do it. Really, when I tell fortunes, I know something at the time and then I forget. I know a lot when I'm doing it, and then I'm even surprised myself at where all the future came from. That's how it is. Then it all comes to mind – humour and understanding. It's like, for example, how a good poet writes poetry when he is in a good mood, and then everything comes to him from his gift and from his skills, so that he is even surprised himself at where it all came from. And then later on he may not even remember. That's what it's like with me too."

Gypsy women tell fortunes from cards *(chuvew fody)* and treat this as their main profession along with magic tricks. There is a wide variety of ways of fortune-telling, and some of them are generally known among the Gypsies and are used by all of them. The Gypsies use the verb *draptey deyw* (to charm, literally, to give herbs) to describe these tricks. Some Gypsy women use a kind of suggestion which is close to hypnosis. Gypsy women with this kind of gift are however extremely rare, and are lost in a crowd of "ordinary fortune-tellers", but they do undoubtedly exist and practice their art. We shall not dwell here on matters like suggestion and telepathy, for there is a lack of scientifically compiled evidence, and our own knowledge of the subject is inadequate. It is however worth devoting a little attention to the properties used in fortune-telling by the Polish Gypsies – extraordinary little figurines which are used to evoke superstitious fear and faith in the magic practices of the Gypsies.

Gypsy Professional Magic and the Native Folk Beliefs

Gypsy fortune-telling and magic, which is the chief source of income of the majority of groups of this people, is based on a skilful exploitation of the superstitious beliefs of the non-Gypsy population amidst which they live. It might seem that people who earn their living thanks to the superstitions of others might themselves be free of superstition, and would be "agnostics" even in matters of primitive folk belief. Such a supposition would of course be wrong. Other people's superstitions, which are made fun of in secret and are made use of to earn money, are simply different from those that the Gypsies keep for their own consumption, which are treated seriously, fully believed in and practiced.

Apart from cards, the properties that Gypsies need for fortune-telling are small figurines and objects known as "little devils", "little corpses", "cubes" and "hairy crosses", which are made of wax, or are compositions from bones, hair etc.

They are not images of any Gypsy demons. And even if they are called "little devils" or "little corpses", these demon figures are produced only for external consumption, their role being to frighten non-Gypsies and evoke superstitious awe. The Gypsies themselves who make these figures have no beliefs attached to them, and do not give credence to their malevolent powers, treating them simply as properties for magic, making it easier for them to earn their living by fortune-telling.

These are therefore understood by the Gypsies themselves as "quasi-devils", "would be corpses" and their aim and pedigree is purely utilitarian. In this lies the heart of the exceptional nature of figurines of this kind in the context of the lore of all other ethnic groups, and the specific significance of these Gypsy products. The fear that they are intended to produce is necessary for the work of the Gypsy fortune-teller: for suitable payment she will offer her services in "removing a charm" or preventing a misfortune which is supposed to be impending. The *bengoro* are sometimes surrealist compositions, showing a one-eyed little devil. His head is made of two hen's eyes closely sewn together, with crooked horns made from hen's claws. One further feature of the *bengoro* is a strand of human hair, trailing down from the hen's eye.

The Gypsies suffer from no shortage of raw material for the production of these things, since chickens are their main game bird, and their favourite dish.

Other little devils are made from wax or paraffin from candles mixed with crumbled charcoal. The Gypsies use this mass which is a little like tar to produce a little devil with horns, four limbs and a tail made from a bunch of hairs. The eyes of a devil like this are red, made from beads or from balls of red paper or thread.

A Gypsy woman will set off for the village with a devil of one kind or another, in order to "charm" *(drab tey deyw, drabakirew).* Sometimes she will take with her a magic "cube" wrapped around with hairs, "a little corpse of wax" or a "cross". And if she has an impression that something is going wrong at some farm or another (illness, fowl pest, crop failure), she will ask the peasant woman for a hen's egg, and wrap it in her shawl, placing it alongside the "little devil" which had been hidden there while the peasant woman was not looking. She asks her client to break the egg, and then unwinds the shawl and takes out of the shell the malevolent little figure. The Gypsy woman will then explain the seriousness of the danger – there is a devil living in the egg. She promises to ward off the "unclean forces" from the house, for an appropriate payment. The "cube", the *kokawo,* can also appear to be "found" at the threshold to the house, in a trough, in a cradle, or in bed linen...

The "little corpses", *mooworo,* are miniatures of a dead man, a wax figure with legs stretched out and hands crossed over his breast. He foretells illness and death, and unlike the "little devil" is not hatched out of an egg, but is born from water on which the fortune teller has cast a spell.

The "hairy cross", *troozoow bawentsa,* is a little cross made from blackened wax, interwoven with human hair. It is used in magic like the "cube" or sometimes like the "little corpse". All these little figurines are

Christian symbols: death, the devil and the cross. The cross is supposed to foretell death and the tomb, and, like the "little corpse", does not symbolize "divine forces": it is interwoven with hair, which gives it negative properties, its extraordinary appearance and its malevolent meaning.

Old documents indicate that many centuries ago Gypsy fortune-tellers were already using these "little devils" or "cubes", and that the procedure was already known in Europe in the 16th century. At the moment, when the native Gypsy demonology is fast dying out, this "money-making demonology" is still alive, exploiting the superstition of the non-Gypsy host society. Practices of this kind might be called exploitation of human ignorance. It is worth citing an account by a young Gypsy woman fortune-teller of something that happened to her while she was travelling around the countryside in 1962. This story indicates that the Gypsy noticed and drew a distinction between human naivety and human misfortune. In a certain cottage, the farmer's wife asked her to cure her son by using herbs and spells. The boy was "completely stupid", according to the Gypsy. He was a mentally retarded child, suffering from epilepsy. His mother explained how much money she had spent on doctors and quacks without any result. And she therefore asked the Gypsy to lift the "evil spell" from the child, promising to pay handsomely. The Gypsy woman gave the child her pack of cards to play with, which pleased him greatly, but refused to help. She gave up a chance to make an easy profit, because she did not wish to cheat this unfortunate mother. "I would have taken too great a sin upon my head," she told me. "I have no mercy for a fool, I'd take his last halfpenny and only laugh at him, but there I couldn't bring myself to *drab tey deyw* (charm)."

The fear by the Gypsies of the evil spirit, and of the devil and the dead, which can be detected in many of their ceremonies and magic practices, in no way comes into conflict with their rites connected with "little devils" and "little corpses", which may be called "the demons of other people's fears". For the Gypsies understand that they have no evil powers. Their task is to arouse fear in the peasant's cottage and not in the Gypsy's tent.

The Gypsy woman, who will smile in her heart at the faith of the Polish peasant woman in these Gypsy "little devils" and "little corpses", and other magical fortune-telling figurines, will nonetheless quite sincerely share the beliefs of her client in the ill-omen of an owl hooting or the calling of a tawny owl. However, the Gypsies consider that fear of bats is senseless and silly, since they believe that the bat is a good omen, and therefore these winged guests are very well-received in a Gypsy caravan. It is very strange that the bat, which lives a nocturnal life, flying only after dusk, is treated quite differently by the Gypsies from the bird of night, the owl. The bat is a personification of happiness and riches, and brings all good fortune. Its appearance over a Gypsy caravan is taken as a sign that the forest where they have pitched their tents is in some way blessed, and that no danger threatens the Gypsies there. The Kalderash call the bat *liliyako,* and some tribes call it *bakhtali* – the "bringer of luck". It is good luck to find a dead bat, so long as it is withered and not decayed. If you keep a withered dead bat in your money bag, you are ensured wealth. The Polish lowland Gypsies, who also believe that the bat is a good omen, sometimes tied the severed wing-paws of the bat to their whip, which was supposed to bring luck to their travel and the horses that drew their waggon.

Another amulet is the *bayero*, which is often given to children – indeed almost every boy – among the Kalderash. This is a small square and flat linen bag. This is hung round a small child's neck to bring luck, ensure health and happiness, and also protect him from illnesses. A piece of iron (*sastree*) and dried herbs (*draboro*) is sewn inside the bag. The iron is to ensure health and strength; sewn inside the *bayero* it will bring the Gypsy child strength to such an extent that he will "become powerful as a knight".

The Polish Kalderash place the herb that they call *strazhniko* in the *bayero*, and this is said to grow only at Częstochowa at the foot of the monastery hill. There has long been a cult of Częstochowa among certain Kalderash clans. This is indicated for instance by the pilgrimage made to Częstochowa by the Gypsy Kirpacz together with his wife and sick son from as far away as Great Britain before the First World War.

The kerchief used to tie up the jaw of a corpse and the *mezoora* used for measurements of the coffin, are highly valued amulets among the Kalderash, and protect them from discovering unpleasant truths and from the police. The magic power of these amulets is derived from the deceased with whom they have come into direct contact. The invisible spirit, through the mediation of the kerchief (*dikwo*) and the *mezoora* passes on the gift of invisibility and of immunity to the object hidden from strangers and to those who are initiated in the matter.

Animals play a leading role as good or evil omens. These, irrespective of whether they are good or evil, are basically taboo and it is therefore not permissible to kill them: in the case of good animals that are friendly towards the Gypsies this is because they bring luck, and in the case of those that constitute bad omens, because this may bring down bad luck upon the perpetrator.

The lizard is an animal that is favourably disposed towards the Gypsies; it warns them of misfortune, and wakes the sleeping when they might be bitten by a poisonous snake. It is therefore forbidden to kill lizards. It is also forbidden to kill birds, since someone who did this would lose his offspring. This is not a rigorous ban, but there are many Gypsies who would not dare to harm a bird. This of course applies only to wild birds and not to domestic fowls like chickens which are killed without qualms. The killing of certain wild birds also sometimes occurs among particular Gypsy groups, for example starlings among the Polish lowland Gypsies.

Snakes, including adders, although they can be dangerous and even fatal, are regarded as sacrosanct by the majority of Polish Gypsies. A harsh revenge is exacted for killing them.

A few decades ago a certain Gypsy man, a horse thief from the Serwa group of Polish lowland Gypsies, was asleep in the forest under a tree. When he woke up he saw a snake crawling towards him. Before he could stand up, he noticed that a whole family of snakes was approaching him. He counted them and found that there were thirteen. He grabbed a staff, and hacking away with all his strength, he managed to kill twelve, while he chopped off the end of the tail of the thirteenth. He did not have to wait long for the consequences. The Gypsy was shortly thereafter arrested and sentenced to twelve and a half years' imprisonment – exactly the number of snakes that he had chopped with his staff.

The Kalderash also recount that a certain Gypsy woman had a dangerous escapade with snakes some years ago. In her tent there was a large wicker basket, which served as a wardrobe. There she kept her clothes and underclothes. In the night, heavy rain fell, and everything in the tent became damp. The following day the weather cleared and the Gypsy woman decided to empty her basket and hang out the contents in the forest to dry in the sun. At the bottom of the basket, to her horror, she found a nest of snakes. Without thinking, she killed them all. But she did not get away with this, and within a short space of time several of her children died.

In order to protect themselves from adders when they are sleeping in the forest, the Gypsies will circle their camp holding a burning rag. They believe that this will prevent any snake creeping into their tents during the nights, for it will not be able to penetrate the enchanted circle delineated by the smoke in the air. Recently, a Gypsy woman brought into a camp a bucket of water from the river, at the bottom of which there was found to be a live snake. One of the Gypsy men was going to kill it with a pitchfork but was warned off by the older men, and spared its life; the snake was carried back to the river in the bucket. It is not only fear of being bitten that dictates the caution of the Gypsies about snakes. They also avoid them because they claim that snakes like to suck the milk from the breasts of sleeping Gypsy women. The Kalderash will assure you that it has often been the case that a snake would creep into a tent, stretch out to its full length alongside a sleeping child and suck milk from the breast of the Gypsy mother.

The Gypsies do not draw a distinction between poisonous and non-poisonous snakes: between the grass snake and the adder. They fear all of them, and are forbidden to kill any. Even to dream of a snake is dangerous, for it is a bad omen, and if in sleep one should say its name, *sap*, ill fortune should be warded off by adding *tye zhaw warachasa* – may he leave with the passing of the night.

To the present day a story is still handed down among the Kalderash in Poland that explains the immunity of snakes: that they are the descendants of the accursed people, and it is therefore forbidden to kill them. The same is true of birds.

Among the majority of Polish lowland Gypsies it would seem that the ban on killing adders has not been maintained. But even those who believe that an adder can be killed claim that to kill the first snake come across in the spring will bring dire consequences.

While living in the forest, some Gypsies are extremely careful not to kill, even accidentally, any frogs. For to kill a frog brings heavy rain and thunder storms. The Gypsy name for the devil comes from India: in Sanskrit a frog is *bheka*, and in Hindi the frog and toad have the same name as the Gypsy devil – *beng*.

The weasel, which plays a very important magical role in the beliefs and rituals of the Balkan Gypsies, is an animal that brings bad luck but at the same time is untouchable for the Polish lowland Gypsies and Kalderash. The Kalderash call it *borory* which means daughter-in-law, the bride, and are afraid of its "blowing" (or "puffing") claiming that it has a habit of throwing itself on men to scratch and bite them. If it only "blows" on people this can bring down ill-luck, illness or even death. The Polish lowland Gypsies also avoid the weasel, and do not kill it, attributing to it malevolent powers. Its name, *phurdini* ("blowing") is actually linked with what they consider to be its dangerous "blowing" on men. Gypsies avoid meeting weasels and if they do see one they try to pass it at a distance.

There are very many things which are ill-omened and whose effects it is necessary to ward off or avoid. The owl, which we have already mentioned, is called the "ugly bird" or the "bird of the dead", and its hooting foretells death. Sometimes, if they see an owl flying overhead, the Gypsies will strike their tents and hastily move elsewhere. There have been cases of the killing of owls by groups of lowland Gypsies, or by the groups of Gypsies of Russian origin, known as the *Hawaditka Roma*. I have heard of the burning alive of an owl in the fire, in order to prevent misfortune. This kind of thing could not really occur among the Kalderash, who do not kill owls. If the Gypsies hear the barn owl or tawny owl hooting, they will reply with curses, wishing the "ugly bird" the very worst of fates.

In the Warsaw zoo, Gypsies will also stand in front of the cages containing owls and hurl curses at them.

The howling of a dog in the night is also a bad sign. The Gypsies claim that Gypsy dogs brought up with a caravan do not howl. Sometimes, however, a Gypsy dog does begin to howl, and then the Gypsies are even prepared to kill it, to avoid ill-luck.

The Gypsies themselves, by carrying out some forbidden action, can call down ill luck on their heads. The incantation *Tye zhaw wa rachasa* (May it leave with the night) is enunciated if after dusk someone says an ill-omened word or does something that is considered an ill omen – for example, to whistle after sundown, or to look in the mirror in the evening.

Some prohibitions of this kind apply only to Gypsy women who are married. They are not allowed for example to walk in front of the shafts of a Gypsy waggon. If this happens, the Gypsies are angry and fear for the fate of the rest of their journey. *Marew wa o dzhew, biebakhtali sas, nakhlas angway hooda!* (May God strike her, bring down misfortune upon her, she went in front of the shafts!)

It is forbidden to pass in front of the tent in the morning with an empty bucket. If you go for water at that time, you have to go round the tent from the back, for otherwise you may "dry up the luck", or bring *shooko bakh* (dry luck) upon those who live in the tent. In order to avert this "drought" from oneself and turn it upon the immediate cause of the problem, that is, the person carrying the bucket in front of the tent, the Gypsies say, *Marew wa o dzhew, nakhli wa shooka bradzhasa! Shuchow wakee bakh!* (May God strike her for walking with an empty bucket! May her luck dry up!).

Warding off spells is a separate chapter of magical practices. According to the Gypsies, these are visited on them not usually by their kinsmen, but by Poles. The first symptom of an evil spell being placed on someone is a headache. It is then necessary to lick the forehead of the afflicted person three times, and then small burnt sticks are thrown into a bowl of water; depending on whether they sink or float, one can tell whether the headache had been the result of a spell. If it is confirmed that someone's "evil eye" was responsible, and that the Gypsy concerned is *dzhino yakhawo*, a triangle is arranged from three needles in such a way that the point of one is through the eye of another. The water that the burnt twig was thrown into is now poured into another bowl through this triangle of needles, and then it is poured out at a crossroads.

To protect themselves from spells, Gypsies wear all kinds of red objects, since this colour is the best protection: it could be a red kerchief, a red ribbon or red beads. Sometimes a *bayero* is made from red linen.

The appearance of certain birds, animals or reptiles is interpreted in diametrically opposed ways among different Gypsy tribes in Poland. For example, the appearance of a magpie, which the Kalderash call *kakaraska*, is interpreted as a good omen by the Polish lowland Gypsies, while the Kalderash believe that a croaking magpie is a sign of bad luck, which will bring the police into their camp, and hand the thief over into the hands of the law.

It would seem that like the vestigial cult of the snake discussed above, the Gypsy beliefs about the moon and stars are also a relic of some extinct myths. It is characteristic that Gypsy amulets, wooden discs, pictures of which were published years ago, usually contain images of snakes, the stars and the moon.

The Kalderash Gypsies greet the new moon to win luck and fortune for their travels. The Gypsies take off their hats to it, bow and ask it to help them, saying, *Tye avyew bakhtawo o son nevo* (May the new moon be happy – happiness-giving). Another version of the moon incantation runs: "A new moon has crossed our path with happiness, so that we should not be penniless, and should be happy, healthy and rich."

The stars are the Gypsies' compass. They have their Gypsy constellations like the *kakhni kakhnyorentsa* – hen with chickens (Pleiad), or *Romano voorden* (Gypsy waggon – The Great Bear). When the "hen with chickens" is high in the sky, luck is not in for the Polish Gypsies. When one star from this constellation is not visible, then it means bad luck for a Gypsy. One old Gypsy woman noted in the period of the Nazi campaign of extermination against the Gypsies in the concentration camps and forests of occupied Poland that one of the stars that formed the "chickens" had fallen. Some Gypsies also say that when one of the three stars from the shafts of the Gypsy waggon falls, then that will spell the end of the Gypsies. Elsewhere they claim that extra stars in the shafts is an ill omen. This belief is however unknown among the Kalderash and is held only by the Polish lowland Gypsies, and not in all groups of them at that.

The old beliefs of the Gypsy demonology, which were still so widespread even a few decades ago in the Balkans, have almost entirely disappeared by now in Poland. There is no trace of the *Roovanoosh* (werewolf) described by Wlislocki in Transylvania in the second half of the 19th century, or of the *Dzhuklanoosh* (dog-man), *Pkhoovoosh* (underground demon), *Khagrin* (incubus) and many others. The *Mamyory* – little old woman – is still however known among the Kalderash and Lovari in Poland. This is an invisible mythical figure, a good spirit who helps the Gypsies. Her presence in the forest, on the stump of a sawn-down tree, which is her favourite dwelling, is attested by a particular kind of fungus, which looks like pinkish or yellowish cream. If a Gypsy finds this kind of fungus on a tree stump, he will collect the "cream" and keep it in a piece of bread. This "cream" carried along in a piece of bread brings luck to the finder. Belief in the three sisters, the three prophetesses of fate to whom we have referred earlier, has also continued to the present day. The *chokhano* and *chokhay* also figure amongst the personae of Gypsy demonology. The *chokhano* is an ill-intentioned ghost of a dead Gypsy which returns to haunt the living; the *chokhay* is something like an incubus. We might add that a moth flying in the night towards the light is also called a *chokhay* by the Kalderash. The Kalderash, along with other Gypsies, believe that sometimes at night an incubus will harass men and horses. Sometimes they even harry horses so much that they cannot sleep, and make plaits in their manes. This is the same evil spirit that harassed the Gypsy horses in Transylvania, and was known to the Balkan Gypsies as *khagrin*. In order to prevent an incubus annoying a man who is sleeping, an axe should be placed under the pillow (so that the evil spirit is frightened by its lethal blade), or a knife and fork (which would make the spirit afraid that it was going to be eaten). The Gypsies have yet another way of discouraging spirits from paying unwelcome visits: before going to bed you should eat something in a place intended for completely different activities – for example near the cess pit. This is intended to evoke in the spirit a feeling of overpowering disgust and revulsion.

While they are camping, the Gypsies are very careful not to pitch their tents on forest paths, even if they are completely unused and overgrown, because *pow droma le vesheskey e rat pkhirehw o byeng* (the devil walks along forest paths at night). Therefore tents are pitched only in places covered with greenery and not beaten down. This devil who walks the paths is probably the same figure as the *roovanoosh* demon known to the Balkan Gypsies. This has been mentioned for example by the Gypsy expert the Archduke Josef Habsburg who wrote: "When they lived in earth cottages built for them on my estates, none of them wished to occupy the last one, lying at the edge of the row, for, they said, an evil spirit – *roovanoosh* – would pass that way." The Kalderash also call the evil spirit *bivoozho* (unclean).

Belief in good and evil omens is especially deeply rooted among the travelling Gypsies and those groups that are less civilized, poorer and more primitive. It has been dying out over recent years, along with other aspects of Gypsy lore, and the post-war generations are already ignorant of many of the beliefs still held and practiced by their fathers. One shocking example of faith in good and evil omens – a faith which in this case constituted a last plank of hope – is the story of the lice in the Auschwitz concentration camp. There is a Gypsy proverb: "Death approaches, the louse leaves", which is based on the observation that lice leave a corpse as the body grows cold. Once in 1943 in Birkenau, when a block was being disinfected, a German who was superintending the Gypsy women in the shower room noticed that one of them was holding something clutched tightly in her fist. She proved to be holding a louse, in a desire to save it from extermination and by so doing also save herself. She explained later that she had done it to bring good luck, "for when a louse leaves man, that means death".

Folk Literature and Papusza
the Gypsy Poet

One peculiar feature of Gypsy lore is the almost entire absence of any of the fine arts, at least at the present stage of Gypsy history. The old professions in the artistic crafts, like metal working or even goldsmithery, have completely disappeared, surviving only in the figurines fashioned mainly from wax as properties for fortune-telling: "little devils", "little corpses" etc. – which have preserved in some residual form the Gypsy traditions of applied art; the colourful costumes of Gypsy women and their love of gew-gaws also still indicate a continuing need to meet certain specific aesthetic requirements.

Folk songs, poetry, fairy tales and proverbs – an unwritten literature – is the only other area apart from music, which has already been discussed, where the folk art of this people has survived.

Gypsy folk poetry still exists in fairly large quantities today, but is undoubtedly by now coming to the end of an era. The old songs are dying out and new ones are only rarely born – they are in retreat before the phenomena of mass culture and the invasion by radio and television – that is by mass media which can overcome even the barrier of illiteracy. The traditional unwritten song, existing only in a form handed down from generation to generation by word of mouth, has no history, and is subject to change and decay. Admittedly the Gypsy song and dance ensembles keep them alive, and their work enjoys success and support, but this applies primarily to the music, while the words sung, which are anyway incomprehensible to the non-Gypsy audience – are reduced in importance and are usually only remnants of what is remembered of the original whole version.

Apart from the works of the contemporary Gypsy poet, Papusza, Gypsy poetry is always sung, is in fact song. All Polish Gypsies sing, each in his own dialect. "You can sometimes find among them," wrote Teodor Narbutt in the first half of the 19th century, "natural poets, who have had no training; some only go so far as to compose songs, while others improvise whole poems, often with dialogue. Usually their verses are set to music, and the music expresses things according to the caprice of the poet. Every song, and sometimes even every verse, has its own music. Their poetry is not made up any differently, it is just that the poet makes up the verses while singing, and when he makes verses he sings. The forgetting of the music sends the verses into oblivion. Gypsies have told me that they have known impromptu poets, who have created completely new songs without hesitation – songs so long that they have lasted for an hour and more. They did not think it possible for anyone to remember the whole of these songs word for word. Nonetheless, they added, there were some young Gypsy women who had such good memories that if they heard something like that only once, they would be able to repeat it at will. They sing recitativo, changing the beat and stress in various ways."

No-one in Poland collected Gypsy poetry: no-one tapped the great resources to be found until relatively recently in the travelling caravans, which still practiced their traditions of song. The only collection made, which is fairly slight and deals only with the poetry of the highland Gypsies, was made by

Izydor Kopernicki in the 19th century and was published before the Second World War. It does not however give a particularly full picture of Gypsy song. Many of the texts recorded then are still alive today among the groups of long-settled sub-Carpathian Gypsies. These are mainly rhymed four-line one-stanza poems. In this respect they bear some similarity to the songs of the local highlanders, which are equally concise. They are sung as individual pieces to a dance rhythm, or sometimes are linked in a chain to the same melody.

The highland Gypsies who create these verses are in a way the Gypsy proletariat, the poorest group of Gypsies in Poland. The main theme in their poetry is poverty and social underprivilege:

> *I am poor*
> *The son of a poor mother*
> *Rich girls*
> *Don't want me.*
> *The rich*
> *Love the rich.*
> *The poor*
> *Love the poor.*

There are still some songs in existence about Gypsy professions – the songs of the blacksmiths and musicians:

> *What do I need coal for,*
> *What do I need iron for?*
> *My black hands*
> *Have not seen work.*
> *My father made me*
> *A hammer and tongs*
> *So that I could work,*
> *So that I'd not get bruised.*
> *In my five tongs*
> *I hold three wires:*
> *From what is broken, what is cracked,*
> *I make what is required.*

Music-making, especially playing the violin, is a way of earning their living for some of the groups of highland Gypsies, and they play in restaurants, at weddings and in tourist centres:

> *They will no longer let us*
> *Play in this inn.*
> *When we played there*
> *They killed my brother.*
> *My little sister ran*
> *Crying so hard*
> *That all her apron*
> *Was filled with tears.*
> *My mother ran after*
> *And gathered up her lost tears.*

It is only playing instruments that the highland Gypsies use as a way of making their living: never singing. They sing only among their own people. But despite the fact that these Gypsies ceased to travel earlier than others, it would seem that here the songs have lasted longer than among the Polish lowland Gypsies who did continue the nomadic way of life. This apparent paradox is easy to explain: the lowland Gypsies, who usually lived and earned their living in towns, were more willing to make use of their songs as a source of income, by singing them to a non-Gypsy audience. In this form of singing, it was the music alone that became important, for the text, incomprehensible to the audience, lost its semantic function, and gradually disappeared because it was no longer essential. This process can be clearly observed over recent decades.

The highland Gypsies, despite their settled way of life, have retained their family and clan communities, and live together in their own isolated groupings. Loneliness, for example as a result of being left an orphan, or being imprisoned, is regarded as the worst possible disaster for a Gypsy. This beautiful duet, which I noted in Biała Woda on the Dunajec river, is a metaphorical plaint and comfort in loneliness:

I no longer have a mother
Or a black-haired father.
I have been left alone
Like a fallen tree.

But that tree
Is not quite alone:
The cold wind blows
And touches its branches.

The lowland Gypsies, who were nomadic and less accessible to outside contact, did not have their songs published in the period when they were still more vital and extensive. However, the fragmentary recordings made by the author after the Second World War indicate that even during the war and shortly afterwards, new works of Gypsy folk poetry were still being created. The old songs were still alive too, and these still remain in the memories of the older generation to the present day. These are usually short songs about life, love, drinking or thieving. The widely-known song of the horse-thief, which begins with what is almost a prayerful invocation is a singular example:

God, send down the black night
So that I can go stealing
So that I can steal two white horses...

In many of the texts of prison songs one can hear the complaint of the imprisoned Gypsy against those who have taken away his freedom, his longing for his family, and threats directed towards his wife who is still at liberty and who is suspected of infidelity. Songs of travelling, which often accompanied a caravan on the move, but which have for years been sung with greatest pleasure during the stay in winter quarters, express joy in travelling in a band, and the wealth which consists in absolute freedom, the Gypsy road, for which no-one would begrudge even shoeing their horses with gold or silver:

The Gypsies are journeying, in many waggons,
Their wheels are creaking,
Their wheels are creaking,
The horses are losing their shoes...
The front horseshoes of gold,
The back horseshoes of silver.

The resourcefulness and thrift of Gypsy women, upon whose shoulders the responsibility for maintaining the family, feeding the children and for ensuring the success of the travelling life of her family usually rests, has been recognised and praised in this song about a mother who manages to cope with unkind fate:

Who is this, who is this
Walking through the woods?
It's my mother,
Breaking branches.
A little rain has fallen,
Put out father's fire.
Who can be found, who will come
To re-kindle the fire?
And my mother came
And fanned the flames.

It is longing for her mother who assures her of care and a feeling of security that this girl's song expresses, as she asks a boy whom she does not love:

I want nothing from you.
Take me back to my mother.
I'm going back to my mother
Like a rose to a garden.

The gradual extinction of the Gypsy folk song has been paralleled in the years after the war by the interesting pattern of the birth of a new song. History touched in the most painful possible way this people who lived, whenever they could, outside history. Condemned by the Nazis to mass extinction, and saved only in part, they managed to bring themselves to accuse their persecutors and bear witness to their fate – in song. This was preceded by another sung complaint:

Where are you? Where are you?
Tell me where you are.
Where has this great war
Driven you?

Songs of lament, the plaints of prisoners and songs of mourning for those who were lost came out of the Nazi concentration camps. These Gypsy songs about the mass extermination differ from other Gypsy music above all in the fact that they contain historical information. The words "Ashvitz" (Auschwitz) and "Oshvientzim" (Oświęcim) are signs of the times and its tragic events. In their traditional, uniform pattern of life, taking place somewhere in the margins of history, it is only exceptional and turbulent events that could enter into Gypsy folk songs, which are normally quite indifferent to historical events. Only a cataclysm that affected their own people directly could leave a new trace in their folk poetry. For the Gypsy folk song is *sui generis* a-historical, speaking of things eternal and ever-topical, like love, death, poverty, flight, loss of liberty, travelling etc. but it does not usually record names of places or concrete events. There are admittedly some grounds for asserting that texts of this kind did formerly at one time exist but that they were short-lived once the facts to which they referred had been forgotten. In the songs about the holocaust one can find certain similarities with many other Gypsy songs which speak of prison and longing for lost freedom. One can already find signs that suggest that with the passage of time, as the Gypsy memory, which easily loses traces of the past, has died out together with witnesses of these events, the concrete details in these songs will also disappear, and they themselves will – if they survive at all in a residual form – become more like the songs from which they stemmed: the songs of prison life, and laments without a historical background of place and time. Today they have almost entirely died out, and although they have not died from memory among the older generation, they are no longer sung. The "black bird" appears in various more or less altered versions – as a messenger between the camp and freedom. In an analogous song of the Slovak Gypsies, this same "black bird" flies as a symbol of liberty which cannot be taken away.

> *In Oświęcim the house is large.*
> *Large is our unhappiness.*
> *Oh! Oh! in Oświęcim*
> *I have a bird*
> *That might take a letter*
> *To my mother, to my father...*
>
> *Lord, lord, Oh dear God,*
> *I'll be lost!*
> *That black bird*
> *Is bringing me a letter,*
> *He's bringing it to where I sit*
> *In Ashvitz.*
>
> *I have dried out without bread,*
> *Without a glass of water...*
> *The star is shining, shining*
> *My candle from the Lord...*
> *Oh, my dear bird,*
> *Bring me the letter*
> *Here where I sit in Oświęcim...*
>
> *I shall never get out of here now,*
> *I shall never see my brother or sisters!*
> *They brought us through the gateway*
> *And let us out through the chimneys...*

The above fragments are taken from several different versions of a Gypsy song about the Auschwitz camp, a place where thousands of Gypsies met their death. This song is falling into oblivion along with memories of those years. The song is fairly simple, concrete and avoids sententiousness, like others of the same type.

The poetry of Papusza, the Gypsy poetess, is quite different from other Gypsy poetry in the richness of its metaphorics, its poetic accuracy, and the colouristics of image and word – and yet it is born of exactly the same parentage as the anonymous Gypsy poetry, and draws its lifeblood from the same source. It is full of brilliance and laconically formulated Gypsy riddles and proverbs. This would seem to offer a fuller expression of the imagination and creative ability of this people than the sung poetry, or at least in those examples of it that are preserved and known to us at the present time. The text quoted above, "I have no mother" is a work of exceptional simplicity and perfection, which perhaps suggests that there may at one time have been more of the same kind of texts in this category of transitory, improvised, sung poetry, and that they may still be taking shape today. We do not however know of any.

Gypsy aphorisms are the embellishments of conversation, serve as an argument, are sometimes improvised, but also include old sayings and proverbs which have been used for centuries and are hallowed by the Gypsy tradition. Here are some of them:

Today's fire is tomorrow's ashes.

Winter will ask you what you were doing in the summer.

Hope allows you to expect, but life does not always allow you to live.

Life is made up of a lot of lies and a little truth.

Don't leave the high-road for a little by-road.

A fly can't get into a closed gob.

A dog that travels will find itself a bone.

Polish ears are so full of the noises of the town that they can't hear what the trees are saying in the forest.

Don't pour water onto ice.

Cut off your tongue before your tongue cuts off your head.

A roast potato tastes better in the forest than meat in gaol.

If the feet don't walk, the mouth doesn't eat.

He bought himself a horse so that he wouldn't have to walk barefoot.

The specific Gypsy sense of humour and laconic style are also shown in the folk riddles:

How can you recognise a Gypsy's dog? (By its singed tail).

The more you cut off it, the bigger it gets (A hole).

What do all living things on earth do at the same time? (Grow older).

Can a one-eyed man see more then a two-eyed man? (Yes, because he sees the two eyes of the two-eyed man, while the two-eyed man sees only the one eye of the one-eyed man).

What can the Lord God not see? (Anyone else like himself).

What goes along with our caravan as a guest, even though no-one took it along with them? (A rumble).

The creative feeling for the comic, for paradox and for the absurd that is reflected in these aphorisms and riddles would seem to be characteristic of the

110

mentality of this people which is reflected in everyday conversations at almost every step; it is a symptom of a particular, subtle ability to interpret the world in a humorous way which even illiterates have.

Apart from the songs, proverbs and riddles, fairy tales and legends constitute another important area of unwritten folk literature cultivated by the Gypsies. Among the groups of urban Gypsies, where their traditions have to a large extent been commercialized, fairy tales are fast dying out. Elsewhere, however, they have survived to the present day. They can be divided roughly into two basic categories. The first are fairy tales about the fantastic adventures of the Gypsies or of kings, princes and other heroes of one kind or another. The second category covers fairy-tale myths of an etiological nature, which might seem to be a fragment of some no longer existent "Gypsy bible". This includes a fairy-tale version of the genesis of the world, the quarters of the moon, a myth on the creation of man, on the origins of fair-haired men, on the origins of the family of snakes, on the birth of the violin etc. In these tales, God created the world from sand taken from the bed of the ocean, and also made the first trees to bear men and animals as fruit. These mythological pieces also include tales which are a kind of parable with their own philosphy. An example of this is the parable known to the Kalderash Gypsies which tells how God tried to graft on patience to the world that he had created:

When God had created the whole and thought that the work was over, he sat down on the seventh day under a tree to rest. Suddenly he remembered that there was one thing he had not done: he had not dealt with patience, and he did not know what would be the best place for her. God started to consider what to do with her. At first he decided to put her into water. So that is what He did. But the water dried up. He therefore wanted to breathe her into a tree, but the tree that received her withered and its branches hung down, it cracked open and turned to dust. God went to a cliff and called, "Rock! Stone rock! I hereby send you the power of patience." But the cliff cracked, and crumbled into sand and stones. The idea therefore came to God that he would give patience to the man who lived in Paradise. And that is what he did. And the man groaned, sighed, and bore it. And from that time on, men have been able to bear more than water, and than timber and than rocks.

The legend about people turned into snakes and birds by a spell is *sui generis* the mythical explanation of the taboo. Gypsies are not allowed to kill snakes and birds on pain of incurring misfortune, illness and even death. The mythical genealogy of these creatures, their human origins, explains the ban which is absolutely binding on the Kalderash. Here is one of the many versions of this story:

There was once a King who had a wife, the Queen, and an only son, the Prince. But the Queen died prematurely and left the King in sorrow and mourning, which he kept up for a whole year. But after the last rites of the year-long *pomana,* the mourning came to an end and the King married again. He took as a wife a widow from the royal family. They lived together happily, but one day the King died. Then the Queen began to try to persuade her stepson to marry her but the young King did not even wish to hear of it. His angry step-mother put an evil spell on him, and changed him into a snake as a punishment to wander in the wilderness for three summers and three winters, living on vermin and never able to satisfy his hunger. The young King, turned into a snake, left his step-mother's castle and escaped into the neighbouring forest. When three years had passed, he became a human being again. He did not return home, for he feared that he would have to marry his own step-mother or be turned into a snake again. So he set off into the world; he walked and walked until he reached another kingdom. He became friendly with the King of that kingdom and married his beautiful daughter. Soon they had two children: a boy whom they called Puyo (Chick) and a little girl whom they called Woowoodzhi (Flower). The mother of these children persuaded her husband to agree to pay a visit to his step-mother, the grandmother of Puyo and Woowoodzhi, together with his whole family. The young King did not want to agree, but finally his wife told him that his step-mother had certainly become kinder in her old age, that she could no longer be thinking of marrying him, and that the children needed a good grandmother. Finally the young King agreed, that they would go to his step-mother's castle but that he himself would not go in, but would wait for the return of his wife and children. They in return had to promise him that they would say nothing about him and would not mention the fact that he was waiting nearby in the forest. They went. The step-mother began to ask questions about her step-son, but she was unable to discover anything. So she promised her grand-daughter that she would give her a great many beautiful toys if Woowoodzhi would tell her where her father was, for she greatly longed to see the young King. The little girl trusted her wicked grandmother and told her the truth, for she did not know that you do not tell the truth to wicked people. The wicked witch then turned towards the nearby forest and called out, "Once upon a time I turned you into a snake for three years! Now I put the same spell upon you for life and for eternity!" At that very moment, the King who was waiting in the forest turned into a great snake, and the coach and horses turned into three juniper bushes. His wife and children fled from the castle, but when they got to the forest, they saw only the snake who crawled out from under the junipers and said, "I am your husband and the father of your children. All this has happened because of you, it is your fault for you persuaded us to come here. I curse you: turn at once into a poisonous adder! When you give birth to children, may you give birth through the throat, and eat them all up. May only those live that you don't manage to gobble up!" At that very moment, the wife of the accursed snake turned into an adder. He also cursed his daughter for not keeping his secret. He called out to her, "You will be a bird without a nest, and you will not have the right to bring up your own children. May they be homeless, brought up by strangers, like orphans." At that very moment, Woowoodzhi turned into a cuckoo. And the snake called out to his son, "Although you are not as guilty as she is, nonetheless, you did not prevent your sister from betraying me. Therefore since your name is Puyo henceforth you will become a real chick, and later a fully-fledged bird. And you will gladden the hearts of human beings with your song for three months of the year!" And at that very moment his son became a nightingale. Then the King who had been turned into a snake crawled into his wicked step-mother's castle and bit her whereupon she turned into an owl.

The Gypsy tales also include accounts of their origins, autobiographical myth, with a legendary version of the genealogy of the Gypsies. They mainly tell of the origins of the Gypsies in Egypt and of the presence of the Gypsies at the Crucifixion of Christ. One of these stories tells of a Gypsy woman who stole a nail from one of the executioners, so that both of Christ's feet had to be fastened with one nail. Sometimes the Gypsies add extra elements to this story: they say that the Gypsy woman, afraid of the theft of the nail being discovered, hid it in a flitch of bacon fat. And until the present day, Gypsy women begging in villages ask first for bacon fat, hoping that one day one of them will find that stolen nail in the flitch that they are given.

The legends about the Egyptian origins of the Gypsies sometimes include accounts of the passing of the Jews through the Red Sea, and at the same time the drowning of the majority of the Gypsies of whom only a small number survived and were scattered over the face of the earth. In another and similar account, the leaving of Egypt by the Gypsies in explained differently:

There was a great Pharaoh in Egypt, and once upon a time he drove all the Jews out of his country. The eldest daughter of this Pharaoh, the beautiful princess Kali Mura (Bilberry) told the Gypsies: "You too must leave here and set off into the world and wander for many years, and even many hundreds of years. There will be many kinds of Gypsies among you: Boiler-makers, Horse-traders, Music-makers, Blacksmiths and Fortune-tellers. But for every thousand fortune-tellers only one will be a true fortune-teller, and the others will pretend. After many years, you will find for yourselves a beautiful, warm country and that will be your homeland." Kali Mura had a golden wand, and she waved the wand. And at that moment the sea dried up to the bottom and the Gypsies crossed the sea with dry feet. And they are still walking to the present day.

Gypsy folk literature which is still alive in the oral tradition, deserves further research of all kinds before it dies out altogether: above all it must be documented, and its transitory pieces recorded permanently. Not only traditional Gypsy suspicion of outsiders consitutes a barrier to this, but also and perhaps primarily lack of knowledge of Romany among ethnographers, the people who would be required to carry out this important work.

Only the poetry of Papusza exists in her own written version, which is something exceptional in the world of Gypsy literature. She is the first conscious poet among the Gypsies whose name is known. Her real name is Bronisława Wajs, but she is known by her Gypsy first name, which is what she used to sign her letters and verses with: Papusza, meaning doll. Papusza was able to give her texts a permanent form because of her ability to read and write which she acquired in childhood thanks to her own determination and to the stolen chickens with which she paid her chance teachers. The present author, who discovered her poetry, persuaded her to write down her poetic improvisations, and then translated them into Polish and published them. He has called them songs, in Romany *geela,* for almost all of them were improvised impromptu to a melody; unfortunately none of the melodies are known, for they were not recorded either by gramophone or by notation.

Papusza's date of birth is not known precisely, and the poetess herself was not sure of the year when she was born. Years ago, she told the present author that it was 1909, but in official documents the date 30 May 1910 is given, and also 17 January 1908. In this generation of Polish Gypsies, the ability to read and write is exceptional. The traditions of the musical groups of Gypsies that Papusza became part of when she married a harpist called Dionizy Wajs, undoubtedly influenced her interest in Gypsy songs, and made possible her poetic spinning of words to accompany music. Her greatest period of poetry writing was in c. 1950, soon after she had abandoned the nomadic way of life, at a turning point in the history of the Polish Gypsies and in a period of growing drama for the whole people. Papusza was a participant in and a mouth-piece for these movements, and her songs are the only artistic accounts given of the drama. As she bade farewell in her songs to the lost nomadic era, and at the same time to her own youth, she became the glorious bard of the whole of her people, expressing their general attachments, habits and longings. This longing for what is lost, which is the *spiritus movens* of her work, is not an isolated and individual sentiment, but was shared with all her Gypsy kinsmen. But her brothers and sisters did not repay her for this with gratitude. She was held to be a "traitor" and was ostracised by Gypsy public opinion for her alleged collaboration with the non-Gypsy host society. She therefore stopped writing for seventeen years, and only in the late 1960s again spoke out for the last time, with a few splendid poems. From that time, ill and much wronged by her own people, she composed nothing; she died on 8 February 1987.

Paper and pen have made it possible for Papusza to record permanently in verse much more and in much more detail than has been the case for the unwritten folk song. The written record has made it possible to preserve her work even though it may already have escaped the author's memory. Papusza was able to give voice to many matters that had never previously been widely expressed in Gypsy folk poetry, and was able to use at times of a much more complex plot, deeper reflection, and verse of a much more expansive nature. On the other hand, Papusza's poetry could not be improved like other folk poetry by constant circulation, by repeated performance, which introduces corrections and sometimes adds new elements, while inessentials which have not passed the test of widespread singing are rejected. Papusza's songs, which have been translated and published twice by the present author, represent the whole of the poet's work: that is, less than 30 verses in all, some long and some short.

One of the first of Papusza's written poems is "Gypsy song composed out of the head of Papusza", dedicated to Julian Tuwim and rated highly by that poet. It is written throughout in a tone of final farewell, an attempt to resurrect in words the lost past of travelling in the forest:

> *I love the fire as my own heart.*
> *Winds fierce and small*
> *Rocked the Gypsy girl*
> *And drove her far into the world.*
> *The rains washed away my tears,*
> *The sun – the golden Gypsy father –*
> *Warmed my body*
> *And wonderfully singed my heart...*
>
> *... the Gypsy horse neighs,*
> *Wakes strangers*
> *But gladdens a Gypsy heart.*

A squirrel on a Gypsy hood
Nibbles a nut...
Oh how fine to live,
To hear all this!
Oh how fine to live,
To see all this...

Oh how fine to live,
In the night go to the river,
Catch cool fish like cold water
In your hand...

In heaven the hen and chickens
And the Gypsy waggon.
They foretell the whole Gypsy future
And the silver moon,
The father of forefathers from India,
Gives us light,
Watches the children in the tent,
Lights the Gypsy woman
That she may swaddle the baby well...

No-one understands me,
Only the forest and river.
That of which I speak
Has all, all, passed away,
Everything, everything has gone with it –
And those years of youth.

The fragments cited above give some picture of her work as a whole. "No-one understands me, only the forest and river," she wrote, and this is not merely a poetic figure of speech. The poet's last verses include two which return to these two confidants, the Forest and the River, and represent a permanent reference to longing for what has been lost – or more, for a congenial element. This is something in which the essence of the Gypsy community has survived, although by now absent from those forests and those thickets. The forest – the father and teacher of Gypsies – which had abandoned its children; the river which no longer meets its wandering neighbours, but follows their custom and itself wanders:

O forest, my father,
My black father!
You reared me,
You abandoned me.
Your leaves tremble
And I tremble like them,
You sing and I sing,
You smile and I smile.
You have not forgotten
And I remember you.

Oh Lord, where should I go?
What can I do?
Where can I find
Legends and songs?
I do not go to the forest,
I meet with no rivers.
Oh forest, my father,
My black father!

The time of the wandering Gypsies
Has long passed.
But I see them,
They are bright,
Strong and clear like water.
You can hear it
Wandering
When it wishes to speak.
But poor thing, it has no speech
Apart from silver splashing and soughing.
Only the horse, grazing the grass,
Listens and understands that soughing.
But the water does not look behind
It flees, runs away further,
Where eyes will not see her,
The water that wanders.

Nature seems to have taken over the Gypsy customs, and will not allow them to perish. It is the forest that has not abandoned its travelling inhabitants, and which cannot forget them. In Papusza's songs the forest expresses feelings, and is the lyrical co-hero. And so: *vesh bagge romanee geelee* – the forest sings the Gypsy song; *khten and khhewen po vesh wen adzha siklakeerdzha* – they are jumping and dancing, for that is what the forest taught them; *(Vesha) keetsi toome romane chhavoren bareeakeerde sir kooshcha toomare tikne* – (Forest, how many Gypsy children have you reared, like your own bushes).

Apart from poetic miniatures, like those cited above, Papusza has also written longer pieces in epic and ballad form – that is in forms earlier employed by impromptu song writers. The longest and most important of them are "Earring of Leaves", "Bloody Tears", and "O My Earth, I am Your Daughter".

The ballad about the earrings requires a botanical and etymological commentary. It deals with the way in which poor Gypsy women who could not afford gold jewellery made themselves ornaments from the golden autumn leaves of the oak tree adorned with oak apples. And these oak apples are caused by insects which lay their eggs in the leaves of the oak tree, forming a round reddish growth on the leaf, like small apples of paradise. They play the role of precious stones, rubies, the Gypsy "leafy earring". Here are some fragments from the ballad:

The poor forest girls
Beautiful as bilberries

Wanted to wear
Golden earrings.

Old Gypsy women and young girls
Went wood-gathering in the forest.
They lit a huge fire by the river
And sang a beautiful song about
Gypsy earrings: O my beautiful earring,
You give me beauty,
You break everyone's heart!

The wind has already blown out the flames,
The river heard the song
And carried it far into the world.
They didn't know how or whence
An oak leaf with oak apples
Fell into a girl's lap...

We'll make with them wonderful
Gypsy earrings!
How beautiful you are,
Earring of leaves!
The oak apples that you bear
Like precious stones!

The second poem is a kind of prolix, rhymed autobiographical tale about tragic war-time experiences in the forests of Volhynia. The full title is "Bloody Tears: What We Went Through Under the Germans in Volhynia in the Years '43 and '44". This deals piercingly with round-ups and executions, murders carried out by bands of Ukrainians, flights through the forest, help given by the partisans. There is also an act of heartfelt solidarity with Jews hiding from the holocaust, mourning for those killed, the death of children from starvation and cold – and finally a prayer for salvation and for the destruction of the enemy. Here are a few representative verses, which as in the preceding examples are literal translations from the Romany original.

In the forest without water, without fire – great hunger,
Where were the children to sleep? There was no tent.
A fire cannot be lit at night,
By day the smoke would give a sign to the Germans.
How to live with the children in the harsh frost?
All barefoot...
When the Germans were to murder us,
They first took us for hard labour.
Some German came to the Gypsies in the night:
"I've something unpleasant to tell you:
They want to murder you tonight.
Tell nobody
For I am a black Gypsy,
Blood of your blood – a real one!

May God grant you luck
In the black forest..."
These words he spoke
And kissed us all...

For two or three days there was nothing to eat
And they went hungry to sleep.
Their eyes did not close,
They looked at the stars...
O Lord, it is fine to live.
The Germans don't let you live.

O, my little star,
O daybreak, how great you are!
Blind the eyes of the Germans!
Draw them along wrong paths!
Don't show them the right way,
Show them the wrong way,
So that the Jewish and Gypsy children can live!..

When the great winter comes,
What will the Gypsy mother do with her children?
Where will she find clothing? a dress?
Everything is falling to rags, leaving the body bare
And you want to die.
Nobody knows, only the heavens,
Only the river hears this weeping.
Whose eyes saw evil in us?
Whose lips cursed us?
Do not listen to them, O Lord,
Listen to us!
The cold night has fallen,
The old Gypsies were singing
A Gypsy fairy tale:

The golden winter is closing in,
Snow is falling to the ground, on the hands
Like little stars.
The black eyes are freezing.
The hearts are dying.

So much snow has fallen,
It has covered the way,
Only the Milky Way in the sky can be seen...

In this frosty night
The daughter died
And four days later
The mother buried their four sons
In deep snow.

Just look, Sun, how without you
Gypsy children die in the winter
In the great forest!
Once at home the moon was at the window
And I couldn't sleep. Someone looking in through the window.
I ask, "Who's there?"
"Open the door, my black Gypsy."
I look, and in comes a beautiful Jewish woman,
Trembling and shaking
And asks for food.
Poor you, my Jewish friend!
I gave her bread, what I had, a shirt.
We both forgot that the police
Were not far away.
But they did not come to us that night...

All the birds
Pray for our children
That they may not be killed by wicked people, wicked snakes
Oh, our fate!
How unlucky my luck!

The snow fell, snow flakes fell as large as leaves
And blocked our way.
Such deep snow that the whole wheel was buried.
We had to make a way by foot
And push the waggons after the horses.
What poverty and hunger!
What sorrow and how far,
How many sharp stones drove into our feet!
How many bullets whistled past our ears.

Papusza's poem, together with the anonymous songs about Auschwitz, (Ashfitz), form a memorial to the years of contempt and extermination. Hers is undoubtedly the most outstanding Gypsy voice, artistic witness to the tragedy of a homeless people – the only one of its kind. One of the last poems that she wrote before her penultimate period of silence, lasting seventeen years, was entitled, "My Land, I Am Your Daughter". This is a major work, and moreover deserves particular attention for non-literary reasons: as a deep and highly individual expression of her own kind of Gypsy patriotism and also attachment to Poland. In a review of the translation of a collection of Papusza's songs published by the present author some years ago, a British Gypsy expert claimed that this poem was false, was unthinkable in the mouth of a Gypsy.

This view is quite mistaken. Papusza is a Gypsy from the *Polska Roma* group, that is the group of Polish lowland Gypsies, who for many tens of generations have never left Polish territory, and are therefore tied to the country of their birth and antecedents. The Polish language is the only one that they speak apart from Romany – only occasionally do they know a little Ukrainian or

German. Papusza herself never travelled outside Poland, and all her experiences and memories concern Polish lands. It is true that a Gypsy polyglot globetrotter could not write and sing poetry of this kind – that is a Gypsy from one of the tribes that travel far and wide, from country to country, never staying for a longer period in any of the places that he passed through. The title of the original is *Phoov meeree me som chhateeree*. This fragment of a Gypsy confession brings to an end our exploration of Gypsy society:

> *O land, mine and afforested,*
> *I am your daughter.*
> *The forests sing, the land sings.*
> *The river and I combine this hymn*
> *Into one Gypsy song.*
> *I will go into the mountains,*
> *The high mountains,*
> *I shall put on a beautiful marvellous skirt,*
> *Made from flowers*
> *And I shall cry with all my strength:*
> *Polish land, red and white!*
>
> *My land, you were in tears,*
> *You were pierced with pain,*
> *O land, you cried in your sleep,*
> *Like a little Gypsy child*
> *Hidden in the moss.*
> *I apologize to you, O land,*
> *For my poor song,*
> *For the Gypsy signs.*
> *Place your body and mine together*
> *When all is over and I die, you will receive me.*
>
> *O land of black forests,*
> *I grew from you,*
> *I was born in your moss.*
> *All living things*
> *Bit and worried*
> *My young body.*
> *O land, you have laid me to sleep*
> *With tears and songs,*
> *O land, you have thrown me into good and evil.*
> *O land, I believe firmly in you,*
> *I can die for you.*
> *No-one will take you from me*
> *And I will give you back to no-one.*

1. *Gypsies,* woodcut, 1689

Paweł Karol Lubartowicz na Białym Kowlu Smolanach y Rakowie Xiąże Sanguszko Hrabia na Wiśniczu Jarosławiu y Tarnowie. Marszałek Nadworny W. X. L.

Znaymuię komu o tym wiedzieć należy osobliwie iednak Ichmm Panom Komissarzom Ekonomom Gubernatorom, pełnią Dispozycyom Dobr moich Zasławskich y Konstantynowskich iz maiąc zalecona skromność Bartosia Alexandrowicza nacion Cygana, y iego sposobność aby miał nad inemi Cyganami zwierzchność. Daię mu to Prawo na Woytostwo tak w mieście moim Zasławiu iako też w Starym Konstantynowie wiele tylko Cyganów znayduie się, wszyscy do tego dependency należeć powinni będą iednak pod surową Karą przykazuię Temuż Bartoszowi Alexandrowiczowi Woytowi, żeby takich tylko Cyganów przyimował do Miast. ktorzy bez żadnego złego Uczynku sprawować się zwykli, y przestrzegac tego Pilno powinien Woyt wyżej Namieniony aby tak w Dobrach moich, iako też Obcych Chłastwa ani Kradzieży nie było, ani Krzywdy Poddanym nie czynili, ale skromnie Handle y Rzemiosła swoie, bez naymnieyszego szukania prowadzili. Cokolwiek tedy Cyganow będzie mieszkało w Dobrach moich Zasławskich y Konstantynowskich, od każdego Gospodarza corocznie odbierać będzie powinien Bartosz Woyt po Talerow dwa bitych dobrey monety, niezaież żadnego, y PP. Gubernatorom moim do Skarbu mego oddawał ~~~~~~~~~~~~ ~~~~~~~~~~~ ~~~~~~~~~~ ~~~~~ żeby PP. ~~ Gubernatorowie moi cokolwiek złych Akcyi postrzegą w Cyganach, takowych Chłastwa zaraz z miast y zе wsiow moich wypędzac kazali. Na co się podpisuię. Dan w Zamku moim Zasławskim Dnia 13. Miesiąca Marca Roku 1732.

Paweł Xiąże Sanguszko
MWM

2. Charter of Prince Paweł Karol Sanguszko
   to the Gypsy Bartosz Aleksandrowicz,
   granting him overlordship of the Gypsies, 1732

3. Jan Marcinkiewicz, King of the Gypsies,
   pays a visit to Prince Radziwiłł at
   Nieśwież, Wojciech Gerson, 1867

4. *Gypsies,* woodcut, 1834

5. *Fortune-telling Gypsy woman,*
   Kajetan W. Kielisiński, etching, 1841

7. Gypsy tinsmith from the Kalderash group in Cracow, c. 1865

8. A member of the Kalderash tribe, c. 1865

6. *Gypsies*, colour engraving, 1st half of 19th century

10. Kalderash Gypsies, c. 1865

9. A Gypsy with a pipe, c. 1865

11. A Kalderash Gypsy, c. 1865

14. Gypsies from the tinsmiths' group (in the centre, their headman, carrying a decorated staff, his badge of seniority), c. 1865

13. A Kalderash Gypsy woman, c. 1865

17. Copper kettle, Gypsy workmanship, 19th century

15. Brass button, Gypsy workmanship, 19th century

16. Ring, Gypsy workmanship, 19th century

18. Detail
    of a bas-relief carved
    Gypsy staff

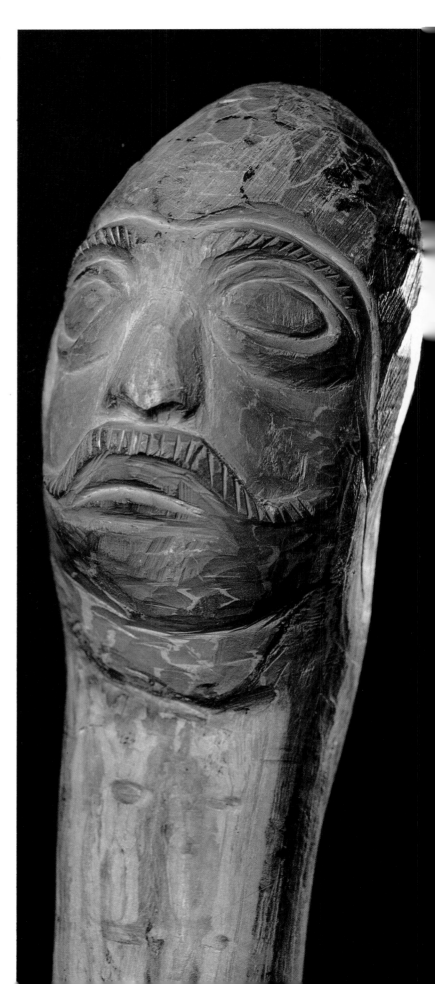

19. Apron with deep sack-like pockets

20. Nails which used to be made
in former times by the Gypsy
blacksmiths in the
Sub-Carpathian region

21. Gypsy property for magic
– the *bengoro* (little devil)
in a hen's egg

22. Gypsy property for magic
    – the *mooworo* (little corpse)
    in a glass of water

23. Gypsy property for magic
    – the *trooshoow bawentsa*
    (hairy cross)

24. Gypsy tinkers at Błonie in Cracow, 1870

25. *Gypsies by the Water*, Wincenty Smokowski, oil, late 19th century

26. *Gypsy camp*, Maksymilian Gierymski, oils, 1868

27. *Gypsies,* Aleksander Kotsis, oils, c. 1860–70

28. *From the Napoleonic Epic* (detail), Stanisław Wolski, oils, 1886

29. *Gypsy Tents,* Zygmunt Sidorowicz, oils, 1876

30. *Scenes from Gypsy Life,* Maksymilian Gierymski, oils, 1868

31. *Gypsies,* Antoni Kozakiewicz, oils, 1924

32. *The Young Virtuoso*, Antoni Kozakiewicz, oils

J. Mien   CRACOVIE
                                                ZAKOPANE

33. The fortune-teller,
    end of 19th century

34. *The Gypsy Woman*,
    Antoni Kozakiewicz,
    oils, 1909

35. *Gypsy camp at Błonie*,
    Juliusz Kossak, water colour

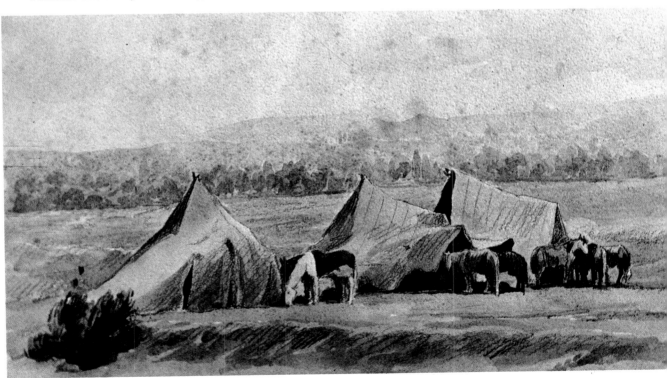

36. *Gypsy Encampment at Saska Kępa near Warsaw,* Wojciech Gerson, engraving

37. *Gypsies,* Józef Brandt, engraving from picture, 1866-67

38. *Gypsies Resting,* Franciszek Streitt, engraving, 1886

39. *The Gypsy Headman,* Tadeusz Popiel, 1898

40. *The Bear-Leader,* Hipolit Lipiński, from oil painting, 1873

41. *The Gypsy Funeral,* Franciszek Kostrzewski, engraving, 1868

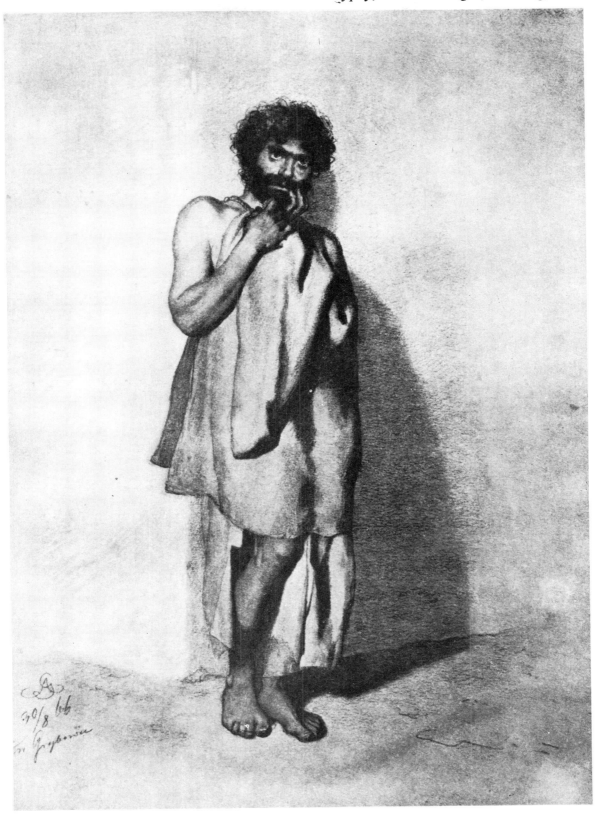

42. *A Gypsy,* Artur Grottger, drawing, 1866

43. *Maternal Bliss,* Antoni Kozakiewicz, postcard from a painting

44. *The Gypsy Caravan,*
Michał Pociecha, engraving, 1878

45. *A Gypsy,* Józef I. Kraszewski,
    engraving from a drawing, 1860

48. *The Gypsy Camp,*
Antoni Piotrowski,
engraving, 1873

49. *The Gypsy Camp,*
Walery Brochocki,
engraving, 1873

46. *The Gypsy Caravan,* Apoloniusz Kędzierski, engraving, 1882

47. *The Gypsy Wedding,* Antoni Piotrowski, engraving, 1873

50. *The Gypsy Camp,* B. Puc, engraving, 1882

51. *The Gypsy Bivouac,* Henryk Pillati, engraving, 1861

52. *The Gypsy Woman*, Henryk Pillati, engraving, 1863

53. *The Gypsy Camp*, Michał Pociecha, engraving, 1878

54. *The Gypsy Camp,* Henryk Pillati, engraving, 1873

55. *Gypsies,* Michał Pociecha, engraving, 1880

Cygany....

... Nędza jest strasznie silną!!! ale i ja!. strasznie silny!! .. czekajmy kto kogo zmo...

56. *Gypsies*, Franciszek Kostrzewski, watercolour, c. 1868

57. *Gypsies,* Antoni Kozakiewicz, engraving, 1887

58. *Gypsies,* Henryk Pillati, engraving, 1886

59. *Gypsies with Bears,* Ludwik Kurella, engraving, 1877

60. *A Group of Gypsies,* Kazimierz Młodnicki, pencil drawing, 1860

61. *A Gypsy Band Settled at Rytro,* postcard photograph, c. 1900

62. *A Gypsy Tent,* postcard photograph, Cracow 1902

63. A Gypsy in front of a tent near Cracow,
photograph from before 1900

64. *Gypsies near Krościenko on the Dunajec River,*
    postcard photograph, early 20th century

65. *The Gypsy Marcin with his Family at Krościenko,*
    postcard photograph, c. 1900

66. *A Gypsy Wedding in the Bolechów Market Place,*
postcard photograph, c. 1910

Wesele cygańskie na targowicy w Bolechowie.
Циганьске весїлле в Болехові на торговици.

67. Gypsies, Stanisławów, photograph, 1919

68. Scenes from a Gypsy camp, photographs, 1908

69. A Kalderash Gypsy in a jacket with silver buttons, Warsaw, photograph, c. 1925

70. Kalderash Gypsies, Todor Czoron with his wife Liza after arriving in England from Poland, photograph, 1913

71. Gypsy women on the porch of the manor house at Worochta, photograph, 1932

72. *The Gypsy Fortune-teller*,
postcard photograph,
c. 1910

73. Gypsy bear-leader in
the Pieniny Hills,
photograph, 1930

74. Gypsy carts,
photograph, 1930s

75. Gypsy encampment in the snow at Leszczyny, photograph, c. 1930

76. Gypsy women by a cart, c. 1930

77. The Gypsy's augury, c. 1930

78. Street musicians, Cracow, c. 1930

79. Gypsy tinkers, c. 1930

80. Kalderash leader, Dymitr Koszor Kwiek, with his family at Marymont, 1928

81. Michał Kwiek,
    the "King of the Gypsies", 1931

82. Michał Kwiek, after his coronation
    at Hajduki Wielkie, 1934

83. Józef Kwiek, the "President of the Gypsy Nation", 1935

84. Matejasz Kwiek, the "Leader of the Gypsy Nation", 1935

85. The visiting card of the "Baron of the Gypsies in all Poland", Matejasz Kwiek, c. 1933

Zjednoczenie
...ganów podlęgających...

Zjednoczenie

...niezale... na
...oespe... wo
Pols...

...owi Rzplitej Pol...
przewodnictwem
...sza Narodu Cyganskiego
...Matejasza Kwiek...

Matejasz Kwiek
Baron Cyganów na całą Polskę

SPECJALNY ZAKŁAD KOTLARSKI
Wykonywa wszelkie roboty kotlarskie dla instytucji
wojskowych i cywilnych. Pobielanie cyną angielską.
Szwejsowanie metali najnowszym aparatem.

Poznań, ul. Kopczyńskiego 31.

86. Funeral of Matejasz Kwiek at Wola in Warsaw on 30 March 1937

87. Coronation of Janusz Kwiek in Warsaw in 1937

I-SZA W POLSCE
WIELKA UROCZYSTOŚĆ
KORONACJI KRÓLA
CYGAŃSKIEGO

WYBÓR i KORONACJA = KRÓLA =

NA STADIONIE WOJSKA POLSKIEGO

Dnia 4 lipca 1937 r. od godz. 18 do 23

30 senatorów cygańskich przybyłych z różnych państw obiera z pośród 5 kandydatów

KANDYDUJĄ:

I. **RUDOLF KWIEK**   III. **JANUSZ KWIEK**

II. **BAZYLI KWIEK**   IV. **MICHAŁ KWIEK**

V. **SERGIUSZ KWIEK**

W PROGRAMIE:

Głosowanie na wybór króla, tłumaczone dla Sz. Publiczności, i nadawane przez megafony. Po czem nastąpi koronacja, której dokona wielebne Duchowieństwo prawosławne na czele z Arcybiskupem.

Po koronacji, wystąpi zespół cygański składający się z 50 osób znanych z filmów: „Oczy czarne", „Burłak z nad Wołgi", „Moskiewskie Noce" pod kierownictwem kandydata na króla Sergjusza KWIEKA.

Kapela cygańska, tańce Cygańskie, Węgierskie, Hiszpańskie i Rosyjskie wykonają słynne cygańskie solistki JADWIGA i TAMARA oraz duet taneczny „WALC STEPÓW" i „CZARDASZ NAD CZARDASZAMI".

Bliższe szczegóły w programach

Wstęp od 99 groszy.

Bilety nabywać można w dniu koronacji w kasach przy wejściu od godz. 11 rano.

Dochód z uroczystości przeznacza się do dyspozycji wdowy po ś. p. Baronie MATEUSZU KWIEKU.

UWAGA: W razie niepogody uroczystość odbędzie się w innym terminie podanym przez prasę.

J. E. Zduneń, Tel. 1.12.42.

89. Protopresbyter Terencjusz Teodorowicz blesses the newly chosen "king", Janusz Kwiek, 1937

90. Decorated royal staff of office, 1937
91. Detail of Kwiek's royal staff of office

88. Handbill announcing the Warsaw coronation, 1937

92. A representative of the French Gypsies and Rudolf Kwiek,
    who stood against Janusz, at the election in Warsaw in 1937

93. Gypsies in Eastern Little Poland standing
    in front of their cottage, c. 1925

94. Gypsy children in hiding during the German occupation
    in the Warsaw suburbs, 1943

95. A Nazi map
    of the "Gypsy camp"
    in the Łódź ghetto,
    1941

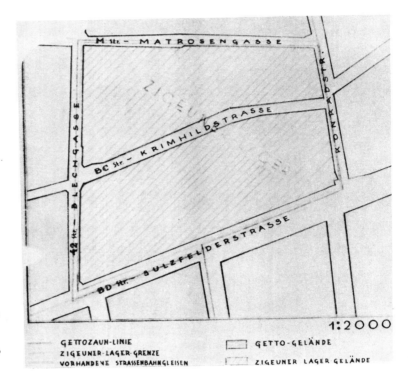

96. Stefania Holomek,
    a Czech Gypsy woman.
    Concentration camp
    photograph, Auschwitz,
    1943

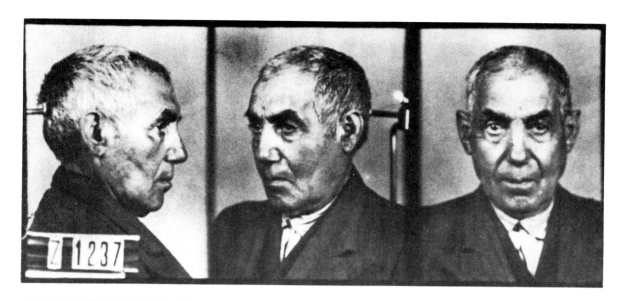

97. Jan Holomek, a Czech Gypsy. Photograph from Auschwitz, 1943

98. A Gypsy in the Bełżec concentration camp. Nazi photograph, July 1940, marked for reduction by the photographer

99. Gypsies in the Bełżec concentration camp. Nazi photograph, July 1940, marked for reduction by the photographer

100. Gypsy prisoners at the Bełżec concentration camp.
Nazi photograph, July 1940

101. Highland Gypsies in the Sub-Carpathian region, c. 1955

103. Gypsy woman with a child from the Nowy Targ region, c. 1947

102. Józef Mirga, a blacksmith, breaking stones in Zakopane, 1950

104. Gypsies around their mud hut near Nowy Targ, c. 1947

105. Gypsy children from the village of Czarna Góra
near Bukowina Tatrzańska, 1949

106. A Gypsy woman from
Nowa Huta, 1952

107. A Gypsy girl from Zakopane, 1955

108. A street fiddler, 1962

109. Door-to-door musicians, 1962

110. A Gypsy workman, c. 1962

111. Sunday in Nowa Huta, 1952

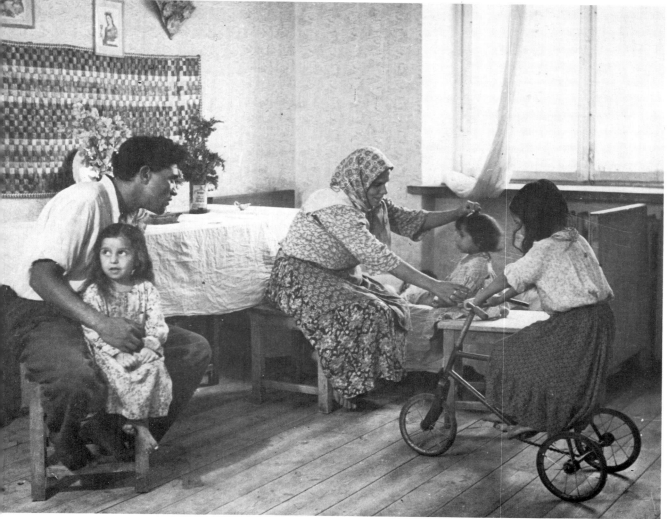

112. Gypsies on the way to work, Nowa Huta, 1952

113. In the flat of Stefan Gabor, a Gypsy foreman,
     at Nowa Huta, 1952

114. Studying under the open sky, Nowa Huta, 1952

115. A broom on a telegraph pole,
a Gypsyroad sign for caravans
passing through, 1948

116. At rest, 1950s

117. Gypsy women at the trial of Rudolf Kwiek, 1947

118. Randia, a Gypsy singer, 1965

119. Sylwester Masio Kwiek, a Gypsy singer, 1966

Gr. Wyrowińska

121. A break in the journey, 1950s

120. Karol Siwak, a violinist from Papusza's caravan, 1949

122. Papusza, the Gypsy poet, 1949

123. A manuscript of a poem by Papusza

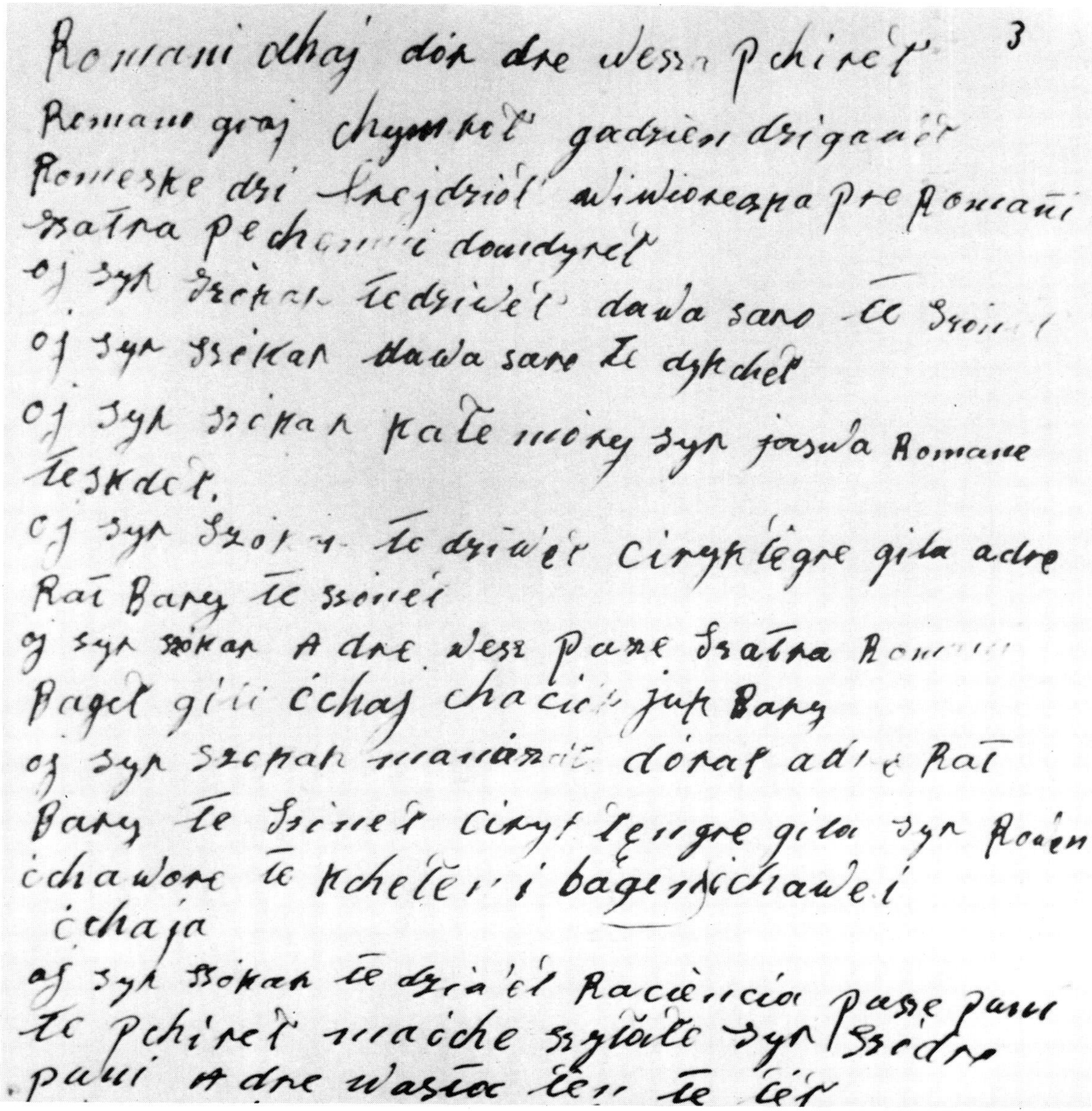

124. A caravan passes through a town, 1963

125. Arriving at the camp, 1963

126. The quantity of pillows and feather eiderdowns owned is a measure of the wealth of a Gypsy family, 1963

127. On the trail, 1963

128. The Gypsy road, 1963

129. A widowed mother driving the family cart, 1963

130. At the watering place, 1963

131. A forest road, 1963

132. Washing the horses, 1963

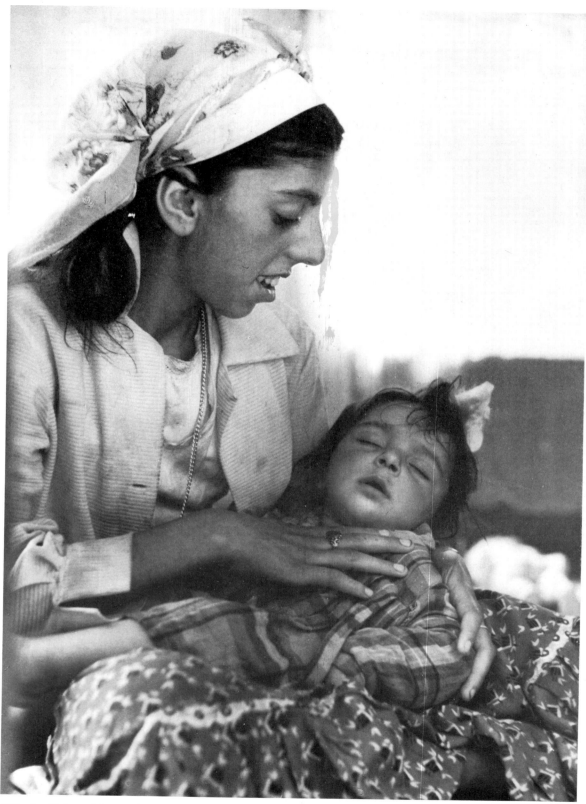

133. Lullaby, 1963

134. A Gypsy beauty, 1963

135. Cooking dinner, 1963

136. Daughters helping with the housework, 1963

137. The elders, 1963

138. Griffin on a cart, 1963
139. Painting on a cart, 1963

140. Entertainment en route, 1963

141. Double-bass player from a Gypsy band, 1978

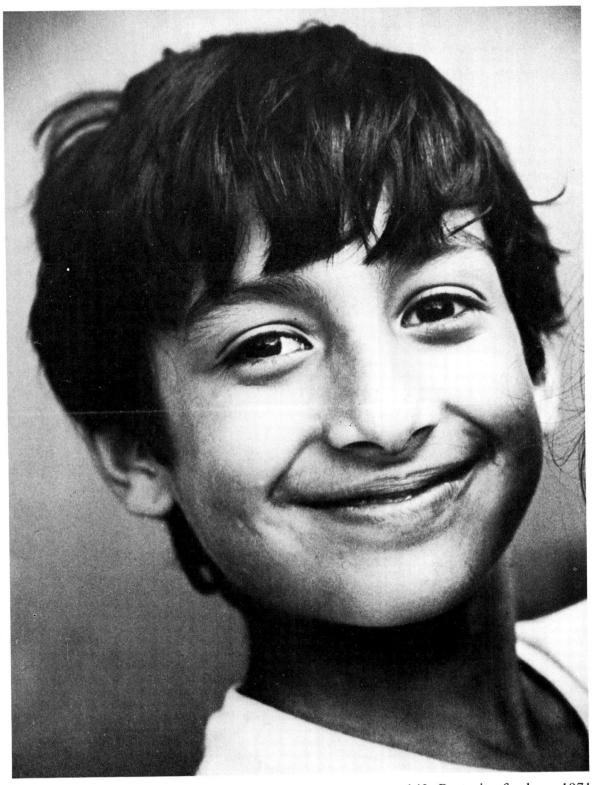

143. Portrait of a boy, 1971

142. Elżbietka, the eldest in a large family, 1971

144. By the camp fire, 1963

145. Portrait of a girl, 1963

146. Gallop by the river, 1963

147. In the tent, 1963

148. A Gypsy doll, 1963

149. The daughter and the horse
of the caravan headman, 1963

150. Music in the caravan, 1963

151. Dancing by
the camp fire,
1963

152. Gypsy
cradle,
1963

153. With mother,
1963

154/155. Plucking hens, 1963

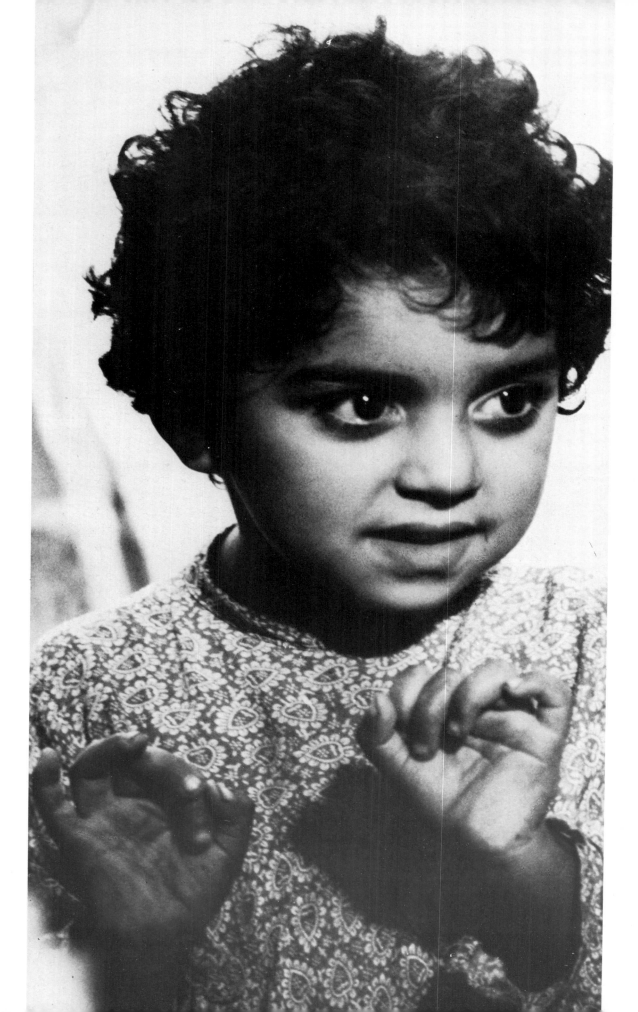

156. In the window of a Gypsy
    waggon, 1963

157. Doing the washing in the river, 1963

158. A meal, 1963

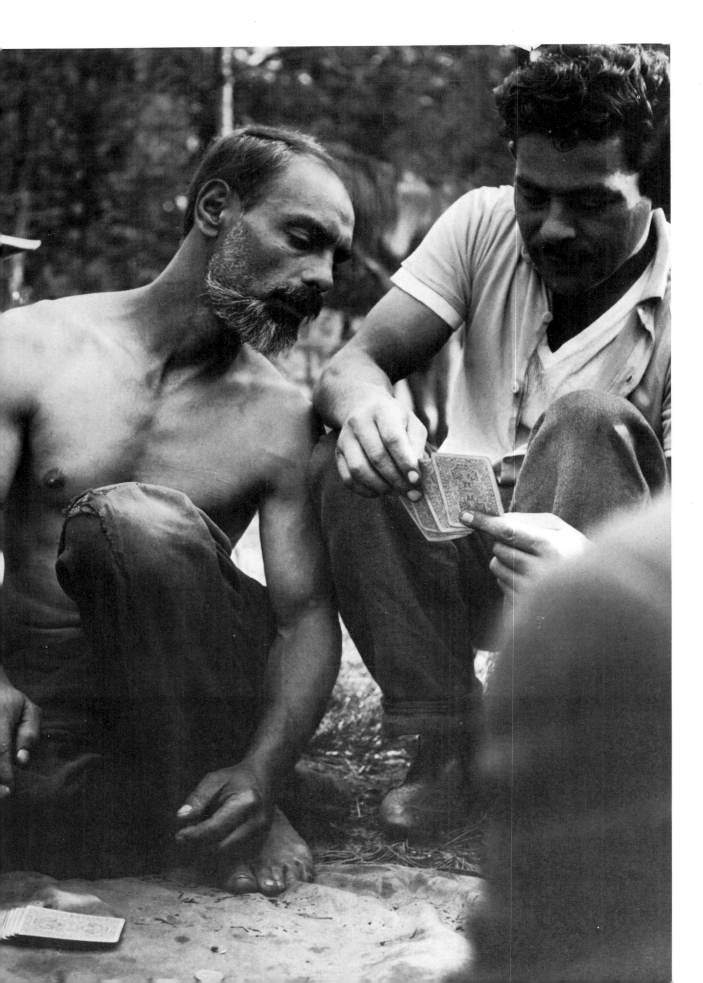

160. A good card, 1963

159. Gambling, 1963

161. Resting, 1963

162. Singeing a chicken over the fire, 1963

163. The caravan sets out, 1963

164. A quarrel, 1963

165. A wedding feast, 1963

168. A poor cart, 1963

166. A nubile girl, 1963

167. Fortune-telling, 1963

169. A forced halt, 1963

170. An offer of fortune-telling, 1963

171. Morning toilette, 1963

172. Before setting off, 1963

173. The Gypsy area in the Bródno cemetery at Warsaw on All Saints' Day, 1983
174. The Bródno cemetery on 1 November 1983

175. A ceremonial feast by Lovari Gypsies on their family graves, 1983

176. The family grave of Tabaczek,
     the headman of the Lovari tribe,
     at the Bródno cemetery in Warsaw,
     1983

177. A cart of the Polish lowland
     Gypsies, 1984

178. Feeding the souls of the dead by
     eating on their graves on All Saints'
     Day, 1984

179. The young people know about
     the era of travelling from the tales
     of their parents, 1984

180. The last cart, 1984

181. A holiday excursion by settled Gypsies, 1984

182. Dancers from the "TERNO" Song and Dance group
in Gorzów Wielkopolski, 1984

183. In a Gypsy cart, 1984

184. In front of the mirror, 1984

185. An accordion player and pupils, 1984

186. Young Gypsies at Gorzów Wielkopolski, 1984

187. A Gypsy cart parked, 1984

191. Gypsies from the "TERNO" group, Gorzów Wielkopolski, 1984

189. Detail of a cart, 1984

190. From a production by the "TERNO" group

192. A performance by the "TERNO" group

193. Granny's tale about the old Gypsy caravans, 1984

194. Fortune-telling with tarot cards, 1984

195. After work, 1984

196. *Bibi*, a Gypsy auntie, 1984

197. Round an autumn camp fire, 1984

198. Edward Dębicki, musician and manager of the "TERNO" group,
with his wife in his flat at Gorzów Wielkopolski, 1984

201. *A Pkhoori-Dai*, a Gypsy matron, 1984

199. In a street in Gorzów Wielkopolski, 1984

200. Pupils at a primary school, 1984

202. *The Gypsy Wedding*, Anna Bińkuńska

203. *The Fortune-teller*, A. Łękawka, 1978

204. *Gypsy Camp*, Bronisława Trzaskuś, 1980

205. *Gypsies in Town,* Zdzisław Bielecki,
    a Gypsy amateur artist, c. 1970

206. *Gypsy Camp*, Maria Mleczko, 1972

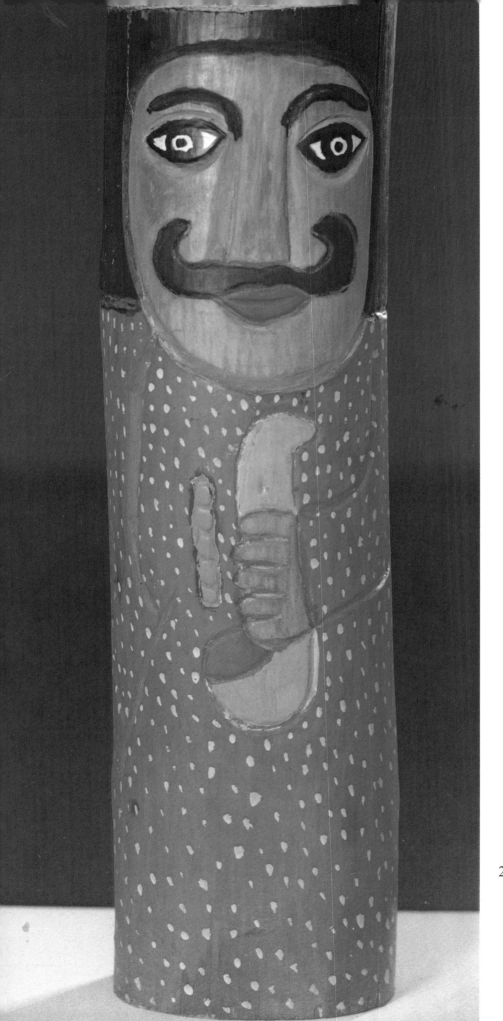

207. *A Gypsy*, Maria Madej, painted wood sculpture, 1961

List of Illustrations

21. Gypsy property for magic – the *bengoro* (little devil) in a hen's egg (from Jerzy Ficowski's collection). Photograph by Janusz Rosikoń

22. Gypsy property for magic – the *mooworo* (little corpse) in a glass of water (from Jerzy Ficowski's collection). Photograph by Janusz Rosikoń

23. Gypsy property for magic – the *trooshoow bawentsa* (hairy cross); (from Jerzy Ficowski's collection). Photograph by Jerzy Ficowski

24. Gypsy tinkers at Błonie in Cracow in 1870. Photograph by Walery Eljasz Radzikowski, Ethnographic Museum in Cracow

25. *Gypsy Camp by the Water*, Wincenty Smokowski, oils, late 19th cent., National Museum in Warsaw. Reproduction: Tomasz Prażmowski, Polish Interpress Agency

26. *Gypsy Camp*, Maksymilian Gierymski, oils, 1868, National Museum in Cracow. Reproduction: J. Ochoński, Polish Interpress Agency

27. *Gypsies*, Aleksander Kotsis, oils, c. 1860–70, National Museum in Cracow. Reproduction: J. Ochoński, Polish Interpress Agency

28. *From the Napoleonic Epic* ("The Gypsy woman"), Stanisław Wolski, detail, 1886, National Museum in Warsaw. Reproduction: Tomasz Prażmowski, Polish Interpress Agency

29. *Gypsy tents*, Zygmunt Sidorowicz, oils, 1876, National Museum in Warsaw. Reproduction Tomasz Prażmowski, Polish Interpress Agency

30. *Scene from Gypsy Life*, Maksymilian Gierymski, oils, 1868, National Museum in Cracow. Reproduction: J. Ochoński, Polish Interpress Agency

31. *Gypsies*, Antoni Kozakiewicz, oils, 1924. From the private collection of Krystyna and Czesław Malczewski, Cracow. Reproduction: J. Ochoński, Polish Interpress Agency

32. *The Young Virtuoso*, Antoni Kozakiewicz, oils. From the private collection of Krystyna and Czesław Malczewski, Cracow. Reproduction: J. Ochoński, Polish Interpress Agency

33. The fortune-teller, photograph by T. Mien, Cracow, end of 19th century (from J. Ficowski's collection). Reproduction and touch-up: Kazimierz Czapiński

34. *The Gypsy Woman*, Antoni Kozakiewicz, postcard reproduction of oil painting, 1909, Ossolineum Institution, Wrocław. Reproduction: E. Wołoszczuk, Polish Interpress Agency

35. *Gypsy Camp at Błonie*, Juliusz Kossak, water colour, Ossolineum Institution, Wrocław. Reproduction: E. Wołoszczuk, Polish Interpress Agency

36. *Gypsy Encampment at Saska Kępa near Warsaw*, Wojciech Gerson, engraving from his drawing (*Tygodnik Ilustrowany*, 1868), Reproduction: Kazimierz Czapiński

37. *Gypsies*, Józef Brandt, 1866–67, engraving from the original (*Świat*, 1888). Reproduction: Kazimierz Czapiński

38. *Gypsies' Resting*, Franciszek Streitt, engraving from the original by K. Olszewski (*Tygodnik Ilustrowany*, 1886). Reproduction: Kazimierz Czapiński

39. *The Gypsy Headman*, Tadeusz Popiel. Reproduction from a copy printed in 1898: Kazimierz Czapiński

40. *The Bear-Leader*, Hipolit Lipiński, 1873. Reproduction from a heliograph of the original: Kazimierz Czapiński

41. *The Gypsy Funeral*, Franciszek Kostrzewski. Engraving by E. Gorazdowski, (*Tygodnik Ilustrowany*, 1868). Reproduction: Kazimierz Czapiński

42. *A Gypsy*, Artur Grottger, engraving, Grybów 1866. Reproduction from a printed copy: Kazimierz Czapiński

43. *Maternal Bliss*, Antoni Kozakiewicz, postcard (Polish Painting printed by A. J. Ostrowski, Łódź-Warsaw). Reproduction: Kazimierz Czapiński

44. *The Gypsy Caravan,* Michał Pociecha, engraving by K. Olszewski *(Tygodnik Ilustrowany,* 1878). Reproduction: Stanisław Senisson

45. *The Gypsy,* Józef Ignacy Kraszewski *(Wspomnienia Polesia, Wołynia i Litwy;* Memories of Polesie, Volhynia and Lithuania, 1860). Reproduction: S. Senisson

46. *The Gypsy Caravan,* Apoloniusz Kędzierski, engraving by M. Różański *(Tygodnik Ilustrowany,* 1882). Reproduction: Stanisław Senisson

47. *The Gypsy Wedding,* Antoni Piotrowski, engraving by E. Boulay *(Kłosy,* 1873). Reproduction: Stanisław Senisson

48. *The Gypsy Camp,* Antoni Piotrowski, engraving by E. Boulay *(Kłosy,* 1873). Reproduction: Stanisław Senisson

49. *The Gypsy Camp,* Walery Brochocki, engraving by K. Neuman *(Tygodnik Ilustrowany,* 1873). Reproduction: Stanisław Senisson

50. *The Gypsy Camp,* engraving by B. Puc *(Biesiada Literacka,* 1882). Reproduction: Polish Interpress Agency

51. *The Gypsy Bivouac,* Henryk Pillati, after J. Lewicki's drawing *(Tygodnik Ilustrowany,* 1863). Reproduction: Polish Interpress Agency

52. *The Gypsy Woman,* Henryk Pillati, engraving by H. Kübler *(Tygodnik Ilustrowany,* 1863). Reproduction: Polish Interpress Agency

53. The Gypsy Camp, Michał Pociecha, engraving by A. Wiśniewski *(Tygodnik Ilustrowany,* 1878). Reproduction: Polish Interpress Agency

54. *The Gypsy Camp,* Henryk Pillati, engraving by P. Dziedzic *(Tygodnik Ilustrowany,* 1873). Reproduction: Polish Interpress Agency

55. *Gypsies,* Michał Pociecha, engraving by J. Krajewski *(Tygodnik Ilustrowany,* 1880). Reproduction: Polish Interpress Agency

56. *Gypsies,* Franciszek Kostrzewski, water colour, c. 1868, National Museum in Warsaw. Reproduction: Polish Interpress Agency

57. *Gypsies,* Antoni Kozakiewicz, engraving by W. Ciechomski, 1887 *(Tygodnik Ilustrowany,* 1888). Reproduction: Polish Interpress Agency

58. *Gypsies,* Henryk Pillati, engraving by J. Minheymer *(Kłosy,* 1886). Reproduction: Wojciech Dudziak

59. *Gypsies with Bears,* Ludwik Kurella, engraving by K. Olszewski *(Kłosy,* 1877). Reproduction: Polish Interpress Agency

60. *A Group of Gypsies,* Kazimierz Młodnicki, pencil drawing, 1860, National Museum in Cracow. Reproduction: Polish Interpress Agency

61. *A Gypsy Band Settled at Rytro,* postcard photograph, c. 1900, Krosno, J. Zajączkowski. Reproduction: Wojciech Dudziak

62. *A Gypsy Tent,* postcard photograph, 1902, Cracow. Reproduction: Wojciech Dudziak

63. Gypsy in front of a tent near Cracow. Photograph dating from before 1900, Ethnographic Museum in Cracow. Reproduction: Wojciech Dudziak

64. *Gypsies near Krościenko on the Dunajec River,* postcard photograph, early 20th century. Reproduction: Kazimierz Czapiński

65. *The Gypsy Marcin with his Family at Krościenko,* postcard photograph, early 20th century. Reproduction: Jerzy Ficowski

66. *Gypsy Wedding at the Bolechów Market Place,* postcard photograph, c. 1910, "Zofia" photographic studio in Bolechów. Reproduction: Kazimierz Czapiński

67. Gypsies, photograph, 1919, Stanisławów, Ethnographic Museum in Cracow. Reproduction: Polish Interpress Agency

68. *Scenes from a Gypsy Camp* (Lovari Gypsies). Photograph by Ł. Dobrzański *(Tygodnik Ilustrowany,* 1908). Reproduction: Kazimierz Czapiński

69. A Kalderash Gypsy in a jacket with silver buttons, photograph, c. 1925, in Warsaw (from Jerzy Ficowski's collection). Reproduction: Jerzy Ficowski

70. Kalderash Gypsies, Todor Czoron with his wife Liza, after arriving in England from Poland. Photograph, 1913, Nottingham (*Journal of the Gypsy Lore Society*, 1912–13). Reproduction: Kazimierz Czapiński

71. Gypsy women on the porch of the manor house at Worochta, 1932. Photograph by Matylda Komorowska. Reproduction: Archive of Mechanical Documentation, Warsaw

72. *The Gypsy Fortune-Teller*, postcard photograph, c. 1910. Published by the Warsaw Photographic School run by the Employment Exchange Department. Reproduction: Jerzy Ficowski

73. Gypsy bear-leader in the Pieniny hills. Photograph, 1930. Reproduction: Archive of Mechanical Documentation, Warsaw

74. Gypsy carts, 1930s. Reproduction: Archive of Mechanical Documentation, Warsaw

75. Gypsy encampment in the snow at Leszczyny in Upper Silesia, c. 1930. Photograph J. Chlebus. Reproduction: Archive of Mechanical Documentation, Warsaw

76. Gypsy women by a cart, c. 1930. Reproduction: Archive of Mechanical Documentation, Warsaw

77. The Gypsy's augury. Photograph, c. 1930. Reproduction: Archive of Mechanical Documentation, Warsaw

78. Street musicians in Cracow, c. 1930. Photograph by Ludwik Bira. Reproduction: Archive of Mechanical Documentation, Warsaw

79. Gypsy tinkers, photograph, c. 1930. Reproduction: Archive of Mechanical Documentation, Warsaw

80. Kalderash leader, Dymitr Koszor Kwiek, with his family at Marymont, 1928. Reproduction: Archive of Mechanical Documentation, Warsaw

81. Michał Kwiek, the "King of the Gypsies", 1931. Reproduction: Archive of Mechanical Documentation, Warsaw

82. At the coronation ceremony of Michał Kwiek at Hajduki Wielkie in Upper Silesia, May 1934 (the grey bearded "King of the Spanish Gypsies" is standing next to Michał). Reproduction: Archive of Mechanical Documentation, Warsaw

83. Józef Kwiek, the "President of the Gypsy Council". Photograph dating from the 1930s. Reproduction: Archive of Mechanical Documentation, Warsaw

84. Matejasz Kwiek, the "Leader of the Gypsy nation". Photograph by Karol Buchar, 1935. Reproduction: Archive of Mechanical Documentation, Warsaw

85. The visiting card of "The Baron of the Gypsies in all Poland", Matejasz Kwiek, c. 1933 (from Jerzy Ficowski's collection). Reproduction: Jerzy Ficowski

86. Funeral of Matejasz Kwiek in Warsaw on 30 March 1937. Reproduction: Archive of Mechanical Documentation, Warsaw

87. Coronation of Janusz Kwiek in Warsaw, 1937. Reproduction: Polish Interpress Agency

88. Handbill announcing the Warsaw coronation, 1937. Reproduction: Kazimierz Czapiński

89. Protopresbyter Terencjusz Teodorowicz of the Orthodox church in the Praga district of Warsaw blesses the newly chosen "king", Janusz Kwiek, 1937. Reproduction: Archive of Mechanical Documentation, Warsaw

90. Decorated royal staff of office, 1937. Reproduction: Archive of Mechanical Documentation, Warsaw

91. Fragment of Kwiek's royal staff of office, 1937. Reproduction: Archive of Mechanical Documentation, Warsaw

92. A representative of the French Gypsies, and Rudolf Kwiek, the candidate who stood against Janusz in the election in Warsaw, 1937. Reproduction: Archive of Mechanical Documentation, Warsaw

93. Gypsies in front of their cottage in Eastern Little Poland, c. 1925. Reproduction: Archive of Mechanical Documentation, Warsaw

94. Children from Gypsy families hiding during the German occupation in the suburbs of Warsaw, near Opaczewska Street in Ochota. Photograph by Jerzy Ficowski, 1943

95. A Nazi map of the "Gypsy camp" in the Łódź ghetto, 1941. Reproduction: Jerzy Ficowski

96. Stefania Holomek, a Gypsy woman from Czechoslovakia, a farm worker, born 27 Oct. 1910. Concentration camp photograph, 1943, Auschwitz Museum. Reproduction: Kazimierz Czapiński

97. Jan Holomek, a Czech Gypsy, born 9 Nov. 1879. Concentration camp photograph, 1943, Auschwitz Museum. Reproduction: Kazimierz Czapiński

98. A Gypsy in the Bełżec concentration camp. Nazi photograph dating from July 1940 ("Polnischer Zigeunerkönig", photographed and marked for reduction by Gensel); from J. Ficowski's collection. Reproduction: Polish Interpress Agency

99. Gypsies in the Bełżec concentration camp. Nazi photograph dating from July 1940 ("Zigeunerkönig", photography Gensel, marked for reduction by the photographer, from J. Ficowski's collection). Reproduction: K. Czapiński

100. Gypsies imprisoned in the Bełżec concentration camp. Nazi photograph dating from July 1940 ("Zigeunertypen im Lager von Bełżec"). Reproduction: Archive of Mechanical Documentation, Warsaw

101. Highland Gypsies in the sub-Carpathian region, c. 1955. Photograph by Jerzy Baranowski

102. Józef Mirga, blacksmith, breaking stones in Zakopane. Photograph by Jerzy Ficowski, 1950

103. Gypsy woman with a child from the Nowy Targ region. Photograph by Bożena Dodenhoff-Romanowska, c. 1947

104. Gypsies around their mud hut near Nowy Targ. Photograph by Bożena Dodenhoff-Romanowska, c. 1947

105. Gypsy children from the village of Czarna Góra near Bukowina Tatrzańska. Photograph by Jerzy Ficowski, 1949

106. Gypsy woman from Nowa Huta. Photograph by Jerzy Ficowski, 1952

107. Gypsy girl from Zakopane. Photograph by Jerzy Ficowski, 1955

108. Street fiddler. Photograph by Jerzy Dorożyński, 1962

109. Door-to-door musicians. Photograph by Jerzy Dorożyński, 1962

110. Gypsy workman, a Polish highland Gypsy. Photograph by Jerzy Dorożyński, 1962

111. Sunday in Nowa Huta. Photograph by Jan Kosidowski, 1952

112. Gypsies on the way to work, Nowa Huta. Photograph by Jan Kosidowski, 1952

113. In the home of the Gypsy foreman, Stefan Gabor, Nowa Huta. Photograph by Jan Kosidowski, 1952

114. Studying under the open sky, Nowa Huta. Photograph by Jan Kosidowski, 1952

115. Broom on a telegraph pole in the Anin area, near Warsaw – a Gypsy road sign for caravans passing through. Photograph by Jerzy Ficowski, 1948

116. At rest. Photograph by Irena Jarosińska, 1950s

117. Gypsy women at Rudolf Kwiek's trial in June 1947. Photograph by Film Polski